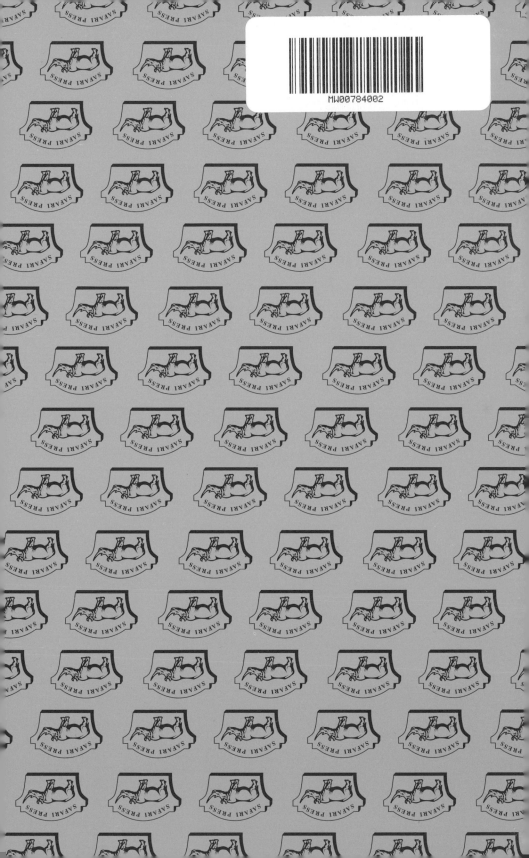

CAMPFIRE LIES
OF A
CANADIAN
HUNTING GUIDE

BY

FRED WEBB

ARTWORK BY
TOM HENNESSEY

Safari Press Inc.

The trademark Safari Press ® is registered with the U.S. Patent and Trademark Office and in other countries.

Webb, Fred

Safari Press Inc.

2000, Long Beach, California

ISBN 1-57157-167-1

Library of Congress Catalog Card Number: 99-66534

10 9 8 7 6 5 4 3 2

Readers wishing to receive the Safari Press catalog, featuring many fine books on big-game hunting, wingshooting, and sporting firearms, should write to Safari Press Inc., P.O. Box 3095, Long Beach, CA 90803, USA. Tel: (714) 894-9080 or visit our Web site at www.safaripress.com.

Table of Contents

Dedication

To the guides of the past who
have shown us the way,
and to our friends, the clients,
who have helped us to follow.

*"There's no sense in going farther . . .
it's the edge of cultivation,"
So they said, and I believed it . . .
Till a voice, as bad as conscience,
rang interminable changes
On one everlasting whisper day and night
repeated so:*

*"Something hidden. Go and find it.
Go and look behind the Ranges . . .
Something lost behind the Ranges.
Lost and waiting for you. Go!"*

—Rudyard Kipling, The Explorer

Foreword

The first time I cut Fred Webb's trail was back in the late '70s, when I dropped my duffel at his Nictau Lodge in New Brunswick, Canada. The occasion was a salmon-fishing trip to the Tobique River with Jim Rikhoff's National Sporting Fraternity, "Rikhoff's Rangers," as Fred referred to the fraternity, and for good reason.

Somehow—probably because I was the most experienced salmon fisherman in the group—Fred had been told that I knew the difference between a Blue Charm and a Green Highlander, so to speak. Consequently, like a couple of unacquainted hounds sharing a kennel, Fred and I kind of smelled each other for a day or so before deciding we could run together. And run we did, all the way from the Tobique to the George River in Quebec's Ungava region.

From firsthand experience then, I'll say that Fred Webb is the most knowledgeable guide and outfitter I ever shared a campfire with; and, without question, the most colorful. But beyond that, and fortunately for those of us who prefer pine-needled rails to pavement, my longtime friend is a storyteller without peer. Accordingly, the tracks he leaves in this book are enjoyably clear, unmistakable, and wonderfully interesting and informative.

Naturally, I was disappointed when Fred told me he was closing his New Brunswick camp and setting a course for Canada's Northwest Territories. "I'm tired of chasing salmon that are so lovesick they can't eat and are getting scarcer all the time," he said in his inimitable way with words. I'm pleased, however, that he has chronicled some of his latest outdoors adventures in the pages of this excellent book.

Sometime in the not-too-distant future, I hope to make tracks to Fred's camp out in Yellowknife. Although I know his stories about that country will be as entertaining as ever, I don't expect that the campfire will burn as long into the night as it did during those younger times at Nictau Lodge and Helen's Falls camp on the George River. It takes years of just hitting the high spots, but old hounds eventually learn they have to pace themselves to keep up with the pack.

Tom Hennessey
Hampden, Maine
January 1999

Acknowledgments

My sincere thanks to the people who have made this book possible:

To my wife, Irene, who after nearly half a century of ups and downs still supports my dreams of adventure.

To Martin, my partner, and Derek, who upholds family tradition in the military.

To Cindy and Janice, who shared the hardships of our early lean years and continue to assist in our business.

To Tom Hennessey for providing illustrations of our memories.

And, of course, to the guides—the ones who have gone before us and the ones still working today—upon whom our sporting industry depends and whose stories have enriched our lives.

A Word about the Title

Before the days of electronic entertainment, one might be greeted around the fire in hunting camps or on the log drive with, "Come on in, have a seat, and tell us some lies." This might be accompanied by the offer of tea or, in the rare lucky instance, a drink of black rum.

Stories told on those occasions were never outright falsehoods or *lies* as described in the dictionary. As a matter of fact, most were 90 percent true, with the balance being a bit of exaggeration or an attempt to protect the good names and reputations of all involved.

Such is the case in *Campfire Lies of a Canadian Guide*. Every story is based upon personal experience, though subtle shifts may have been made in locales or names to protect the innocent.

For those of you who were there, it will bring back memories . . . for those of you who were not, I hope these "lies" will give you some insight to the life and times of a Canadian guide.

Preface

AN ARCTIC EPISODE WITH
MY FRIEND FRED WEBB
by Harry Tennison

Back in what we now call the Good Old Days, there developed a group of people we called The Winchester Irregulars. This was a crew composed of people who for some reason had voiced opinions about hunting and fishing that caught the ear of one James Rikhoff. Mr. Rikhoff, then in charge of promotion for Winchester, became the head of a sort of rat pack of fishing and shooting companions whom I considered the elite of the hunting and fishing world at the time.

Included were such truly famous people as Connie Ryan (*The Longest Day* and *A Bridge Too Far*) and his buddy, the senior member of the board of the famous 21 Club, His Excellency Pete Kriendler. Along for the trips to many places was one of the greatest outdoor writers of all time, the one and only Gene Hill, referred to as Hilly among friends and Gene when you talked to him personally. Grits Gresham and another truly famous writer, Ed Zern, became part of the group, as did people like Guy Coheleach and Bob Kuhn, those finest of outdoor artists. We had the captain of the Olympic equestrian team, Bill Stinekraus, and Col. John Ray, kicked out of Bulgaria because he was a true CIA-type spy.

Tim Hixon from San Antonio, along with Stan Studer and Jim Midcap, made up the allotment for Texas. Of course, I am from there, too.

From The Winchester Irregulars came the nucleus of the famous National Sporting Fraternity Ltd., an exclusive group, limited to 1,000 invited members, with like interests in the better things in life: hunting and fishing, and books and other arts devoted to these pursuits. Jim Rikhoff, president and founder, became the leader of what became known among poor, set-upon outfitters around the world as Rikhoff's Rangers.

Although the Irregulars had many get-togethers in many exotic locales, the very first trip under the newly organized National Sporting Fraternity Ltd. was to member Fred Webb's grouse and woodcock lodge in New Brunswick. The summer Atlantic salmon group and the autumn birdshooting group became a tradition, so when Fred became involved in helping operate a salmon camp in northern Quebec, Jim was not long in getting a group together to visit.

One day Jimmy called and said we should go to a place called Helens Falls, as it was a great salmon river, and that Fred and his son Martin were involved in helping the local owner, Sandy Annanack, with the operation.

I had been on this river before, with very bad memories—everything had been misrepresented, and they did not like Americans. No one wanted to go into that sort of deal, so I told Jimmy that it had better be damn good or he would go into the water himself, headfirst.

We met in Montreal, as best I remember, and flew the next day in a rather cramped jet to a place called Fort Chimo. There we met the crew that was to fly us to the George River, seventy or eighty miles to the east, to join Fred. I didn't know whether or not the airplane would get us off the ground, since there were nine of us plus a ton of gear and all sorts of other things that had to be flown into the camp for our pleasure.

We had brought our own liquid refreshments and were told to hide them or lock them up, or by the last night everyone, including the Inuit ladies of the camp, would likely have a party with our whiskey! Good advice!

We landed on a runway made out of logs, and if we hadn't stopped in time, it was a 150-foot drop to the George River. The ability of those bush pilots flying in and out of such places was fantastic.

We were met by Fred and his son Martin, who helped run the camp with their Inuit partners, the Eskimo of Canada and Greenland. The camp was pretty nice, better than I expected, although there was a small tear in the tent right above my head, and it did rain a little every so often. I just moved my head to one side and went back to sleep.

The river looked great. Right in front of the camp was a rather steep set of rapids that we rode through twice a day on the way upriver to the main falls.

From where we landed, a footpath progressed from Beat One clear up to Beat Ten about a mile above. There were acres of blueberries along the way, and we had those for our after-breakfast and after-lunch dessert.

This year the river was in fine shape, with lots of fast water and large pools, some over a hundred yards across. Everyone had a certain beat for each morning and evening, and it worked out fairly well for me as I had my sixteen-foot Spey rod along and could reach just far enough to where we would see salmon rising as they came upstream to the falls. The steepest part of the falls was most difficult for any salmon to get over, but we saw lots of them doing just that.

To me the river looked beautiful, and with the rush of water over the rapids in front of our camp, I could see all of us catching a lot of fish, although a few did better than others.

The blueberry pancakes every morning helped out, and certainly the walk upriver was always interesting for no one knew when a bear might also be interested in those ripe berries.

We were soon into good fishing, and with my long Spey rod I started catching salmon. They were hard fighters and certainly pleasing as they went through a series of jumps, just as it says in all the angling literature.

My favorite beat was Number Seven, and for the rest of the week everyone wanted to fish that beautiful stretch of water, for it did seem to hold the largest number of fresh salmon. Most of the other pools, however, also held a good number of salmon.

By the luck of the draw, I was once again assigned to my favorite Number Seven on the last day. One member of the party had not been too successful and started bitching about it.

I simply said, "OK, that beat is yours for today. I will take yours, Number Three." So he went off very happy on his way to number seven. I landed three very nice salmon before noon, and as we all gathered back by the boats to return to camp, I learned that my unhappy fellow fisherman had not even had a rise to any of his attempts. I stayed out of the conversation as the other guys gave him a hard time.

During the week the group landed an even one hundred prime George River salmon and released probably four times that number. An excellent week in any salmon camp in the world!

Alas, the last night at camp turned into a mess, any way you look at it. Some of the Inuit ladies had stolen some of our liquor, notably the half-gallon of vodka belonging to Gene Hill and Jimmy Rikhoff. When we came in to have a shot ourselves, we found that we had company. Four women were in our tent, and all of them had liquor and love on their minds. I didn't mind the liquor, but looking at toothless Salema headed for my bed made me put my feet up in the air just to let her know that that was as far as she was welcome. They weren't really being bad, just wanting to have a good time, and my friends seemed to have pointed me out as the main target.

My friends Jimmy and Gene, Dr. Whit Smith, Dr. Wayne Grayson, and his wife, Donna, were having a good laugh at my expense until a couple of the ladies, rubber boots and all, decided to climb into their beds as well.

Thank the good Lord we ran out of whiskey and they finally went back to their own tents or over to bother Fred and Martin. That night one of them jumped into the rapids and Fred rescued her with the landing gaff. Slightly punctured but sober, she survived and was there when we returned the next year. I'm not sure where Fred hit her with the gaff, but these people are truly tough, and she came out of it all ready for another party.

The Inuit are truly magnificent and wonderful people. We hope they can always be happy as the world goes on.

Taking off from this camp in the Twin Otter was a remedy for any hangover or bad nerves. As a pilot myself, I knew this airplane was the strongest in the North, but I had a few nervous moments as the pilot revved up the engines to full power, then turned the brakes loose. We were off. Loaded with nine passengers and our luggage, its takeoff run was rather sluggish, but the fifty-foot freefall when we hit the end of the runway made us airborne. It was exciting, and obviously we made it or I wouldn't be writing this story. Upon landing in Fort Chimo I was assured by the pilot that today's was one of the easy trips—most of his flights carried much more weight and used worse runways.

My friends Fred and Martin Webb ran a wonderful camp with their Inuit friends. It was all the good fishing that had been promised, and the hike upriver through the ripe blueberries was an added treat. We had a wonderful time and made some great friends. Although the membership list is dwindling, we still share fraternity trips and talk about the visit with Fred at Helens Falls. Wish you had been there!

Introduction

LIFE OF A GUIDE IN REVIEW

Considering the era in which I grew up and the opportunities available, I have managed to survive a fairly free and varied existence—especially, as my wife says, "for someone who has been married for most of it." As I once told an audience at a Safari Club International gathering, "Irene and I have the typical teenage marriage that wasn't supposed to last six months. I guess the secret is that out of the past forty years I have been away about thirty-five of them."

One hesitates to divulge too varied a resume, but the truth is that anyone who makes a lifetime's living from the business of guiding is just bound to have had a lot of short-term employment at a variety of jobs. Such was my lot for a good many years, until we had our family outfitting business at the stage where we could claim to be totally self-employed.

All of my work experience has been outdoor-oriented. As a kid I worked on farms, in the lumber woods, and at guiding whenever I could escape school. Busting out of the hated classroom somewhere around the middle of high school, I first found employment as a truck driver. Then I joined the army, trained to jump out of airplanes, acquired a tattoo, got married, and started a family . . . in one eventful season. All of this was well before I'd reached the age of admittance to the bars and liquor stores.

Coming out of the army, I hurried home to Irene and our daughter Cindy and went back to driving trucks, working in the lumber woods, and guiding. Barely surviving on this kind of short-term employment, I spotted a government poster at the post office in town one day. It asked ex-service personnel to enroll in a course in communications, for employment in the Arctic. Off I went.

Away from home again, learning the skills of a radio operator, I was called to the phone one day and informed that we had a brand-new daughter, Janice. Less than a year later, on a radio station in the middle of the wilderness of Labrador, a passing airplane en route to the DEW Line informed me that Janice was learning to walk, that Irene and Cindy were well, and that they hoped I would come home sometime.

For a little over ten years I led what I term my "other life." I was employed first as a radio operator on ships, then as a communications specialist on exploration and scientific expeditions. As a lady journalist doing an assignment on my travels back in the seventies termed it: "A life that took him from the Arctic to the Andes and some interesting places in between."

During this "other life" I was able to keep my touch with the forest by trapping and guiding whenever possible. My main aim was to lay the groundwork so that I could become my own boss as a full-time outfitter in northern New Brunswick. By this time Irene and I had added to our family with first Martin and then a year later, Derek. Now with four children, I saw the growing importance of changing the lifestyle that had kept me away from home for months and months at a time.

By the late 1960s I had partly achieved my goal. We were building up our own guiding business, but it was a hard, uphill fight. I had to run the traplines, work on the stream drives, cut and truck logs, guide for other outfits, and still take occasional contracted jobs on expeditions to foreign places as guide and communications man.

About 1972, having returned from a prolonged trip abroad, I received a bit of advice from my partner: "Either stay home, starve or not, and build up our own business, or move us out of this hole in the woods and go back to sea."

The choice was easy: I gave up the traveling life—or so I thought at the time—and devoted full time to the outfitting business.

For years we always seemed to be on the "leading edge" as we strove to expand our employment season. Some things worked and some did not; all were hard work and worry, and required reinvesting every penny we managed to earn.

We were the only "year-round" operation in eastern Canada, hunting bobcats in winter and black bears in spring, running canoe trips and Atlantic salmon fishing camps in summer, guiding woodcock and grouse shooters in early autumn and whitetail hunters in later autumn. We even dabbled in accommodating cross-country skiers and snowmobilers in the winter. In between we somehow found time to keep up the traplines and do the necessary marketing of our services. It was a busy and exhausting period of our lives, but with the kids all home, it was a happy time as well.

I had always dreamed of returning to the Arctic as my own boss, engaged in the sporting business. The opportunity arose through working with the Inuit-owned Federation of Cooperatives of Nouveau Quebec. The FCNQ developed, supported, and marketed the native-operated camps—the only ones allowed north of the fifty-seventh parallel at the time under the terms of the James Bay Agreement.

Bill Tait was the Director of Tourism for FCNQ, and through our friendship the Webbs became involved as independent operators assisting with developing, operating, and marketing new camps.

At the same time, we were working in Newfoundland part of the season, hunting moose and woodland caribou. Not content with working ourselves nearly to death, we then became involved in the western part of the Northwest Territories (NWT).

For a period of about five years, we worked a schedule that had us in the United States on marketing trips from December to March, and in the Arctic hunting from March to mid-May. Then we headed across the continent to New Brunswick to run bear hunts from late May to the end of June, then to northern Quebec for July, and in the NWT during August and September. I would leave Martin in charge of the NWT camps in early September, drive across Canada, fly to northern Quebec, then back to Montreal and on to Newfoundland. The season ended in Newfoundland around the end of October.

I would go back to New Brunswick, Martin would return from out west, and we would run November whitetail hunts, then hit the road for the States again. Needless to say, we could not keep up this kind of an operation forever. Finally we had to sell out everything in the East and settle in the West, investing everything in the NWT.

Our family by this time had all ended up in western Canada. The facts of life in New Brunswick, province of our ancestors, included high unemployment, especially for unilingual English-speaking job seekers, and a generally depressed economy. The outfitting industry there was essentially terminated—for anyone who required a full-time living—by forest-cutting practices and government support for ever-increasing numbers of newcomers to the profession.

Our daughters Cindy and Janice, with their families, live in the lower mainland area of British Columbia, as does Martin—at least part of the year, as he remains a partner in our outfitting business. Derek opted for a career in the military, including peacekeeping duties with the United Nations in various world trouble spots, but he hopes someday to retire and get back to the guiding life.

It has been a long, hard trail, but we still face our changing seasons with expectation and excitement. In the Arctic a brand-new territory is emerging—*Nunavut,* "Our Land"—and we are part of it. There are many new clients to meet, and many new places to hunt.

THE GUIDES

A few years ago, about the time a serious heart operation reminded me of my mortality, I was persuaded to make an effort to write down reminiscences of a lifetime spent guiding in one place or another. The result was the publication of the mostly autobiographical *Home from the Hill.*

When I started the project, my publisher advised me that most books contain three hundred pages or so. Having no idea of how much writing that involved, I asked him to translate it into how many beer boxes of paper this would fill . . . something to which I could relate. Someone miscalculated somewhat, for we ended up with about twice as much as would fit conveniently into one book.

I guess that is as good an excuse as any to publish a sequel. One obvious problem with a sequel is to choose a title. I was not too happy with calling it "Home from the Hill Two" or

"Home from the Hill All Over Again." The publisher, being of a more gentlemanly bent than I, dashed my hopes of calling it "More of the Same Old Bull——"!

I have therefore settled upon *Campfire Lies of a Canadian Hunting Guide* as the most appropriate name for a collection of tales that revolve around the profession of leading the way, whether in the pursuit of fish and game or guiding of a different sort on far-flung expeditions.

These are stories of days gone by and circumstances that can never be repeated. However, our companies are still engaged in guiding and we look forward to future developments in the new northern territory of Nunavut.

As I stand at the window of our home base in Kugluktuk, on the edge of the frozen Arctic Ocean, I am still looking north after nearly half a century.

With our Inuit partner, Charlie Bolt, my son Martin is building a new hunting venture at Nagyuktok, on the far-off shore of Victoria Island. There is still room to move around in the central Arctic, a fitting land for the next generation of "The Guides."

As you read these pages, I hope you will agree that although guides very rarely die rich, they at least do not expire from boredom.

Kugluktuk, Nunavut Territory
October 1997

Author's Note

I have never been quite sure how to properly define a person who dabbles in the business of writing. It always seems to me a bit presumptuous for amateurs and part-timers such as myself to aspire to the title of "author" when there are professional full-time writers about who are much more deserving of the designation.

It is a fact that in our sporting industry, as in the prostitution industry, the professional who does it for money must face unfair competition from the eager amateurs who do it for fun and entertainment. I always feel a bit guilty for putting myself in the latter category as it applies to writing.

However, I am probably worrying for nothing. It has been my privilege to have guided, at one place or another, many of the best-known outdoor writers throughout the past thirty years and more. Without exception they were true experts, both in the sport and in writing about it, and invariably a joy to be with in the field. In many cases, what started out as onetime visits turned into friendships that have endured for years.

As the reader will soon become aware, this book is written not by an "author" but by a guide who has managed to make a living without the benefit of much formal education.

Some of the language employed herein is that of the working woodsman. Unlike the obscenities used in much of the present-day literature, film, and television, however, it is not put in for shock value, but reflects reality in the lives we lead.

Pull up a stump by the fire. I'll pour you a cup of tea from the old black kettle, and with the help of my friends I will tell you some campfire lies.

YOU CAN TAKE THE BOY OUT
OF THE WOODS, BUT ...

WEIRD AND WONDERFUL PROJECTS

In a book written primarily about my life as a professional hunting guide, it is probably wise to mention other employment only in passing. Most of the jobs abroad, in what I term my "other life," were of varying duration. Some meant months away from home, others just a few weeks at a time. They fit in very well, for the hunting business was seasonal at best.

Around the coast of Canada, I worked with a team that did everything from seismic survey work on the Grand Banks of New-foundland in support of oil exploration, to studying the sex life of copepods (immature shrimp) in the Gulf of St. Lawrence.

Many specialties make up the science of oceanography, and most of the work was international in scope, involving scientists from various nations.

Most voyages I was on covered a wide range of programs, all concerned with "gathering pertinent data" for both peaceful and more serious purposes. On one ship, for instance, we sailed on a three-month journey in the Atlantic, where we operated "mid-water trawls" to collect all sorts of sea creatures for study. Pretty routine and boring, except for a couple of side trips to the islands of the Azores.

On another trip I sailed to the Sargasso Sea. I found that trip particularly interesting because we eventually discovered where all the freshwater eels in the Western Hemisphere go to spawn. On the San Pablo and Kelvin seamounts, submerged mountain peaks, we attempted to drill core samples out of the ocean bedrock. In the Mid-Atlantic Deep we sent down devices to capture species never or rarely seen by man. Various probes, core-sampling drills, and dredges went to the ocean bottom to recover both living creatures and samples of mineral deposits.

It was an extremely interesting business and exciting to anyone who enjoyed confronting the unknown. The fact that in some cases the data gathered had uses other than purely scientific was taken for granted. I also made connections on these trips that resulted in offers of employment on other, less publicized projects.

Many of the "scientific" programs I was involved in were based upon the need for early detection of anyone approaching the continent with hostile intent. The emergence of new political forces throughout the Americas and other parts of the world helped keep the pot boiling and my interest up.

Over the course of a few highly eventful years I found my-self involved with what we termed "mad scientists" on some weird and wonderful short-term jobs. I spent a couple of very interesting months in the Azores and Madeira Islands, mostly assisting with the training of what were termed "counter-insur-gency units." Our job was supposedly to help balance the in-volvement of Cuban and other "advisors" in bush wars that are probably still going on.

We monitored and recorded military radio transmissions to enhance the information gathered by U-2 flights over Cuba. Somewhere there probably still exist warehouses full of half-inch magnetic tape and 16mm film from those days. We always speculated that when the codes were broken and the Russian was translated, it would probably be some guy saying, "Send five pounds of bacon, a dozen eggs, a carton of Lucky Strikes, and two rolls of toilet paper."

We spent several weeks working on Barbados, where a team was building and testing a truly awesome weapon, which later gained international recognition as the "Super Gun." This won-derful invention by a Canadian engineer was simply an immense rifle barrel that was supposed to shoot data-gathering satellites into low orbit. Twenty-some years later, the Super Gun showed up as part of the arsenal of Saddam Hussein. The scientist be-hind this project was subsequently executed by the intelligence arm of one of our allies.

On another trip to Barbados, working on a different project, three of us enjoyed ourselves playing tourist. There was plenty of amusement in Bridgetown, including the famous Harry's Place, where one could sample the excellent island rum drinks and eat flying fish, curry, and other exotic dishes. Slightly shocking at first was the fact that the waitresses were all stark naked. Hardy souls that we were, it would take more than that to drive us away.

One evening, along with a group of foreign scientists, we attended a party at a private estate up in the hills. For the occasion we had rented a new Ford Comet—a tight squeeze for six people, but we managed. When it came time to leave, a New Zealander working with us asked to drive. I sat in the middle to help navigate and pass the rum, while a young lady scientist named Eadie sat next to the door. In the back seat were Paul, one of my crew, and a couple of other scientists.

Broad Street in Bridgetown runs right down one of the main docks, and at the end turns abruptly right. We were doing fine until it came time to turn, and then we went straight over the cap of the dock, nose-first into the harbor.

I can see it all in slow motion as if it were yesterday. Car going down into the water like a submarine, headlights still on. In a flash Eadie was out the window. I was immediately behind her, and as I struggled for the surface, I had the ridiculous thought that her fancy party dress, all ballooned out, looked like a giant version of the poison jellyfish we had to avoid while diving.

Treading water, we were vastly relieved as the rest of the party, one after another, popped up to join us. That was as close to a miracle as I will ever witness, proving once again that the Lord looks after fools and drunks.

Up on the dock after a difficult scramble, I fished the card from the car-rental agency from my dissolving wallet, dropped a BeeWee (British West Indies) quarter into the dockside phone, and after several minutes of ringing woke the agent. The conversation went something like this:

"The agreement was that we could leave the car anywhere?"

"Yes! Yes, Mon! Why you wake me up with such a dumb question?"

"Well," I replied, probably spoiling his night's sleep, "the car is at the bottom of Bridgetown Harbor!"

So much for keeping a low profile while working at what was supposed to be a sensitive project.

As if this wasn't bad enough, the following evening my assistant, Paul, brought himself to the attention of the locals in a spectacular manner. With a few rums aboard and wanting to impress one of the American "scientists" with his inventiveness, he hot-wired a big Link Belt mobile crane, drove it through a chain-link fence, and started uptown with it. Unfortunately, upon leaving the dock area, there was a customs checkpoint. As Paul drove up to the building, he ran the projecting crane through the roof—about like poking a stick into a hornet's nest. This little indiscretion led to three extremely uncomfortable days and nights in the local dungeon. Only the intervention of some fairly high-level diplomacy made it possible for us to discreetly ship him out, to avoid any further international embarrassment.

On another fairly interesting multipurpose job, I was based in Bermuda during the autumn hurricane season. Our ship was docked in St. George, a few miles from Hamilton, right in front of the White Horse Tavern. Behind us was docked an immense, rust-covered, Russian factory ship. One look at the antenna arrays decorating her masts told me that part of her job involved fishing for more than fish. Her name in Russian script was something like, Arkhanjelsk. We called it Archangel.

The "mad scientists" on our side were developing another tool for the arsenal of the antisubmarine forces. This new gadget, termed a radio thermometer, was to be used along with sonar buoys to improve the submarine detection capabilities of the aircraft patrols.

Two of us flew with the crews of a specially equipped Argus out of Kinley Field. Spending ten to fourteen hours a day droning along at a hundred feet or less over the ocean is like riding a bicycle up the railroad tracks. I found it bumpy and boring as hell, except for the occasional burst of excitement as we did "pretend" attacks on both our own shipping and the ever-present Soviet and East German spy ships working within their fishing fleets. We always hoped that the enemy appreciated the bit of variety we brought to their likewise boring existence.

Most nights, as I returned late to the ship, the coxswain on gangway watch would tell me that the radio officer from the Archangel had dropped by to invite me to visit the Russian ship. This is fairly common among radio operators around the world. In the middle of the Cold War, odd as it may seem, this sort of fraternization sometimes occurred in neutral ports, as each side thought that its guy would learn something of value from the other side. With the schedule I was maintaining, however, I just didn't have the time.

The aircraft crews, just kids in our eyes, flew every other day, so they were free to party three nights a week. The other "technician" and I, old experienced drunks that we were, could not keep up for long, especially as we flew every single day. Thank God for tomato juice and aspirin.

Toward the end of October, just as the weather was beginning to make low-level flying even rougher, we wrapped up the project and prepared to sail. About an hour before departure, the skipper asked me to go ashore to the White Horse Tavern and round up any of the crew still hanging around the bar.

I was on my second hasty beer, talking to Roland King, who had the evening gangway watch while in port, when in walked a group of officers from the Russian ship. We were aware that women often sailed with the fishing fleet, but few, certainly, were as attractive as the blonde with two rings on her uniform sleeve.

Recognizing Roland, she walked over and in only slightly accented English said, "I see you are departing. Too bad I missed your radio officer. Tell him I would like to show him my equipment if he would show me his sometime."

Three blasts of our ship's whistle ended any further conversation. We made it aboard with the gangway and sailed into the tail end of the latest hurricane.

FRONT-PAGE NEWS

On a voyage intended to be carried out somewhat discreetly, we sailed after Christmas for what is certainly one of the most inhospitable pieces of ocean in the world at that time of year. A project was to be carried out along the route that killed so many men and ships in the convoys sailing to supply Russia during World War II. When one talks to seamen who survived the horrendous conditions, it is apparent that only part of the threat came from German submarines and the aircraft flying out from occupied portions of Scandinavia. The weather and the sea conditions alone were enough to sink many a ship.

Our job was to lay subsurface current meters and recording devices in Denmark Strait, between Greenland and Iceland, and in the Norwegian Sea north of Iceland. As oceanographers and submarine skippers are well aware, these waters are fairly shallow relative to the deeper ocean to the south. Submarines coming from the north, headed for the open Atlantic, had to traverse this area before being able to descend into the safety of the Atlantic Deep. Anyone looking or listening for these submarines paid a lot of attention to that part of the world.

One of the hazards to shipping in winter is the buildup of ice on a ship's superstructure, caused by freezing spray. A vessel can become sufficiently top-heavy and roll over. The only remedy is for everyone from the cook to the captain to work topside, actually breaking up the ice and heaving it overboard.

During one such dangerous incident, we took temporary shelter inside the edge of the ice pack off the east coast of Greenland. Unfortunately, as we maneuvered in the ice, one of our rudders and associated steering gear became seriously damaged. The prudent decision was made to head for shelter in Iceland before another storm occurred, which would have put us in grave danger indeed.

The captain instructed me to make contact with any nearby vessels, in case we needed emergency assistance. In about a minute on the Morse key, I raised the Icelandic fishing factory ship *Narfi*, just over the horizon. They were about to head for port themselves, so her skipper obligingly agreed to escort us in safely.

You Can Take the Boy Out of the Woods, But . . .

In the hope of remaining at least a little bit anonymous, our captain decided that instead of going into the capital, Reykjavik, we would dock in the smaller harbor of Hafnarfjordur, a few miles down the coast. Perhaps repairs could be completed there without drawing any more attention than necessary. Within an hour of making port, we were tied up and repairs on our damaged gear were under way.

The *Narfi* docked behind us, and our captain sent the navigator and me to extend our thanks for the assistance. As a small token of appreciation, we carried along a half-gallon of our best West Indies rum.

We were well received. After a few toasts and a number of sea stories, a most remarkable coincidence began to come to light. The radio officer on the *Narfi*, Ollifur Bjornson, ten years previously had been on an Icelandic trawler. They had run into an iceberg in Davis Strait, and he had sent out a call for assistance.

In what had to be the fluke of the century, it turned out that I had been the operator on the Canadian icebreaker that came to their assistance and towed them into Gothaab, Greenland. This, of course, led to toasts and pledges of undying friendship. The Icelandic people, descendants of the original Norsemen, have a strong affinity for tales to do with survival in the icy seas surrounding their homeland. Seamen are held in the highest esteem, heroes on the level of the North American cowboy.

Sometime during the afternoon, a representative of the press showed up. Pictures were taken despite my modest pleas to remain in the background. By this time we were well-launched on what turned out to be a party of truly epic proportions. Despite our feeble protests, the navigator and I were whisked off ashore for further celebration.

In the lead taxi heading for Reykjavik, the Icelandic captain insisted that we simply had to visit the president of their fishing company. Graciously received by the gentleman and his wife, we were soon drinking another round of toasts to Canadian-Icelandic friendship. The party by this time included the Icelandic skipper, my buddy Ollafur, the radio officer, two other ships' officers, and the photographer from the newspaper, who had tagged along.

The rest of the evening is something of a blur, but upon visiting an office somewhere along the line, I was presented with a silver pin, which I had the presence of mind to place inside the pages of my passport. It attested to the fact that I was a radio officer first class in the Icelandic Maritime Service. More speeches, handshakes, and drinks, of course, were in order.

Our numbers by now had increased from two to six taxis full of revelers, both male and female. Sometime after midnight, while we were helping to close one of the big clubs, either the Porscafe or the Saga, it was decided that all and sundry must proceed to another party at the home of one of the participants.

Icelandic people must certainly rank among the friendliest and most hospitable in the world, if they happen to like you. There are some historic grievances against the United States and Britain, going back to Iceland's occupation by the allies during World War II. However, once they know you are Canadian, and a seaman at that, all the barriers are down. Since being Canadian brings very little benefit in Canada, the navigator and I were pleased to know that we were appreciated somewhere in the world.

When the clubs closed, a whole convoy of taxis wound its way down the coast to a private home somewhere in Keflavik. Here the party continued unabated until most of the participants staggered off to go to their various places of employment. We later came to realize that although we were the excuse for this particular blowout, merrymaking of this magnitude is pretty routine during the Icelandic winter.

Delivered to the dock in a none-too-steady condition, we decided to drop into a little cafe in hopes that a cup of coffee would settle our nerves before we undertook to sneak aboard the ship. Upon spying my face, the lady behind the counter grabbed up a copy of the newly delivered daily paper. "Look! Look!" she shrieked. "Yesterday was Krushchev, today is YOU!"

Sure enough. There was I, taking up nearly the entire front page of the *Morganblad,* the Icelandic equivalent of the *New York Times.* Accompanying a couple of excellent pictures was the epic tale of two heroic radio operators and how we had battled the dangers of the Arctic seas. So much for maintaining a low profile on a delicate mission.

When we were safe and sober, back at sea, some fairly serious messages were received from the upper levels of the outfit we worked for. However, it soon blew over; one advantage of being on an "unofficial" project is that things tend to get swept under the rug fairly quietly.

Once in a while I look at the silver radio officer pin and my souvenir edition of the *Morganblad*, and wonder what else I might have talked about besides the radio business. Fortunately, few of us know anyone who can translate from the Norse language. The exact contents of the article remain a mystery to this day.

SOMETIMES IT PAYS TO BE POLITE

Three of us were in Antwerp in the early sixties on a discreet errand. It involved the acquisition and shipment of some badly needed equipment to friends in a West African country. After accomplishing the job in less time than expected, we had a couple of days to kill, waiting for our ship to make port.

We were staying in a modest little old-fashioned hotel just off the main square in the middle of the city. Across from the big central railway station on Stadesstrat was a real going concern of a nightclub, the Lauchen Cou (Laughing Cow). Outside hung a great carnival-type mockup of a gigantic moving cow head, which actually gave out with a plaintive *MOO* at the passersby. It was a great place to spend some leisure time, full of seamen from all over the world, so strangers were taken for granted. The beer and the polka music were great, as I recall. Things can get a bit rowdy in this type of place, but everyone was simply having a great time when in swaggered a couple of Slavic-featured drunks, probably off some German canal boat.

For an hour or so my mates and I had been watching a little old guy in a funny-looking suit, sitting alone quietly, drinking his beer from one of the big, slim, one-liter glasses for which the bar was famous. On the table he had reverently placed a brown paper bag, which he seemed to be guarding, for he reached out and took hold of it every time the waiter came by. We were amusing ourselves by speculating on what could possibly be in that bag when one of the big blond drunks sat down in the chair opposite the little man. After some loud words, the blond drunk lunged across the table to grab for the paper bag. Bad move! In a flash the beer glass was shattered, then jabbed right smack into the face of the drunken bully. Tables were kicked over while other patrons jumped into the fray, mostly bent on dragging the crazed and blinded drunk out the door and kicking his struggling friend out along with him.

After the police had examined papers, of which we fortunately had plenty, and took statements, the tables were set back up, the beer and glass were cleaned up, the band struck up another rousing polka, and all settled down again.

Buying a new round of beer, I sent an extra one to the table of the little man with the paper bag. As the waiter delivered it with our compliments, he beckoned me over to his table. After a toast, "À votre santé," he handed the paper bag to me, said something in Flemish, and indicated that I should open it. Somewhat gun-shy after the previous performance, I very cautiously opened it up and peeked inside.

You could guess for a million years and never come up with the right answer. It was a harmonica, what we call a mouth organ. He passed me an elegant business card, which I later figured out said that he was a professional classical musician. He invited my two friends over to the table, and we later went out to dinner, for which he insisted upon paying. It turned out that as a young man he had been in the Belgian resistance when Canadian soldiers had liberated Antwerp after the bloody fighting up the Schelde Estuary in the closing months of World War II. We left the next day, so could not take him up on the invitation to visit his family.

It occurred to me later that it cost me only ten Belgique francs for a beer to find out what was in the paper bag. By the looks of things, it had cost the other guy at least one eye and a hell of a pile of stitches . . . and he never did get the bag open.

GATHERING PERTINENT DATA

Following the years spent on Arctic exploration, I was transferred to employment in a more international arena. This was during the coldest part of the Cold War, and events all over the world provided jobs for an entire industry engaged in what one might term "defense-related scientific exploration."

Working initially as radio officer on a foreign-going oceanographic research vessel, I was in effect an employee of the Canadian government. In addition, I was soon working, part of the time, on programs for which the source of funding was somewhat more obscure. With a young family to support at home, I welcomed this "ask no questions" income.

Most of the time the work was entirely legitimate research, open for all the world to see and share, useful for both peaceful and other purposes. For example, the weeks we spent in the North Atlantic—hove to in horrendous weather, heaving your guts out while lowering instruments to the ocean floor to measure temperature, salinity, and oxygen content at various levels— had, we were told, some benefits pertaining to fisheries. On the other hand, accurate mapping of ocean currents, temperature, and salinity levels is very useful when engaged in submarine detection or evasion, depending upon your particular viewpoint.

Some projects called for a high degree of discretion. The standard explanation offered to those without a definite need to know was that we were "engaged in gathering pertinent data." The phrase became a sort of motto, around which many jokes developed.

Now that the Cold War is officially over and peace supposedly exists between the East and the West, one can view those tense and sometimes dangerous times with nostalgia, tinged with a certain amount of humor. At the time, however, everyone seemed to take each situation quite seriously.

With the benefit of thirty-odd years of hindsight, it is obvious that despite the gravity of the times, most of our clandestine projects bore much more resemblance to the adventures of the Coyote and the Road Runner than they did to those of Agent 007. Thankfully, our opponents were just as susceptible to fumbling and bumbling, so things pretty well balanced out in the long run.

Although every "secret" has long since been sold to the enemy or published in best-selling novels, to avoid any embarrassment I will here add the disclaimer that anything in this book to do with what I call my "other life" is entirely fictional. Besides, like all my contemporaries, I enjoyed the occasional beverage in those days and probably imagined much of what went on anyway.

A BELLE OF BELFAST

We were going into Belfast after a couple of rough months in the North Atlantic, and Bobby McGraw, my second operator, was a bit worried. Coming from a strict Irish Catholic family in St. John's, Newfoundland, he had been pumped full of tales of the Civil War and all the religious strife in both the Republic and Northern Ireland.

"Bob," I advised him, "in any port in the world you simply act like a gentleman. Sit with your back to the wall, drink your beer, mind your business, and always go along with the majority."

Not such good advice, as it turned out. Late that night, in the Ferry Boat Inn, known among seamen around the world as the "FBI," Bobby found himself with a difficult choice to make:

> I spent the evening wining and dining a charming young lady named Bernadette. She's as pretty as an angel. My mother would really like her, except for the way she talks. To be safe, I didn't even mention religion. At midnight the band played "God Save the Queen," and everyone in the place got up and stood with their hand over their heart, so, taking your advice, I did the same. Looking down, I saw Bernadette frowning and keeping her seat. "What is the problem?" I whispered. "Sure and she's noo my fookin' Queen!" was the reply.

A bunch of us were sitting around the FBI a couple of evenings later when we heard sirens as police and fire vehicles rushed down the street. No one seemed to get too excited about it, so we finished our beer before leaving for the ship.

Back aboard, we were having a nightcap in the officer's lounge when in rushed Bobby and his lady friend. Looking like refugees from a war zone, they were half-dressed, dirty, and disheveled. Bob had his eyebrows and most of his hair burned off and what we later found out were some fairly extensive flash burns all down the front of his body. Full of whiskey and adrenaline, he was not as yet feeling any pain.

"What in hell happened to you?" we all blurted at once.

The story went something like this: They had taken a room at the old Crown Hotel a few blocks away from the FBI, for what purpose I cannot imagine. Sometime during the festivities, they paused long enough to notice that the temperature in the room was only a few degrees above freezing. There didn't seem to be any temperature control on the wall, but there was a fireplace. Coming from the "New World," our Bob had never before confronted a fireplace that didn't burn wood. Gingerly tiptoeing around in his bare feet on the cold floor, he discovered above the fireplace a black box with a slot into which Bernadette instructed him to drop a sixpence.

All of a sudden there was a hissing noise and a funny smell filled the room. Scurrying around, he at last found a box of matches in his lady friend's purse and struck one. *BOOM!* The resultant explosion hurled him back, almost through the window, the drapes of which instantly burst into flame. With remarkable presence of mind, he tore down the drapes, grabbed blankets off the bed, and smothered the fire. Jumping around amidst smoldering fabric and broken glass, they frantically half-dressed and, carrying the rest of their belongings, scampered down the back stairs into the alley. At that moment, the first emergency vehicle pulled up in front of the hotel.

"My goodness!" moaned the burned and trembling second operator. "I made the taxi driver promise not to tell anyone about picking us up and gave him a good big tip. Mother would never forgive me if she found out I was in any trouble. What do you suppose will happen?"

"Not to worry, me luv," assured the much calmer Bernadette. "Sure and they'll blame it on the fookin' IRA."

Turned out she was right, and we sailed with fond memories of Belfast.

A LITTLE BIT OF RELIGION NEVER HURT ANYONE

The above pretty well sums up my approach to the spiritual. One of my grandfathers told me as a child that rum and religion have at least two things in common. As he put it, "A little bit is probably good for you, but too much will drive you crazy."

I'm far from begging for success in hunting or wealth in business, but I have been known to sneak in the odd "Oh, Lord, please don't let this boat sink." And on a couple of occasions, "Oh, please, Lord, make sure this parachute opens." Aside from that, I have taken a fairly casual approach toward whoever can make any sense out of it all.

In the course of my travels I have had the honor of associating with many truly "good living" persons. Some were Christians, many were not, but all shared the goal of doing the right thing.

Many of the most "religious" people I have been associated with have had a commonsense approach on selected matters. One such was the chief engineer of a ship on which I sailed for a short time.

"Scotty," as the name might imply, was of Scottish descent and a strict adherent to the teachings of the Presbyterian Church. On all matters religious, he was considered the ship's top authority; at all meals in the officers' dining room, he was in charge of giving the blessing. A fairly young man at the time, I regarded him somewhat as the Ayatollah was viewed years later in Iran.

A more human side of the man emerged one evening as we shared a taxi, going ashore in Dunkerque, France. French customs officials are known as some of the most bureaucratic, insulting, and ignorant to be encountered anywhere in the world, a fact that we would soon have confirmed.

On this occasion, although neither Scotty nor I was a smoker, we were held for two hours while our papers were checked and double-checked on suspicion that we were involved in smuggling cigarettes into France. I later learned why they were so afraid of the invasion of foreign smokes. Their own tasted like donkey sh-- rolled up in a newspaper.

At last we were released, our passports were returned, and we stood out on the road in hopes that another taxi would come along to take us to town. Having successfully kept our cool so as not to bring more bureaucratic attention down on our heads, we congratulated each other on seeing it through. Scotty was philosophic about the experience and as usual found refuge in the teachings of the Holy Bible.

"Sparky," he told me seriously, "it is quoted in the Scriptures: 'Love thine enemies, but hate a f--kin' Frenchman'."

I could only agree. After all, Scotty was the expert.

GUIDING . . . THE PROFESSION

Tom Hennessey

The history of North America, like the history of the world, reveals the fact that man originated as a hunter and has remained so in one form or another until the present day. As long as there have been hunters, there have been guides.

If present theories are proved correct, one of the greatest guides of all time was the first man to venture across the land bridge from Asia to spread his followers and their descendants throughout the Americas. Even in those days the people lived by following the migrations of animals, and there were always those who led the way to better hunting. Over the centuries, exploration of all the wild places of the earth has depended upon leaders, guides who will go where others have not. Sometimes called scout, trapper, or professional hunter, these guides have shown the way to new lands, new resources, or exemplary trophies of the chase.

Yes, if guiding is not the world's oldest profession, it must come in a close second. Since Adam was brought out from the Garden of Eden, some men have led and others have followed.

I have been privileged to belong to this profession, and honored to have been acquainted with so many fine men, including a few whose memories went back to the early days of the century. Most of the men I guided with on the Saint John and Tobique Rivers of New Brunswick had worked as loggers, stream drivers, trappers, and guides in the years between the World Wars. Nearly every one of that generation had served overseas in World War II, many as scouts and snipers attached to combat infantry regiments. Guides in war as in peace.

Working for other outfits as well as for our own company, I have known literally hundreds of guides. Some of them have been Whites, notably those in New Brunswick and on the island of Newfoundland. Others have been native North Americans—Micmacs and Malecites in the East, Cree and Naskapi in Quebec, Dogrib and Chipewyan Dene in the West, and Inuit in both Ungava and the central Arctic. They may come from different areas and widely different cultures, but all true guides have much in common.

They make their living out-of-doors. Due partly to circumstances but mostly to choice, they are available for part-time seasonal work as guides. Though they seldom put it into words, one thing they all share is a high degree of pride in their abilities. At times they may assume the role of servant, but when the chips are down, they are the boss. Whether the person in their charge is a millionaire, a member of royalty, or a truck driver from Pittsburgh, he is well advised to be aware of this fact if he is going to have a safe and rewarding journey.

All successful guides are personalities in their own right. The ones who do not realize that they are really engaged in the entertainment industry despite the serious aspects of the job, are often soon forgotten. The ability to be a bit creative is sometimes deemed an asset, especially when game is scarce, and tall tales around the campfire are well received. However, I have met a few guides who always told the absolute truth, and they were well regarded because of other aspects of their personality.

It sometimes amazed me when I would meet previous clients at sports shows down in the cities. They would always remember with fondness some flashy and entertaining guide despite the fact that he might be the laziest guy in the crew. Meanwhile, the hardworking plodder might go unnoticed when it came time to pass out the tips. Sometimes human nature is fickle. Fortunately, a majority of the experienced and perceptive guests appreciate the worth of the truly great guides.

In Canada, from the Atlantic to the Pacific and even in the Arctic, various interfering government agencies have devised schemes over the years to train and certify and regulate the guiding profession. These programs seldom do anyone any good, and it has always been a struggle to make sure they do not ruin what has worked properly since time immemorial.

Guiding ... The Profession

Guides learn to be guides by working with experienced guides, not by sitting through some course taught by a college-trained schoolteacher. Most of the very best guides have limited formal education, and indeed a good proportion of the older native guides do not even speak English.

Fortunately, there are signs that the people involved in establishing the new self-government of Nunavut are willing to try the old ways—learning from the elders. The old ways are the best, and we hope this becomes the way of doing things once again across Canada. Otherwise the tradition and the ethic of guiding will be lost forever.

I believe that as long as there are people wanting to travel the wild places, there will always be guides to lead them.

THE EDUCATION
OF A PROFESSIONAL BEAR HUNTER
(or, Attaining the M.B.E.)

Tom Hennessey —

When we first started hunting bears, as opposed to trapping them, the consensus in the country was that you began with a dead horse. Horses were still being used in the lumber woods, and in those pre-Humane Society days dead ones were in good supply, especially around camps employing Frenchmen. Transporting an animal weighing two-thirds of a ton was something of a problem, so the ideal was to secure one that was still breathing and mobile. We were rarely that lucky, and it was usually necessary to invite a teammate to the funeral.

It occurred to me fairly early in my career that just because our forefathers had worn themselves out at an early age was no reason to continue the folly. Surely, something lighter and more portable would entice Old Bruin to show himself so the fearless dude could get a shot into him.

One winter when I was trapping with Ab Higgins, I received a call from a farmer downriver. He had lost a cow to the dreaded shipping fever. At that point our hardscrabble outfit could not yet afford a truck, but Ab was the proud owner of a big pre-war hearse. I think it was a Cadillac, and he used it as a family car and general runabout. Getting a full-sized, stiff-legged, rangy old Holstein cow into that hearse was a job in itself. Little did we know that our journey was only beginning.

The logging company had a road plowed up into the mountains bordering the Mamozekel River; the snow anywhere off that road was at least eight feet deep. We had a hell of a job winching the cow out of the hearse and atop the snowplowed rim of the road, and only managed to accomplish the task with a set of blocks and tackle. Naturally, the next time the plow came down from the camps, the cow was rolled under. Out of sight, out of mind, at least for a while.

When the snow started to melt in mid-April, lo and behold, the cow surfaced. Although no one had ever heard the term "environmental pollution" in those days, we began to receive complaints about littering. The complainer was a local resident famous for maintaining a house and yard that would put a Los Angeles landfill to shame. As with a lot of other "concerned environmentalists" I have known, this guy had plenty of time to stick his nose into other people's business. Having, as rumor had it, twisted his back while stealing a skidder tire from the lumber company, he lived quite comfortably on welfare and worker's compensation.

When the snow finally melted and after about six aborted attempts, we managed to haul the accursed critter a couple of miles up a ridge, where we hoped to bag a bruin. In a country full of bears, that thing lay there for a solid month, swollen up to four times its original size and nothing bigger than a blowfly touched it. Finally, on one visit with an old sport named Pete, from Lancaster, Pennsylvania, Ab decided that not enough odor was escaping. He soon rectified the matter, giving the carcass a good rip with his belt knife.

An hour later we were boiling the kettle down by the brook. After the sport's bread was nicely toasted on a forked stick, Ab pulled out the very same belt knife used a bit earlier and proceeded to lay on some margarine. "Whoa! Stop! NO THANKS," the guest cried. "My doctor says I'm not supposed to eat any butter!"

We never did kill a bear on that bait, and I vowed to never again accept the gift of a dead cow.

A few years later, and not much wiser, I was working with Rudy Richter. A large pig operation sixty miles away called to see if we wanted a truckload of well-deceased swine. Good old Rudy—never one to turn down a bargain—went over and completely filled the camper body of our four-wheel-drive truck.

After letting it sit in his dooryard for a week at temperatures down to minus forty degrees, he called me over. Seems he was having difficulty unloading. The pigs had most inconsiderately frozen solid in a cementlike lump with their darling little trotters wedged in behind the frame of the end door on the camper.

We tried axes, sledgehammers, and crowbars. We could not move one single grunter. Eureka! I had a bright idea.

Wrapping a top chain around the first candidate, I hooked it to a telephone pole out by the gate and butted ahead in four-wheel-drive. Great move—I broke the pole off at the level of the frozen ground and knocked out half the telephones in that country for nearly a week.

Back to the drawing board. We finally managed, after many unpleasant hours, to buck up the frozen corpses with a chain saw and remove them a piece at a time. If you have never worked inside a truck camper on your knees in the guts and gurry, being choked by carbon monoxide and showered with pig sawdust, you will not attain your Doctorate in Bear Baiting.

We had no option but to keep learning on the job. Unfortunately, there was no one to ask for advice; the other local outfitters were even dumber than we were. They were still back at Lesson One, the Complete Dead Horse.

For several years thereafter, we would go "down country" to the farms and slaughterhouses and fill our truck with the various leftover bits, pieces, and by-products. Hauled in an open truck, our loads did not gain us a whole lot of friends, but we did notice that when we pulled up for lunch at any of the fast-food joints along the route, we usually received quick service.

Tommy Everett and I were stopped at a gas station with a full load one day when an ex-schoolteacher of mine pulled into the next lane. After he'd carefully scrutinized the load, recognition dawned as he looked over at me. "By Jesus, Webb," he said. "I always thought you would end up doing something like this." My reply will not be printed here.

Progress being inevitable, even in the hunting business, sometime around 1970 I decided to start hauling bait in metal barrels.

This would at least make the process a little more efficient.

I will always remember the pronouncement by one of my veteran Riley Brook competitors: "Jesus Christ, what does Webb think he's doing now? Bears will never come near those barrels." Seeing as how we annually killed more bears than the rest of them combined, it soon became impossible to obtain empty barrels within three hundred miles.

For the next fifteen years or so, the hauling of slaughterhouse offal in forty-five-gallon drums became the accepted modus operandi for everyone in the bear-hunting business. It continues to this day among the less-informed, which takes in most of the current crop of operators.

Unlike many of my colleagues who believe in tradition—meaning that as long as father and grandfather screwed up, the only course is to screw up ourselves—our outfit continued to experiment. Having the benefit of experience in other areas of the North, where attracting grizzly and polar bears is definitely not viewed in a positive manner, I began to revise my thinking about bear baiting.

Although we have always considered and advertised the black bear as an elusive and cunning foe, it finally became clear to me that in 99 percent of the cases, he ranks on the intellectual scale somewhere between the raccoon and the groundhog. Though clever, perhaps, when compared with some of the people hunting him, he is not even in the ballpark with critters such as the wolf, wolverine, fox, white-tailed deer, elk, and a dozen other animals.

No, the truth of the matter is that the poor old black bear, trying to scrounge a living, does not need a whole lot of encouragement to come to dinner. Like a freelance outdoor writer locking onto an inexperienced outfitter, as long as it is free and available, he is going to take it.

That old bear, often existing on a diet of vegetation and ants, when hit with a jolt of high-carb sweets or high-energy fat is about as much inclined to give it up as your average inner-city pharmacology fan is inclined to give up Needle Alley. Lest anyone wish to argue, I realize that there are exceptions, but they are few and far between. In all probability, once a bear has indulged on the right offering, he is going to return. If by chance he is a bit clever, he may come in the dark, but aside from that, the only way to keep him from the bait is to put some dude there who refuses to do what the guide tells him.

For a half-clever bear, you must at least sit still, watch the wind, and not go for walks so that you spread man scent all over the area. Fortunately for professional bear guides, even if you persist in doing everything wrong, a certain percentage of bears are so determined to commit suicide that they will stroll in despite all efforts to the contrary. One has only to experience a camp-raiding bear to realize that once Old Bruin has sampled the Good Stuff, it is very difficult to keep him from coming back.

From the late 1970s onward—first for economic reasons and later because it was the proper thing to do—we cut down drastically on the amount of bait used.

I am not at this late date going to bother educating my smart competitors or arguing with the stupid ones, but by the time we quit black-bear baiting, we were accomplishing better results with bait carried in our hip pockets than we ever did with a boxcar load. Although we never, ever broke a game law, we occasionally hunted areas where certain people made it clear we were not welcome. We did it with methods so subtle that no one, except the bear, ever knew we were in the country.

It took thirty years in the College of Hard Knocks, but we graduated with a doctorate in Bear Baiting and achieved the pinnacle in the profession—the title of M.B.E., Master Baiter Extraordinaire.

CAN'T WIN 'EM ALL

I was guiding in a deer camp one time for Lenny Waters up on Serpentine, and we got in a bunch of Long Island Italians. Eight of 'em there were, which in those days meant eight guides, cook, cookie, and the boss outfitter—quite a crew. Pretty nice set of camps, once the chinkin' between the logs was tightened up and the mouse shit shook out of the mattresses. We had a real good cook, nicknamed Old Pig Lips. He was known around the country for liking boys too much, but I didn't give him any chance to prove it.

These Italians were a pretty nice bunch; seemed awful loud to us, though. But then, most of us guys were pretty quiet. The first night in camp they got in a big row over who would kill the first deer and the biggest and all that stuff, kept pushin' us guides for answers, but all we could tell them was that we would get out there in the woods and look around the best we could.

They put up prizes, and the biggest prize of all was going to be a full half-gallon of Wild Turkey whiskey to the guide who got his sport the biggest deer.

We guides talked it all over in the guide shack later, and as Tommy put it, "Jesus, I would dearly love to get my hands on that whiskey, but you know the woods are awful dry and noisy, and did you get a look at the size of the feet on these guys?"

"Yup," Blake chimed in, "and they all got them swishy rubber pants you can hear comin' for three miles. We'll be goddam lucky if even one of us gets a deer so we can split that bottle!"

"Well," spoke up Eddy (a young guide that Blake described one time as a "nice enough young feller, but he don't know nothin'!"), "don't you old bastards worry. I'm goin' to win that jug, and it is goin' home with me for Christmas."

"Guess that lets us out, boys. Blow out the goddam lantern or none of us will be up at five o'clock." My partner, LeRoy, had the last word.

Next mornin' the boss outfitter lined us up, and we drew straws for which sports we would take out. LeRoy and I drew two old brothers. At least they looked in half-decent shape, though both of them wore glasses thicker than Coke bottles. "Christ, Fred," said LeRoy, "do you think them guys can shoot anything? At least we didn't draw that big pussy-gutted old feller that Eddy got. Maybe between us we can get that Wild Turkey—what do you think?"

We decided to hunt together, so as to be able to travel a bit farther and have help handling the deer if we shot any. LeRoy's man, old Dave, drew the straw to shoot first.

Can't Win 'Em All

Weather stayed good for picnics, lousy for deer hunting—clear and sunny with dry leaves underfoot. First day, nothing killed. Second day, one guy gave in and shot a button buck. Third day, a little forkhorn and a spike buck came in. Fourth day, two trophy hunters broke down and killed two does.

All week, me and LeRoy had been mostly sittin' around on ridges. It was impossible to still-hunt. Every time we tried, it meant sloggin' along like a freight train and diggin' them big-footed old dudes out of blowdowns. If we had any hope at all, it would be watchin' some of the half-growed-up timber cuts or around a lick.

Just before lights-out that night, old Blake spoke up in the guide tent: "Well, boys, that just leaves three of you to kill somethin'. That little forkhorn my man paunched is startin' to look bigger and bigger."

"Don't worry," said Eddy, "big one comin' in tomorrow, and me and the old woman will have that Turkey for Christmas."

LeRoy and I looked at each other and didn't say nothing.

Next mornin', we got started an hour before daylight hit the swamp. Just us and Eddy still deer huntin', rest of them goin' to sleep in, play cards, and maybe go out later for some birds.

Me and LeRoy had made it up that we would walk right from camp with lunch in our packs and give the old guys a good workout. We figured to travel the ridges for the mornin' while it was still a bit damp, then come out on the edge of a three-year-old clear-cut on the head of Five Mile Brook to sit for the afternoon. We had figured for the boss to drive around by the road and meet us at dark on the other side of the cut.

Middle of the afternoon we were layin' on the sidehill, lookin' across at the other slope, which had been cut, roads crisscrossing back and forth, covered in new growth—good deer feed. I had an ace in the hole that I never mentioned to anyone. Early in the season I had found a small mineral lick in a little spring on the side of one of the bulldozed roads. There were lots of tracks around it. It could be all dried up this late in the season, but what the hell, might as well look at this hillside as any for the last afternoon.

We'd been layin' there quite a spell. The old sports were snorin' away, me and LeRoy scannin' with binoculars. All of a sudden I spotted him, biggest goddam buck deer in the country. He was pickin' his way along the side of the bank and then stopped over there about three hundred yards straight across, and began pawin' around that little lick. I pointed him out to LeRoy.

"Boy, oh, boy, I can taste that Wild Turkey right now," he said and got old Dave woke up and squared around. Great big magnum rifle, scope on it big as the headlight on my truck, no problem to hit that deer from a dead rest.

But Dave couldn't see the buck. "Jesus Christ, man, do you see that big pine on top of the ridge?" Dave nodded excitedly. "OK, now, come right down the hill from there to that big stump on the side of that road." Dave nodded. "Now, come left along that road and there stands the buck!" Poor old Dave, try as he might—took off his glasses and cleaned them, squinted through his scope—he just couldn't see that deer.

My sport, even though it wasn't his turn to shoot—and he couldn't see the deer anyway—was squirming and a sort of whining sound was coming out of him. I dug him in the ribs and shut him up.

"Jesus, LeRoy, let me try—we gotta kill that deer." I squared old Dave away and pointed again. "You see that little clearin' with the white birch around it?" Dave saw it. "OK, now you come down from there, about two fingers wide, and there's a rock. You go left from the rock and you'll see a leanin' popple that didn't get cut, then straight down from that is a piece of the road, and there is the deer." Goddamned if he could see it.

Just then I glassed uphill, searchin' for more landmarks, and was horrified to see two figures comin' out at the top of the slope. I pointed them out to my partner. "Holy Christ!" exploded LeRoy. "That's that goddamned Eddy—must have drove in from the other side. Now that fat old bastard will kill the deer and we'll never get a smell of that bottle."

He grabbed old Dave by the collar, looked him straight in the eye: "Now, by Jesus, you're the only man can save us now." Took him by the ears and aimed him at the hill, tried once more, but Dave couldn't see the buck. In a few minutes it would be history. They'd be comin' around a turn in the road just fifty yards from the deer. With a sigh of disgust, LeRoy grabbed his sport one more time.

"Now, you see that big lightnin'-hit spruce at the foot of the hill here right in front of you?" Dave nodded. "OK, go right up the tip of it and right straight up the hill. You see a big white rock on the edge of that bulldoze rim?" Dave nodded again, all excited. "Now, you go to the right about a hundred yards, then up the hill to that white birch." Dave, peering through his scope was right on track. "OK, now you go straight up that birch to the next road, then go left . . . do you see that fat guy in the red teddy-bear suit?"

"Yes! Yes! I see him. I see him plain as day!"

"All right, then," roared LeRoy, *"Shoot the son of a whore!"*

LONE TRAPPER

It's three in the afternoon on a mid-December day and the light is beginning to fade, even here on the open lake. Third day away from home base, including one night in an abandoned logging camp and one in a brush wigassee with an all-night fire in front. Now this part of the line is tended, and I can almost taste the good hot supper my wife and partner will have waiting at our main camp in Nictau.

A good night's sleep in a bed warmed by a lover's presence is incentive enough for any kind of journey. Sure beats choking on smoke when the wind shifts, watching for sparks on your sleeping bag, and shifting to keep the knots on the spruce-pole bed from digging into your bones. Winter camping on the trapline may seem exciting to the person who only reads about it, but in reality it is definitely not that much fun.

Gear is packed and wrapped in the tarp, and lashed on the sled along with the frozen pelts of a dozen beaver and three otter, skinned at the last two nights' fires. Eight marten, one fisher, and a snared bobcat, all still in the round, remain frozen solid and lashed on top of the load. A couple days spent at home will provide time to thaw them out, flesh them properly, and get them on the stretchers to dry.

That'll be just about time for the fur buyer to come through the country, hopefully before Christmas or it will be a slim one for the kids.

The 1967 model sixteen-horsepower Skidoo has certainly made it easier to cover a wide-ranging line. In the old days, on snowshoes alone, the round trip would have meant at least a couple of weeks away from home and family. The $650 it cost brand new seemed like a lot of money, but it has been paid for and then some. It has been a reliable, if somewhat impersonal, partner on the trapline.

Choke set, ignition on, one good pull, and the starter cord breaks halfway through the pull! As I stand rubbing my strained and fast-freezing right hand inside the mitten on my left, I look to the sky to see if anyone is watching. Better modify my cursing, just in case. May need help before the night is over.

Across the high blue bowl of the heavens, a white trail arcs from the north toward the south. Probably one of the big nuclear bombers from the Strategic Air Command base in Limestone, Maine returning from patrol across the Pole. Guarding our freedom, or so we have been told.

"Mr. Pilot," I say to the silence, "you are sure as hell going to be warm and full of supper long before I am tonight."

Darkness is almost on me now, and the temperature has dropped to about twenty-five below. The wind is starting to kick up the snow a bit. It is damned tempting to unload the gear from the sled, get out the ax, dig a hole in the snow at the edge of the thicket, and get a good fire going. Easy enough to have ice melted and water boiling for a hot cup of tea within ten minutes or so.

No! To hell with that! Darkness, windblown snow, and forty miles or not, I am going to have my feet on the oven door at home sometime tonight. Digging out the little tool kit, I find the flat wrench. The sizes are in metric, which I don't pretend to understand, but the end that says 10mm is the one that fits the little bolts on the starter housing. A few minutes' struggle, a few curses, a skinned knuckle on my frozen right hand, and the starter falls away. Carefully I save the bolts; surely I can fix it later at home. The cord is broken in two nearly equal lengths, neither long enough for a good pull.

The nylon rope that closes the top of my knapsack is just about right. With the last bit of feeling in my hands, I wrap it around the end of the engine shaft and around my wrist. Snow has been blown out of the carburetor intake; the choke is closed again. There! A long, smooth pull and the engine catches. The little one-cylinder Rotax idles roughly, rocking in its mounts. A little nudge on the gas trigger—partial and then full opening of the choke—and she levels out. Music to my ears for sure.

Now there is time to repack the sled, after which I put the skinned and sprained hand inside my shirt to thaw out on my bare belly. Sled hitched up, parka pulled tight to lessen the bite of the wind, and I am ready to hit the trail. Full dark and the wind is dropping; the stars are out. Not that I need it for guidance in my home territory, but the old North Star up there over my right shoulder is comforting anyway.

There's been new snow since I've been out, but with any luck I'll see the light in the kitchen window in less than four hours. The kids should be just about finishing their lessons; supper will be warming in the oven. Couple or three days, and I will be back out on the western part of the line. Fur is bringing a good price this year, and it's a long time until spring bear guiding.

Trapping pays the bills.

ENCOUNTER WITH A SLIPPERY CUSTOMER

As a young man I had been told by a guide whose experience went back to the turn of the century that there were only four basic rules every guide must remember:

1. Always keep your ax sharp;
2. Keep your matches dry;
3. Don't sleep with the old sport's wife; and
4. Never get into a pissing match with a skunk.

I had done pretty well sticking to those rules, but one memorable summer about forty years ago, I very nearly backslid on at least a couple of them. It came about like this:

Since the dams were built on the river, the Atlantic salmon runs had been badly disrupted, despite the promises of the government biologists and the advocates for more hydroelectric power. With the loss of this, our most valuable resource, most of the outfits were trying to convert to trout fishing and family vacation parties, an enormous step backward in both prestige and economics. The Glory Days were over, never to return.

Before the launch of our own outfitting business, I was guiding for anyone who had a job to offer. That year it was to be for Jim Hayden up on Little Tobique. Four dollars a day for all the daylight hours—about eighteen of them during July. Meals and a bunk in the guide shack, but bring your own canoe and riggin'.

The previous winter, all the guides and outfitters had been invited to a meeting in Plaster Rock, the nearest town, thirty miles downriver. Some guy had come all the way from York, Pennsylvania by train and was installed in the old Valley Inn. He wanted to talk to all of us about being our booking agent.

This was the first time any of us had ever heard the term "booking agent." The sports had always come to the big clubs and outfits for as long as anyone in the country could remember. Some had come through two World Wars and the Depression, and were into third and fourth generations.

About twenty-five of us showed up for this meeting, as everyone in the valley was either a guide or an outfitter in those days. It didn't take long to find out that this guy had a real line of what I will charitably term "salesmanship." In fact, he was so good that old Jim Hayden and at least three others fell for it hook, line, and sinker.

Encounter with a Slippery Customer

My first impression was that here was a real slippery customer. In our part of the country a slippery customer was a wheeler-dealer around whom you would be well advised to hang onto your wallet. As it turned out, before the year was over I would become familiar with two different slippery customers, one of them much more closely than intended.

On the way back upriver that night with four of us jammed into the cab of a half-ton truck, the vote was split on whether or not this guy could be trusted. Old Jim, who had lined me up to guide for the summer, had been the first to go along with the guy and had signed a contract.

He told us, "You know, boys, it's hard to pick up sports nowadays, and this is a foolproof plan. You notice that he only asked to take 10 percent as his share. Why, all I have to do is add 20 percent to my price and I'll be in clover."

Although I was still guiding for others, I had plenty of plans to become a big-wheel outfitter myself. And even at that age, I had few illusions about getting something for nothing. I was also very doubtful about guiding someone who had been booked by an agent who had not even seen our country.

As the season approached, I would run into old Jim once in a while, and he told me that he had heard from the agent; there were plenty of promises but so far no deposits. I was beginning to wonder if I had made a mistake. Maybe I should have stuck with guiding for the other club, where the people at least always came on time, even if the wages were lower.

"Maybe I was too greedy to fill the camps up," Jim told me. "Maybe I made a mistake with this guy. I hope to hell I haven't put us all into the hands of a slippery customer."

"Sure hope not," I replied, "but come to think of it, at the time, I thought he might turn out to be a slippery customer. I never met a used-car salesman who wasn't, and he said that was his main line of work."

As it turned out, the very first party to arrive convinced us that our friend the booking agent was indeed a slippery customer in the extreme. Not only had he wheeler-dealered the price down, then taken his 10 percent off the top, he had also lied outrageously in order to sell the trips.

We had people arriving expecting far more in the way of fishing, accommodations, and facilities than we could provide. He had sold them everything from the scenic seacoast to the Rocky Mountains and most of what lies between.

Accustomed to guiding affluent Atlantic salmon fishermen, we were now down to family vacation parties. There is no doubt that it is easier to guide people who do not expect miracles for their money and who can afford to be there in the first place.

There is a saying in the guiding business that in dealing with the public you will always run into a certain percentage of pricks. And it is always better to guide rich pricks than poor pricks. No doubt about it!

Naturally, everyone at our end, especially the guides, was stuck with trying to make up for the fact that the booking agent had ripped us off. Week after week we did our very best to make the clients happy. Finally, about the first of August, a party arrived that pushed us to the very limit.

The guy, Tom, was about fifty, his newly acquired wife, Nancy, about thirty-five. They had with them two boys of around ten and twelve, the result of his former marriage.

Within two minutes the other guide, Wallace, and I knew what we were up against.

Family relations were already strained after a three-day drive up from Maryland. It didn't help matters that the booking agent had told them they were coming to a resort with a swimming pool and horse rides when actually it was a bunch of log camps in the woods with a smudge fire to keep the flies away and mouse sh-- under the bunks.

It was also apparent that poor old Tom was caught, as we used to say, "between the ledge and the top of the falls." Anyone could see that he was trying to please the kids, who had been poisoned by their mother, while attempting to provide a honeymoon for the new wife at the same time. I could tell this was going to be a great week.

On the first day we sailed downriver together. Wallace took Tom and the oldest kid, and I put Nancy and the other brat in my canoe. This simply did not work out. The little darlings thought we were in some sort of competition during the fishing and in a race when traveling, and in general did their best to infuriate their parents.

When they got to wrestling and kicked over the boiling kettle and knocked the frying pan into the fire, Wallace and I decided that we would do things differently for the rest of the week.

The new wife put up with the shenanigans but made no effort to hide the fact that she didn't think the family had much of a future if it included the two nose-pickers.

It was decided back at camp that Wallace, with his bigger canoe, would take Tom and the monsters, leaving it up to me to entertain the lady. This did not hurt my feelings too much.

The water level was going down in the midsummer heat, and I didn't mind having a neat and compact companion instead of old, fat Tom and his two tubby kids.

Next morning, having split up the gear and lunches, we took off on different sections of the river. The lady seemed to be a lot more interested in the fishing and the country once away from the rest of the family.

We guides always had a policy that if the guest wanted to talk, then we would listen. If they didn't, that was fine with us also. In this case, within half a day I acquired more than enough information about the entire family—all of its history: personal, financial, medical, and otherwise. As a guide I was used to being a companion, a servant, or a babysitter, but this was my first experience as a marriage counselor.

Confession apparently is good for the spirit, because the next morning she was down waiting by the canoe before I had the lunch packed and ready to go. The day being bright and sunny, the trout weren't biting too good, but it didn't seem to matter to my customer. Having given up sitting looking toward the bow, she arranged the seat to face me while she told me more about life in suburban Baltimore.

It seems she had been a receptionist in Tom's law office when they'd started "fooling around"—a quaint description for what turned into quite a torrid affair. At that time he was fit and successful with a wife and two small kids, but apparently lacked something or other in his marriage.

"I should have quit while I was ahead," she confided. "It was the perfect setup—romantic lunches, trips to faraway cities as his assistant. Then his wife found out about it."

Encounter with a Slippery Customer

I tried to make sympathetic but noncommittal comments. After all, my main job was to pole the canoe, stay off the rocks and bars, and keep out from under the sweepers. If my guest wasn't too interested in fishing, no problem; the week has only so many days one way or the other. She appeared to be enjoying herself, and aside from running the boat, getting lunch ready, and helping her apply suntan lotion, life wasn't too strenuous.

That night in camp old Jim came down to the guide shack to complain to me and Wallace again that he had really been taken in by the booking agent. "Boys," he said, "it sure looks like I have been flummoxed by that slippery customer of an agent. He was supposed to have twelve paying customers here, and all we have is this one cut-rate family special." It didn't take much brains to figure out that with all his other expenses, old Jim would be hard put to come up with our wages at the end of this most interesting week.

"I'm doing okay with Tom and the boys," Wallace told me. "Just as long as the little bastards can catch fish and throw rocks at the birds and squirrels, they're happy. Maybe I can get through the week without kicking their asses after all."

Wallace, older and wiser than I, then added, "You better be careful how you handle her. Any goddamn fool can see she's taken a shine to you, and even old dumb Tom will notice sooner or later."

"Oh, sh--," I laughed, "she's just feeling her oats now that she's clear of those boys for a few hours a day. And besides, I always remember that rule about not sleeping with the old sport's wife, no matter how good lookin' she happens to be."

"Well, seeing as I've been around a lot longer than you have, I'm goin' to give you some more good advice," Wallace said as he pointed his old black-stem pipe at me. "Whenever in danger or in doubt, I have always gone to the scriptures for guidance. And you might better do the same."

The next couple of days were pretty routine. In the morning Jim would haul Wallace and his share of the party upriver to Red Bank, where they would put in and fish down to the camp. Nancy and I would leave and sail downriver, to be picked up again in the afternoon at Little Cedar Bridge.

Weather remained perfect, hot during the middle of the day, with an upstream wind developing late in the afternoon, but nothing to give me any trouble poling the canoe. As always, "no-see-ums" were around early in the morning, but out on the river there was always breeze enough to keep the bugs away.

The customer was still enjoying herself. Not much interested in fishing, she brought along a book and spent half her time reading passages to me while taking the opportunity to acquire a suntan. I ran the canoe, always content to expand my education by whatever means. By the fifth day, her uniform had gradually become scanty enough so that she needn't worry too much about having any white streaks to spoil her new tan.

As old Jim said after picking us up at the landing, "My God, that woman hasn't got enough cloth on her ass to pad a crutch!"

I had to agree, but wasn't in much of a position to complain, especially with only one day to go.

As we got the canoes ready next morning, Wallace kidded me, "You mind what I told you about quoting the scriptures and looking out for that woman. I wouldn't want to lose our tip for the week—especially as Jim probably isn't going to pay us after that slippery customer held back the money on him."

I was starting to regret having mentioned any worries I may have had around Wallace and Jim. After all, we were right down to the last day on the river, then the guests would all go home and forget they ever heard of this bunch of bushwhackers on the Tobique.

"Well, it's sure nice to have so much good advice from you old bastards, but yesterday, after she got me to rub on her suntan oil, I really had to look sharp to see the rocks in the channel."

"But did you remember what we told you?" old Jim butted in. "One time I broke my pole right on the brink of the big falls on Serpentine, but my faith in the Bible saw me through—I grabbed up the paddle, and we sailed clear to the Narrows."

"Yeah, I tried that yesterday. Got clear through the Psalms and halfway through the commandments, but somehow or other I started to choke when I got down to that one that says, 'Thou shalt not commit adultery'."

Here the conversation ended as our guests came down from their cabin. Tom and the boys were all geared up for another day's fishing, while my sport came lugging a little bag, two pillows from the camp, and a gallon thermos jug.

"How about your fishing rod and raingear?" I asked. "It's going to be a long day. I've got extra lunch, and we'll sail right on out to the Forks."

"Perfect," she said. "I've brought along a new book, and the cook has made us a whole jug of iced lemonade. You might have to let me out once in a while to go to the ladies' room."

Wallace and old Jim rolled their eyes heavenward, and I replied more gruffly than intended, "Well, there ain't a hell of a lot of those between here and Nictau, but we'll do our best." I pushed off before getting any more good advice. We were down around the first turn when I heard the truck heading upriver.

Tom and the boys would work Wallace to death releasing trout and retrieving their hooks from the bushes all day, I figured. Probably I was lucky. All I had to do was stay between the banks and off the rocks and make polite conversation.

Little Tobique, when there is a decent pitch of water, is the nicest stream in the world for a guide who can pole a canoe. It mostly meanders along scenic banks, but is sometimes tricky on the turns as bars tend to form out into the curve, and every so often trees blow down across the channel—what the old-time stream drivers called "sweepers." Minor hazards to avoid. The whole stream from Nictau Lake down to the Forks is a joy to run.

On a beautiful day in summer, with a bit of a breeze to keep the flies at bay and a pretty lady for a customer, no guide in his right mind should be complaining. Having to stop on a sandbar once in a while, since the lady didn't wish to attend the "ladies' room" in the tall grass ashore, was not too much of an inconvenience. I could always look up at the sky or check the canoe for leaks or something.

By noon we had passed Little Cedar and had lunch on a bar just below. My companion had been enjoying the sail and reading me passages from her new book. From the standpoint of what we see nowadays, it was a pretty tame book, but for those days in our part of the country, it would have been called "kind of racy."

Encounter with a Slippery Customer

The title was *Lady Chatterley's Lover*, and the story, as she explained it, was about a lady who fell in love with an English gamekeeper. Although I thought a gamekeeper was some sort of game warden, she insisted that it was really about the same as a guide. News to me, but who am I to argue.

At the head of the ledges, I put her ashore on a narrow beach so she could once more visit the ladies' room. As good a term as any, I thought, given the fact that she was terrified of going into the bushes but made do with some grace behind the bow of the grounded canoe. I studied the clouds going by and remembered what the boys had told me about thinking of the scriptures.

Up until this point she had been wearing her skimpy shorts and a shirt that looked like it was made from two handkerchiefs. Now, with the sun beaming down, she said she would like to change into something new she had brought along for special occasions. Would I mind turning my back for a moment?

Naturally I complied—the customer is the boss, after all—but I wondered where in hell she carried a change of costume in that little bitty bag that held her suntan oil, book, and camera. When invited to turn around again, I saw instantly that what she termed her "new bikini for special occasions" would have fit nicely in my shirt pocket, with room left over for my tobacco and sunglasses.

"OK," I suggested, "let's get going. It's starting to cloud up a bit in the west, and I wouldn't be surprised if we got a thunderstorm in a few hours."

"Would you mind helping me one more time with my suntan lotion? Then I won't bother you again for a while."

51

That done, we set sail. Running a canoe with a pole is a bit of an art and a science. Standing up in the stern gives the boat runner a good view of any obstacles, around which he can turn or snub up and swing over, when running shallow water. In this case, I was getting about all the view inside the boat that I could tolerate.

Most ladies of my acquaintance shaved under their arms in the summer, and a few of the more daring had started shaving their legs. Our fashion up here tends to lag behind that of the cities by quite a bit, but this guest had the cities beat by miles!

The best of canoe men occasionally bump a rock. *Bang*! Now I hit a boulder barely under the water dead-on. Off-balance, I was launched in two giant steps the length of the twenty-foot canoe, cracked my shins on the crossbar, and landed on top of my guest, upsetting her lemonade.

Scrambling up, cursing and embarrassed, I grabbed for the canoe pole that was floating away and tried to ignore the blood running down my skinned legs. At last I regained my composure and my place in the stern.

"Look," I managed to croak, "would you mind sitting up and looking to the front? Maybe you can help me spot the rocks or something." I returned to poling the canoe, keeping one eye on the clouds that continue to blacken and trying to recall the scriptures that are supposed to help during such occasions.

"I think we are in for a real bad thunderstorm here pretty soon," I said to break the uncomfortable silence. "These things blow up pretty fast this time of year, and you have to get in off the water when they do."

Encounter with a Slippery Customer

"Oh, that's OK—I know you will take good care of me," she said, arranging herself facing me once more. "I'm not afraid of a little rain. I haven't got much on to get wet anyway."

With that I heartily agreed.

We were drifting down a long, straight, slow stretch below the mouth of Lunch Hole Brook when the upriver breeze turned into a hard, gusty wind and the first big drops of rain started to bounce off the water.

On one shore was a low swamp with tall green grass, stinging nettle, and no shelter. On the west side for most of a mile there was nothing but sheer clay bank with trees hanging over. No doubt about which side to head for. I soon had the canoe grounded on a two-foot beach at the foot of the clay bank. It was now raining so hard I could barely see the length of the canoe, and the thunder was deafening. We were soaked. The rain so far was as warm as dishwater, but I knew it could turn into hail within minutes.

"Come on," I hollerd over the noise of the downpour, "we've got to get up over the bank into the thicket before this gets any worse!"

Quickly I tied the canoe to a root—it might fill up and sink, but I could always dump it. Grabbing my ax and raincoat, I heaved them up over the bank. Now to get up the slope ourselves!

It was a sheer clay cliff maybe eight to ten feet high with a few tree roots sticking out of it, seemingly impossible to climb. There was only one way to do it. I told my customer I would try to boost her up so she could grab a good solid tree root and shinny on up, then give me a hand.

I am going to tell you right now that trying to hoist a 125-pound nearly nude female up a sheer cliff is not something every guide has attempted. To begin with, there are only so many handholds on the human body, and this one seemed to have fewer than usual. You may have heard the terms "slippery as a greased pig" and "slippery as snot on a doorknob," but until you have attempted lifting a warm, nude body covered in fly dope, suntan oil, rainwater, and mud over your head, you ain't seen anything slippery!

They say that adrenaline kicks in during times of stress. Some way or other, after trying several angles of attack, we got up over that muddy bank. Grabbing my ax and raincoat, I led her into the woods. I chopped the limbs out from under a big newly downed fir tree and we crawled underneath just as the first hailstones started to rattle off the branches.

Nothing to do but huddle there like two drowned muskrats, sitting on my shirt, holding my raincoat over our heads to protect us from the stinging hail, and watching the lightning strike the mountain across the river. I tried to drum up some recollection of all that good advice and all those psalms and scriptures, but somehow or other my mind was a total blank.

All storms eventually end, and as this one subsided and moved off upriver, we crawled out of our den. I dug out my watch and discovered that over an hour had passed since we made the run for shore. The canoe sat half full of water, and my pack basket containing dishes and food was floating around, keeping company with my customer's pillows. Lady Chatterley had survived, but like her reader, in a somewhat sodden condition.

The air had cooled down several degrees, making the river water seem warm by comparison. Good chance for a quick swim to wash off the mud, pitch, and fir needles before heading off down the river.

"Too bad I didn't bring along more clothing," my shivering companion now admitted, "but thanks for letting me use your shirt and raincoat."

"We'll go ashore again down below Whitefish Brook where there's lots of dry wood," I said. "We'll build a fire and have a chance to get dried out and make a pail of tea. Plenty of time before we meet old Jim. With that storm, he's probably going to be cutting trees out of the road on his way down to the forks anyway."

Next morning they were leaving for home—just one more canoe ride across the river to where their station wagon was parked on the road. I took lots of luggage and my sport in one trip. As we waited by the car for the others to come across, she told me that this had been her best vacation ever, and she slipped a folded-up envelope into my shirt pocket.

An hour later, over coffee in the cook house, old Jim was still moaning and complaining about having been robbed by that agent, that slippery customer. I was thinking about the note that read, "To my gamekeeper for a wonderful vacation" and the $20 bill that had been wrapped in it. Hell of a tip for those days! Especially as old Jim was getting ready to tell us that he couldn't pay our wages.

"Well," said Wallace, "slippery customer or not, I guess he sent us some pretty nice people. Old Tom turned out to be a good tipper, and I was even getting to like those two little bastards." Turning to me, he said, "Did you remember all that good advice I gave you?"

Thinking it all over, I guess those old rules cover a lot of situations, and there's one more I really like . . . the one that says the customer is always right. And talking about slippery customers, someday I'll tell you a story about a REAL SLIPPERY CUSTOMER! But of course I never did.

IN PURSUIT OF THE GOOD, CHEAP HUNT

Tom Hennessey

As a professional hunter, I travel and work in various areas of Canada. Some of them are wild, remote, Arctic regions requiring hours of jet travel, and some are like our New Brunswick operation, a day's drive from New York. The island of Newfoundland, or "Newfie" as it is affectionately known, contains what I call "accessible wilderness" and remains one of our favorite hunting grounds. Its interior for the most part is true wilderness, a mountain plateau with a subarctic environment of scrub, bogs, and rocky ridges. For the serious big-game trophy hunter seeking eastern Canada moose and woodland caribou, this is the best place to start looking.

Although I had ten years' experience guiding when I first looked to Newfoundland for hunting prospects back in the '60s, I was still naive enough to believe in the myth of the "good cheap hunt." Looking back on it from a safe distance of many years, it seems like it must have been fun. Fortunately, we were blessed with a series of relaxed and understanding clients. Otherwise some of our fiascoes would have led to our being shot, or worse, sued.

At that time it was still possible to purchase non-resident licenses for just about any part of the island. In some areas there were established outfitters, and in most places any number of local "guides" were available. Getting off the ferry at Port Aux Basques, one was besieged by people offering everything in accommodations from sleeping on a living-room floor to a berth on a schooner. Most could genuinely show you a good time and lots of game at rates so low none of them could possibly make a living. We were certainly no smarter than the rest, though perhaps more adventuresome.

One trip in particular sticks in my mind. It was typical of this era. The client flew in from Philadelphia to one of the island's major airports. The plan was to travel by motor canoe up a great long lake, then pole up the watershed to where we would camp and hunt on the plateau. For this trip I had charged the client the princely sum of $400. The trip involved myself and another guide driving a thousand miles and included an overnight boat trip, bringing along canoes and gear, and purchasing supplies. We arranged for the services of one of the famous local Micmac Indian guides, supposedly to call moose and satisfy the licensing requirements. Three guides looking after one client should have assured him a great trip; I, poor mathematician that I am, should have known I couldn't make any money on the deal.

On the appointed day, good old Pete the Client stepped off the airplane in shirtsleeves and blue jeans. He had departed Philly with temperatures in the 80s and immediately found that it was at least 40 degrees cooler in Newfie. Unfortunately, some cretin masquerading as a baggage handler had managed to put his rifle, duffel bag, and sleeping bag on a plane to Los Angeles. We were faced with the chores of borrowing clothes that did not fit; purchasing a cheap, inadequate sleeping bag; and assuring Pete that he could use my rifle, brought along for just such emergencies. We overlooked the fact that Pete was left-handed and cross-eyed, while my rifle wasn't tuned for either. This would show up later in his shooting.

After such a fine start, we proceeded to pry our keen-eyed native guide out of the local gin mill, loaded canoes and gear, and headed for the launching site. Anticipating at least a two-week trip and not willing to endure undue hardship, I had included a goodly supply of beer to lessen the pain of the portages. Bouncing along on the back of the dust-smothered truck, old Jim, the Micmac guide, was suffering the pangs of sobering up for the first time in a while and spied the telltale label on the boxes.

"Wibb," he called, "isn't that a box of beer yer sittin' on there?" I had to admit it was. Another mile bounced by. "Wibb," he tried again, "this is one hell of a load for two canoes. Maybe we should drink up some of that beer, eh?"

Knowing I was beat, and half-choked with dust myself, I gave in, and we polished off the first case before reaching the boat landing. Somehow or other, when we were loaded and launched, the rest of the beer ended up in Jim's canoe. However, we were off on the great adventure, despite a headwind and threatening skies. We were used to weather changing in the fall, usually from bad to horrid.

Good old Pete the Client was quiet as a mouse, rolled up in his borrowed raingear in the bow, when the first rain-filled squall nearly blew us out of the water. Those shallow northern lakes are not long in getting up. Soon we could only glimpse the shoreline while cresting the six-foot seas that were trying their damnedest to swamp us. Pete didn't open his mouth all through the next hour as we struggled for the shore. Perhaps I did see his lips moving a little as he bailed furiously with the frying pan I had thrown at him, his eyes on heaven. In the last few minutes of failing light, we made the lee of the hills and weren't long in getting ashore.

There are things more cheering than making camp in a wet spruce thicket, but this was one of the times it sure beat the hell out of the alternatives. Unfortunately, the cardboard beer boxes had pretty well dissolved in Jim's canoe. Fortunately, they seemed to be the only casualty. As any fool could see, there was just no way to repack the beer with no boxes, so it became our sad duty to eliminate that part of the cargo. By this time, I had figured out that the expedition was stalled until this chore could be taken care of anyway.

Four men sleeping in a two-man tent made it pretty chummy. But when I awoke to someone groping under my sleeping bag, I figured things had gone too far. A flashlight in the face revealed Jim the Guide. "Wibb," he said, "wasn't there one more bottle of that beer left?"

The rest of the trip was the standard ten days of continuous late-September rain, nights in wet sleeping bags, meals standing on your head around the fire with smoke in your eyes, and days spent struggling over shallow rips with canoes that should have had wheels on them. We portaged through blowdowns, bogs, and tuckamore thickets without benefit of beer, and old Pete missed every moose we encountered. Round it out to your good old-fashioned "economy-type moose hunt." Probably Pete still treasures the twenty-eight-inch moose he eventually managed to murder. Jim the Guide, I am sure, remembers me with kindness for having bestowed upon him most of Pete's four hundred bucks plus all my beer. As for myself and the other guide, I guess we gained some expensive memories.

Although I was slowly becoming a little smarter, consequent trips over the next decade still involved seeking the unattainable "good cheap hunt." By this time the Division of Wildlife, following a period of decline in the moose population, wisely brought in a program in which hunt zones were set up and licenses issued based on sound management practices. Licenses started to be available only through registered outfitters, so it made sense for us to work in tandem with local operations.

Not wanting to become too smart too fast, we again started from the bottom, price-wise, and entered a period of wondrous adventures along the J-5 trails. The J-5, for the benefit of the uninitiated, is one of the inventions of Bombardier of Quebec, the people who brought us the original Skidoo. This tracked, all-terrain vehicle performs miracles in many lines of work, from plowing city sidewalks to yarding pulpwood in some of the worst geography in the world. It is ideally suited to carrying men and moose meat over rough, boggy ground, which describes nine-tenths of the Newfie hunting areas. Some of the machines were fitted with welded-on racks and handholds so the victim-client could cling to the sides and avoid trekking along behind, where muddy bushes would spring back up into his face from under the tracks. The client might be lucky enough to avoid falling off or getting scraped or bounced off; he might even arrive with rifles, scope, cameras, and other valuables intact, if they were well protected. Rarely did the beer supply, even if contained in cans, survive the trip to camp.

The "accommodations" enjoyed during this phase of our education ranged from terrible to nonexistent. During bad weather, we gave new meaning to the term "roughing it." Keeping meat, especially during the warm early week of the season, was difficult in the extreme. Capes and antlers posed somewhat less of a problem, but occasionally even these were lost due to the inevitable black bear finding them.

Black bears are fairly numerous on the island. They are always hungry and occasionally quite aggressive. Every culture has its folklore and demons. We lowlanders fear the mountain heights, and the coastal Eskimo never ventures far inland without feeling a bit of unease. In the case of the Newfoundlander, the common black bear assumes a temperament and proportion unheard of in any other area we hunt in. Men who have endured the hardship and danger of the seal hunt for four hundred years, and who routinely trust body and soul to a fourteen-foot wooden dory in the gales of the North Atlantic winter, will become unhinged at the prospect of encountering a bear. Many are the "bear stories," and a few of them are even true. Anyone who has witnessed the damage black bears can inflict upon meat houses and unattended camps will never doubt their agility and strength.

At one camp, an unusually persistent bear had been attempting for a week to clean us out, and the party of New York clients insisted that the guides and I sleep in the meat house to protect the trophies. The guides, being a bit shy of this solution, waited until they heard snores, then quietly deposited all the capes and antlers on the roof of the guest cabin.

The guest cabin in this case, as with most "good cheap hunt" operations at the time, was a logged-up section of Newfoundland measuring about eight feet by twelve, sleeping six visiting Yankees in bunks under a roof of poles and tarred felt paper. The guides' accommodation was somewhat less luxurious. One member of the party—a foreman on the docks of Hoboken, New Jersey, which should have guaranteed that he feared nothing in the world—was a bit nervous in the solitude of the wilderness. He always wired the door securely shut, leaving a two-foot-square plastic-covered window as the only possible entrance or exit.

Sometime between when the rain quit and when I would have had to get up anyway, having drunk eighteen cups of black tea laced with Newfie rum to celebrate this last night of the hunt, one hell of a row erupted from the direction of the guest cabin. Screams, curses, banging around, and at least one shot had the guides out in underwear and bare feet, stumbling around the stumps and muskeg.

When at last a lantern was pumped and lit and a damage assessment made, we began to gather some information as to what had disturbed the slumber of our clients. Apparently, a grizzly bear weighing at least one and a half tons had torn off the camp door and entered with the intention of devouring the occupants, sleeping bags and all. This could not be substantiated, but our examination showed that a black bear—probably weighing less than a hundred pounds, judging by the track found the next morning—had climbed up to dine upon the moose capes and had fallen through the tarpaper roof into the cabin. This set off a reaction akin to hollering, "Time, gentlemen" in an Irish tavern. The only exit being the plastic-covered window, it should have been simple for the bear to escape, except that six hunters, all outweighing the bear by at least a hundred pounds, had the same thing in mind. As one of the steadier hands commented later, "If we had just stood back and let him go instead of fighting over who went out the window first, we would have all got out of there sooner." Over the years, I am sure that bear has become much too large to have scrambled out through a two-foot window.

By the mid-1970s it started to dawn on me that the "good cheap hunt" does not exist. The term itself is a contradiction, as in the "surefire method of birth control," "the good honest used-truck dealer," etc. Education comes hard in this business, even for the people doing it for a living. I despair for poor old Joe Client, who these days casts his bread upon the waters, blithely sending out his deposits to people offering exaggerated kill statistics and "bargain" rates.

As for us, we finally wised up and have for years now been operating with a partner who offers the finest hunts in Newfoundland. We now hunt only the fly-in areas, working out of our own float base. Camp staff is made up of excellent cooks and topnotch Newfie guides. We have convenient airport pick-ups and the area's only outfitter-owned walk-in freezer facilities to take care of meat and trophies. Nearly every client has the opportunity to take a legal male moose, a high percentage of which are trophies. A check on the Seventeenth, Eighteenth, and Nineteenth Boone and Crockett Awards books will show we rank in the top three consistently on woodland caribou, with the Nineteenth Awards book showing our Number 1 taken by Gordon Birgbauer of Michigan.

Although we have learned that "good cheap hunts" are a myth, we have shown that excellent hunts at prices reflecting the expense and effort involved are surely available.

THE WORLD'S OLDEST OUTDOOR STORY

Tom Hennessey —

Every so often there appears in one of the outdoor publications an article entitled "How To Choose an Outfitter" or "How To Plan Your Hunt."

As an outfitter and guide, this never ceases to amuse and amaze me. I'm always wondering just what sage advice is going to be given on this oldest story (with the possible exception of the Holy Bible) in the world.

Once in a great while, these things are written by well-known, well-traveled, and experienced big-game hunters and thus are worth consideration by anyone in the profession. Even old dogs can occasionally learn new tricks, including this old dog.

However, most of these pieces are the sad tale of some neophyte "sportsman" on his first venture into the great big world of Away from Home Hunting. Usually it is someone who started out pumped full of impossible expectations and then stumbled through the entire experience with his eyes and ears closed and his mouth open. He ends up himself the victim of articles entitled "How To Choose an Outfitter and Plan Your Trip of a Lifetime."

One such article appeared a few years ago in one of the "Big Three" outdoor magazines. I have waited this long to comment to avoid hurting the author's feelings or upsetting the magazine's legal staff.

The gentleman relates his horrific experiences encountered on a high-country hunt in one of the western states. His tale of woe starts with how badly he was taken in by the outfitter, who was attending a sports show in the East. As he goes along, his story becomes more and more typical of what every guide has encountered at one time or another.

Upon his arrival at the jumpoff point, the writer wonders why he is greeted with something less than enthusiasm by the guides and wranglers. The fact that he has brought along four times the amount of gear specified, including an old-fashioned steamer trunk and a double aluminum rifle case as big as a coffin, might provide a clue. It seems to have escaped him that everything must somehow be loaded onto packhorses.

As an afterthought, he informs the outfitter that he has also brought his wife along, despite having made no prior booking for her. Although neither of them has ever been on a horse, they have always liked western movies and know that you sit facing the ears. They have no boots suitable to fit the stirrups, or raingear, but they do have a new cowboy hat apiece. The hats are big ones, of course, guaranteed to blow off and stampede the stock.

Arriving at last at the tent camp in the mountains, our hero finds that he and spouse are to sleep in a hastily erected tent. He then proceeds to complain about the stove smoking while the wrangler tries to get it started with wet wood. He doesn't realize, of course, that they are thus bivouacked because he has inflicted the Old Dragon upon the outfit and the entire sleeping arrangement has been thrown out of whack. Two of the guides will have to sleep under a tarp because he and his bride have been given the guides' tent.

The food, naturally enough, is not up to his wife's expectations. Nor is the room service, the after-hours entertainment, or the bathing facilities. With three other male hunters in camp bent on enjoying a return trip with friends they made the year before, the talk around the table becomes a bit exotic for the lady's delicate ears. She departs the cook tent in a huff, with, one presumes, our buddy in tow.

When the hunting begins, he questions why everyone else has departed for the peaks while he and the missus are parked at the end of an easy trail, watching a meadow. For this he blames the guide's inability to find a "good place." Of course, the fact that they couldn't ride and wouldn't walk had nothing to do with it.

The crowning indignity comes when the cook shoots an elk right out of the tent door, then refuses to let our sport tag and claim it. The Old Millstone coming down with double pneumonia, diarrhea, chafed thighs, and what she perceives as body lice comes almost as an anticlimax. Nowhere does our sport appear to be aware that even a small portion of his troubles is directly attributable to his own stupidity.

Now, to compound the idiocy, this expert proceeds to advise others on matters of which he knows so little himself. A special gem is his perception of "How To Handle the Guides"—guides apparently being something requiring "handling." It seems that you take the guide aside at the first meeting and tell him, "Look, I am prepared to bestow upon you my rubber boots, or some other such exorbitant gift, if you will just make sure we kill something." This approach implies, I gather, that without promise of a bribe, the guide is going to screw him around. This approach to any guide on my crews would get you at best amused tolerance, or more probably, advice upon where to stick your secondhand rubber boots.

Another real winner is the gentleman's recommendation on how to handle liquor around the staff. His theory is that though you never offer anyone a drink while in camp yourself, it is entirely appropriate on your departure to give the guide the bottle instead of a tip. This guarantees that the guide can piss it up on the outfitter's time and ruin the trip of the incoming guests.

The article goes on in similar vein until the nauseating conclusion that you should present the outfitter with a clever list of questions a mile long. This interrogation is apparently designed to trip him up should he stray from the narrow bounds of the Truth as perceived by the Inquisitor. Then you should be sure to check, double-check, and cross-examine every single past client who has been kind or dumb enough to volunteer his name and phone number. Be sure to disregard the time zones so that you do this at the least appropriate time of day.

For a week or two after this article appeared on the newsstands, I received a rash of inquiries based upon this gentleman's

"List of 375 Questions To Ask Your Outfitter." Given my tolerant nature, I did not book many of these people. Most were the type who go around begging to be lied to, and when confronted with the truth about what to expect on a hunting trip, do not know how to deal with it.

I have finally figured out that this kind of suspicion is a product of one's environment. The dog-eat-dog urban lifestyle, in which you are robbed, raped, and ripped off every day, does not engender faith in your fellow man. You can see the same thing in animals. The Arctic fox will eat from your hand, while his southern cousin is so trap-shy and suspicious that he will circle and sneak around, thinking about how smart he is, until he gets flattened by a truck on the freeway.

Fortunately for the hunting sports and the sanity of all concerned, the great majority of people we deal with are smart enough to recognize quality and honesty in their dealings with our profession.

Years ago I learned that by telling the truth the outfitter is able to weed out the great majority of dummies who expect to be run down by herds of caribou or devoured by a grizzly upon stepping off the airplane. In the case of truly difficult hunts, I will reverse the process somewhat and ask the prospective client some questions of my own.

Once in a while, despite every effort to the contrary, the professional hunter will be confronted with someone who just plain refuses to believe what he has been told. In the stories that follow, names will not appear. They are, however, engraved in my memory.

In the mid-1970s, part of our yearly operation involved running black bear and white-tailed deer hunts in the wilds of northern

New Brunswick. Here I had the misfortune to accept a group, whose leader turned out to be one of those unfortunates who, after being told the truth, stood there with his mouth hanging open as if there just has to be more to come. This self-appointed pope had come from St. Paul, Minnesota. With him were four nice-enough young men who might have been transformed into real sportsmen except for the braggart's overbearing influence.

We were working out of a bunch of old log camps up the Mamozekel River, right in the heart of what was at that time the best hunting territory in the province. Having written several letters to this guy and endured hour-long phone calls from him, I thought that he had been told everything the English language is capable of expressing on the subject of November bear hunting in New Brunswick. In some years, with a good crop of beechnuts on the ridges, it can be terrific. In others, with no nuts and early snowfall, the bears may go to den in October and your hunt will be mostly for deer.

On arrival, over the first cup of coffee, he told us about the lousy hunt he had had the previous year in Maine, and of the three times he had been screwed by outfitters in Ontario. He described a hunt on which his party saw only four bears and killed two. I truthfully assured him that that sort of statistic was not too bad in eastern woodland hunting. He had heard, however, that the Webbs were mighty bear guides and knew that we would "really stack 'em up." This statement was accompanied, of course, by Number 987 in the Guide's List of Famous Last Words: "You guys just show us the game, and our gang will kill it." I said I most fervently hoped things would turn out that way.

In camp that week there also happened to be a Welshman named Steve who had come clear across the Atlantic to hunt with us. Steve had hunted extensively in Africa and, while with the British Army, in India and Burma. This was, however, his first visit to the wilderness of North America, and he was enjoying it immensely. He was, that is, until the Loudmouth from St. Paul and his disciples showed up. Steve's accent, his clothing, and most of all his Purdey double shotgun and .404 Rigby immediately became the butt of numerous ignorant remarks and feeble jokes.

Our heroes, naturally, were clothed and armed with what they considered the "right gear": L. L. Bean gum rubber boots, "Elmer Fudd" suits in red-and-black-checkered splendor made by Woolrich, and armament consisting of matching .308 Remington automatics and pump-actions with high-power telescopes. In a country where all the guides preferred to see .30-30 lever-actions or any decent bolt-action with iron sights, the pumps were known affectionately as "burp guns" or "jerk-off guns." With few exceptions, they always seemed to be favored by people who believed in firepower rather than accuracy.

What followed was one of the worst weeks in a lifetime spent guiding hunters. We used to say that any good guide could put up with the devil for a week and send him away smiling. With this bunch I soon began to wonder. The hunting conditions were hard enough—cold, windy, and noisy. Even with good hunters, it would have been difficult; with poor ones it was impossible.

They wouldn't sit still when put on stands, and they couldn't walk without sounding like a herd of elephants. They turned down most of the deer and two bears as being too small, and they missed or wounded the ones they thought were bigger. Every evening in the cookhouse, the tasteless jokes and pointed remarks became harder and harder to swallow, especially their harassment of Steve the Welshman, who was still enjoying what he considered a good hunting trip.

It all came to a climax on the final evening. After exhausting all of my legendary diplomacy, I finally blew up, called the Leader of the Pack everything except fit for service, and told his gang that "You will never, ever have a good hunting trip if you follow this old prick around." Then I challenged the big bastard to come out into the dooryard where I would tramp his guts into a mudhole. This seemed to put a damper on the party. As Steve remarked later, "My word, I thought you were coming to blows."

LeRoy, one of the guides, summed it all up: "The best thing I saw all week was that son-of-a-whore's taillights going around the corner." Thus ended a trip that started with the would-be client asking the outfitter to answer a list of questions taken from one of the many "How To Choose an Outfitter" stories.

Other examples of the apparent futility of trying to tell people the truth about hunting conditions occurred frequently in the days when we hunted bobcats with dogs. This winter hunt, carried out on snowshoes in mountainous deep-woods country, was physical in the extreme.

With a high cat population and great dogs, I could have guaranteed the result after we took a track. The dog was going to put that cat up a tree, nearby or twenty miles away, and come hell, thickets, or thin ice, I or the other guide would get there with a shotgun. But the client got there and saw the cat alive so seldom that it certainly proved to me how absolutely phony these advertised "guaranteed cat hunts" are.

The same applies to bear hunts where dogs are used and the hunting must be done on foot, not by vehicle. I would estimate, based on our experience, that perhaps 10 percent of the clients ever see the critter when it is still breathing.

Telling people these hard facts while booking them proved to be impossible. Basically, they wanted to be lied to, and the famous claim always was, "Don't worry about me. I'll get there if I have to crawl." They showed up in every shape and size, including one fellow who probably would have dressed out at a hundred pounds to the quarter. Not once in ten years did anyone turn up with the type of clothing recommended, the weapon recommended, or boots that would keep your feet from freezing while also fitting into a snowshoe harness. As a sport for the guides who had trained the dogs, it was the finest in the world, but as a business, it was a nightmare.

On the subject of "planning your hunt," certainly there are sensible preparations that should be made, but some people take it to such an extreme that there is nothing left for fun, luck, or spontaneity. Such was the case of the Long Island Planner.

This guy had an occupation in which plenty of "planning" was probably required just to stay alive. He worked for an organization that controlled pinball and gambling machines throughout the New York City area. His job was to go around and collect the money, probably in surroundings that would make gorilla hunting with your bare hands safe by comparison.

His hunt-trip planning took two years. He wrote to me, called me, checked and double-checked every reference, read every book, and ordered maps to cover most of eastern Canada, all before coming on a spring black bear hunt. Equipment lists alone went back and forth for months. He arrived at last about the first week of June 1975, complete with gear, weapons, maps, and photocopies of every letter I had written to him, just as a triple-check.

That spring we were hunting out of a spike camp reached only by a thirty-mile, four-wheel-drive truck journey. We always offered the client three options: Bring in your vehicle, walk, or ride in the back of our tough old woods trucks. Needless to say, we didn't get any takers on the first two choices, so into the back of the truck they went.

On the first day, after sighting-in rifles and packing lunch, we were off for the bear stands. Coleman McDougall, my chief guide, and I had four eager bear slayers, each of them, of course, wanting to be put in the best place. No one ever listens to my protestations that no one in the world knows where the best place is until the bear comes, and this includes the bear, who makes very few long-range plans.

Our Planner was the most agitated of the bunch as we traveled the trails, working our way through an area that had been hunted earlier in the season toward what Coleman and I considered the best range of high ridges to start hunting. The Planner, as it turned out, hadn't planned on how rough a 4x4 truck rides. About six times, he banged on the cab and halted us to complain that it was too dusty and that he got car-sick riding backward.

With my renowned patience wearing thin, I told Coleman, "If that guy opens his goddamn mouth again, he's going on the first stand we come to even if there hasn't been a bear there for three years." Sure enough, again came the banging on the top of the cab, and out went our Planner on the very next stand, one that had not been touched by anything bigger than a raven all season.

Naturally, about eight o'clock that evening a big old male bear strolled right past that stand with never a thought on his mind except munching dandelions along the side of the trail— biggest bear of the season.

Back at camp, over midnight coffee, our Planner was congratulated on his good luck bagging such a great trophy the first day out. Enjoying center stage, he informed his admirers, "Boys, there is no such thing as luck in hunting. What you have here is the result of hard work and expert knowledge by the guides, and most of all, careful, precise planning on my part."

So having destroyed your faith in advice from the experts, I guess I should now become an "expert" myself and give my own advice, most of which I assume will be disregarded in any event: Consider the species and the type of hunt you are contemplating. Consider your own abilities, your physical condition, the time you have available, and your financial resources. See if they all are compatible.

The booking information provided by any well-established and reputable outfitter will answer 99.9 percent of the sensible questions about anything over which the man has any control. The problem forever seems to be that the only one who reads this stuff is the proofreader at the print shop.

Make sure you understand the operator's policy regarding the refund of deposits. When you make the deposit and receive the contract, take time to read it. Send back any medical forms or questionnaires the outfitter provides. Take his advice regarding travel, licenses, export fees, and other government requirements.

Then come to camp prepared to hold up your end of the deal and equipped with the attitude that we are all going to enjoy your visit whether we kill anything or not. Somehow, this outlook seems to produce the trophies that you see listed in the record books. Leave your worries back where they belong, and enjoy a fine vacation in the northern wilderness.

The great majority of clients who come hunting with us or any other recognized professional seem to go home happy, and friendships are forged that last forever. We want to add you to the list.

STREAM DRIVER

Tom Hennessey —

(Appeared in the *Victoria County Record*, May 1977)

In our area of eastern Canada, for generations men made a living for their families by guiding, trapping, cutting logs, and stream-driving. We spent the winter cutting, then the logs were hauled by sled and horses to landings on the streambank. In my generation, when the ice went out, the logs were driven to the mill in Plaster Rock on the Tobique. In my grandfather's day, logs were rafted and driven down the Tobique and the Saint John to tidewater and the shipyards on the Bay of Fundy.

The last big drive I worked on was in the spring of 1969. The following year, stream-driving on the Tobique was over forever; changing times in the form of union wages, roads, and mechanization had ended an era. There are still men along the river who can tell you stories of how it was in the days of sleds and horses. The following is dedicated to these old drivers and the ones who have gone before us.

Stream Driver

When you're sailing down the Serpentine and you run the
    Narrows Falls
Where the icy rushing water flows between those granite walls
On the bank you'll see a cedar with a mark that's nearly hid,
It marks the grave of one they called the wild White Water Kid.
They say he wandered into camp in the spring of Thirty-five
They were waiting for the ice to run so they could start the
    drive
To the Boss he says, "Now, sir, I hear you're looking for recruits
Well, I'm the kid they say was born in a pair of high corked boots."
In a day or so the ice is gone and they start to fill the brook
The stranger steps upon the bank and the boys all stand and
    look
With peavey, pole, and dynamite they see he knows the game
And when he springs out from the shore they see he's earned
    his name.
For here's a man can board a log and ride her through the rips
And when he dogs that peavey in you know it never slips
He used to say, "One trade have I and that one I know well
And when it comes my turn to go I'll ride a log through Hell."
Then came the day the Narrows jammed with logs from shore
    to shore
She ran, then jammed and piled that wood to forty feet or
    more
The Boss said, "Boys, it can't be done, it's suicide to try."
The Kid said, "Pass that dynamite, I'll pull her plug or die."
With a peavey and two dozen sticks he skipped out on that jam
The boys stood up upon the hill and heard the mighty slam
"She pulls, she goes, she's running free!"—the thunder shakes
    the ground
The lumber's headed for the mill, but the Kid cannot be found.
The Boss says, "You can't drown that Kid, he'll walk back in a
    while."

But next day his sole possessions come ashore at Seven Mile

Some claim it was a miracle, others say it was a trick

But his corked boots and his peavey were still standing on that stick.

So then back up to the Narrows and the boys all gathered 'round

And they buried boots and peavey 'cause that's all they ever found.

He played the cards that Fate had dealt and the Devil took the bid

But we'll always love the memory of that wild White Water Kid.

WOODLAND ROMANCE

Tom Hennessey —

Alfonse Sonpreel, or Fonsus as we called him, was one of the most famous moose guides ever to work for our company. Depending upon the audience and the level left in the bottle, old Fonsus would claim to be anything from pureblood Swampy Cree to French aristocrat. The truth was that he was of mixed heritage, like a lot of us Canadians.

When we first signed him up on the payroll, we needed proof of his birth to satisfy the goons in the tax department. The only record I could find was that of a son born in 1922 to a young native lady who worked as a housekeeper for the French priest at the mission. No mention of her aboriginal name, but she was baptized as Lucy Sans Pareil (without equal)—a recommendation of some sort, I assume.

Around our country there were many guides who claimed to be expert callers of the moose. The truth is that during the rut anyone can call a moose with a chain saw, a train whistle, or any sort of whine or grunt. On the other hand, to call in a bull before the cows come into season, when they are hiding coyly

Toill Hennessey —

in the thickets awaiting the enticements of the amorous bull, is an entirely different matter. Fonsus Sonpreel was known as one of the few who could bring the bull under the sights of his client's rifle during this early part of the season.

In the fall of 1960, Fonsus and I were guiding two sports from Boston, and we were having a dry old time. These guys—big, bulky, and awkward, dressed in noisy rubber rainsuits—would never get within miles of any game while trying to still-hunt.

Although we knew the country to be full of moose, not very many tracks were in evidence, which is quite common in

82

the pre-rut period when nothing seems to move for a week or ten days. We had gone out early and stayed out late—watching clearings and ponds and long stretches of the river—all to no avail.

Now, on the last day of the hunt, I called upon my partner's legendary talents. It was do or die. No moose, no tips!

"Fonsus," I told him, "I have always heard that you can call a moose when there is no moose. Now is the time to earn your wages. We have to get at least one bull for these two guys or they'll cry around my booth at the sport show forever."

"OK, Boss. I know de country where one big bull live, all right. Ee's never meet no cow before, but if this a real emergency, I try de secret call da fodder of my mudder tell to me long time ago."

In late afternoon we landed the boat at Fonsus's secret place—a long, sweeping bend in the river where alder-covered banks went back half a mile into black spruce so thick you couldn't beat a weasel through it.

Looks just like every other bend in the river we have tried all week, I thought to myself, *but what the hell, only one more hour before darkness. May as well be here as anywhere.*

After carefully testing the wind, Fonsus placed the two Boston dudes so that they could not shoot each other or ourselves should a miracle occur. When all was in readiness, Fonsus whispered, "Now I show you the secret. Now Fonsus make believe ee is da cow, and I talk to da bull hiding in the forest."

Cupping his hands over his mouth, nose pinched shut, he let loose the first call—"*Nnnnnairrrrruh, nyuuh*!" Fonsus translated, "I say I am de pretty cow, come and see me, I want very much da lover."

We strained our ears for a reply. Half-an-hour and nothing.

"*Nnnnnnnairrrrruh, uuh!*" He tried again, "Talk to me, my big, strong bull. I am waiting."

There—at last! From the depth of the thicket we heard "*Nnnnyyyuh, nyyyuh!*" An excited Fonsus translated, "Here! Ee say, I am da big bull, talk to me, pretty cow, I am coming."

"*Nnnairruh nnnairruh nyhh!* "Come to me, my love, I must see you!"

"*Wahuuuuh wahuuuh unnuh!!* "There, ee say, I am come, my darling, it is you alone that I love!"

Time stood still. Ears and eyes strained. It was almost dusk now. White knuckles on the Boston boys, rifles up, thumbs on safeties!

Fonsus stepped to the edge of the river, splashed with his hands, filled his hat and let it pour loudly into the water. "There" he whispered, "I am the cow—so hot I am pissing into the water."

"*Nnnnnairrrr nnnairrruh uuh!*" "Come to me, my handsome bull, I am ready for love you!"

From the alders right in front of us, not thirty feet away, came a great crashing and shaking of branches. "*Waaahh waaahh unnnuh unnnuh unnnuh!!!*" He was coming—immense antlers waving above the bushes, mud flying in all directions! A monster, and he was right in our faces!

At that point we heard the final advice from the guide as he dashed for the boat: "Now, my frens, you shoot fast and you shoot good, or one of you is goin' be da cow!"

Kabang! Kabang!

Moose liver for supper! Heroes all! Lots of rum and big tips! All's well that ends well!

THE UNMENTIONABLE TOPIC OF TIPS

Tom Hennessey

Of all the million questions asked of an outfitter, one of the most difficult to deal with is the topic of tips. Tips, gratuities, or whatever you care to term them seem to be a fact of life all over the world, and are usually given automatically, whether deserved or not. Everyone accepts them, and everyone expects to pay them.

For some reason, this doesn't always carry over to hunting-camp situations, perhaps because the relationship between guide and client is usually a closer one than in most service situations. Most outfitters, myself included, when asked about tipping policy, will squirm, shuffle, look at the ground, and mumble something like, "Some do and some don't."

Wherever we travel down south we tip, usually too much for the service involved. Cabbies, doormen, bellhops, redcaps—they all have their hand out. Everyone in, on, or around an airport, except the pilots, stands in line. Around the convention hotels it never ceases. The show electrician, the freight guy who rolls in your booth, the girl who brings you a phone message, the shoeshine guy, the barber, and the person of questionable sex who hands you a towel in the sauna all expect to be taken care of.

Do you notice the cute little notes left in the room by the maids, and the fact that the girl who turns down your bed doesn't leave you the little peppermint patty on your pillow if you haven't coughed up the night before? And how come the room-service menu says a 15 percent service charge will be added to the already exorbitant prices, and then the kid delivering the food stands there with his hand out?

Bartenders, of course, just automatically get tipped, usually beyond 20 percent or so and regardless of the quality of service. In restaurants it is worse. The *maitre d'*, or whatever the modern unisex label is for the "sitter-downer," looks at you expectantly. The sullen waitress who spills the coffee into your saucer, mixes up your order, and arrives with her thumb in your soup will coast by with the smirking, inane question, "Is everything fine here?" How many of us have the guts to tell her the truth? How many, after suffering through it all, wait patiently for the bill and then still overtip? Most of us, I'd wager.

So, if tipping, right or wrong, is an accepted fact, how does it apply to the guiding business? And why are we so reticent about it? Oh, yes, some of us may mention it discreetly in our brochure. Some feature statements like "Our rates cover everything except personal items, booze, tickets to the World Series, and gratuities." Most don't mention it at all, so at the risk of being judged crassly commercial, I will lay down a few thoughts on this forbidden subject.

To begin with, forget the myth that friendly natives and we simple rustics will somehow be insulted if offered a gift. This is a cop-out. Years ago I overheard a New England deer hunter telling a veteran New Brunswick guide, "I would leave you my worn-out L. L. Bean rubbers, but they probably wouldn't fit you." To which the guide replied, "Don't worry, I can wear anything from a size six to a thirteen."

All guides like to receive gifts, especially if they are something practical and not locally available. However, one guy can wear only one pair of sunglasses at a time and carry only so many jackknives. Good gear costs like hell up north, but guides from even the most remote Eskimo villages nowadays order from Bean, Dunn, and Cabela's, and would probably like to pick out something for themselves.

One time in a camp in Arctic Quebec, the leader of the party, Jim Rikhoff, was canvassing the gang for tip money. He patiently explained to one guest that his Eskimo guide would not really appreciate the significance of a little pin from an exclusive New York sporting club that he intended to give as a tip.

The gentleman was at a loss:

"Oh, I never know what to give as a token of my appreciation."

"Goddammit," Jim exploded, "the Phoenicians solved that problem about three thousand years ago when they invented money!"

In some camps it is perfectly all right to pool the gratuities and leave them for the manager to distribute. However, unless you know the people concerned, this is not always the fairest policy. My son worked all summer in one camp up north where the owner divided the tips among his myriad Eskimo relatives, so some guys who deserved recognition received next to nothing.

I have been unfortunate enough to experience a few instances in which clients wanted to tip in advance. This is a lousy policy, and worse manners. When a guy gets off the plane, takes me aside, and whispers, "There'll be something in it for you if I get the best guide, the softest bed, the biggest bear, or the new world-record caribou," he is telling me a lot about himself. For starters, he knows even less about hunting than he does about guides, and apparently thinks that we are going to screw him around if we aren't paid off in advance.

A gratuity should be a gift given in appreciation of a job well done—no more, no less. A guest who recognizes true effort expended, regardless of whether or not game was taken, and shows that appreciation, ranks high in the memory of any guide. On the other hand, if service has been terrible, food worse, facilities non-existent, and some total incompetent has by sheer luck stumbled onto an animal and you have taken it doesn't necessarily mean that you are obligated to set him up for his old age.

It is also nice to remember that the guide, regardless of how good he appears, is not the only person contributing to your safety and success. Other people—the cook, camp attendant, skinner, and, yes, I am reluctant to say, even the camp manager—all contribute to making the guide look good.

The Unmentionable Topic of Tips

When it comes to the big question of how much, like all of my peers I am going to chicken out. It all becomes a matter of personal choice, one's perception of the quality of service, and how much an individual guest feels comfortable paying. We have all enjoyed guiding many, many fine people who for one reason or another did not tip at all. I don't think that anyone in our profession expects the 15-percent-plus that is demanded of travelers down south, and you should never feel obligated to pay extra for a low-quality experience.

The viewpoint of most guides I know is similar to that expressed by one of the finest and oldest guides in our operation. Coleman McDougall—seventy-four years old, lifelong guide, and born-again Christian—puts it this way: "We guide for our wages and because we love it. We don't depend on tips for a living, but certainly appreciate any we get." For good service and that kind of attitude, I think you'll agree that tipping is justified.

THE DREAM VS. REALITY

Tom Hennessey

I am in the middle of my umpteenth caribou season in the Barren Lands, and wondering if maybe I have been at this job too long. I am reminded of the old story of the tomcat making love to the skunk, when he says, "Honey, I don't know how much more of this ecstasy I can stand."

I have just been somewhat less than diplomatic to one of my newfound clients. Landing back in camp unannounced in the middle of the day, when the cooks are trying to steal a few minutes' rest from the grind, he wants to know if they would mind firing up the stove and cooking the liver from his freshly killed caribou. "No," is my first reaction. "They will cook the meat during regular mealtime if everyone in camp agrees that they want caribou loin instead of pork chops, but they don't cook the guts. Take it back out to your guide. He will be happy to prepare it, up the lake, while you glass for your second caribou."

I see his face fall. Undoubtedly I have punctured his dream of the genial, carefree hunting-camp host and staff who keep the coffee pot on twenty-four hours a day and prepare à la carte meals at the client's whim.

Thinking it over later, perhaps I was too hard on him, but I have never figured that the truth was an unkindness. A solid hunter/outfitter footing, where everyone knows the difference between dreams and reality, ends up producing safe and happy hunts, at least most of the time.

All of us, on both sides of the equation, are subject to dreams, but all of us also must be willing to put up with the reality. The way a person views anything is greatly influenced by his position relative to whatever is being looked upon. This applies both to how the client perceives what goes on in a hunting camp and to the cold, hard reality faced by the outfitter.

Though I've never had the opportunity of being the client, I have indeed met quite a few of them. As for being a guide and an outfitter, I have done little else in my lifetime. Every outfitter should be aware that the most important thing he is selling the client, aside from fresh air and scenery, is the dream. Without the dream, there would be no sport of hunting and no professional hunters, guides, and outfitters. Above all, regardless of what some think, we are NOT in the business of selling animal carcasses.

It is up to the guide to make reality conform as much as possible to the client's perception of the dream. Perhaps a bit of explanation can help the client understand just how far the outfitter can go in this direction.

To begin with, one must realize that the outfitter, if he is a professional earning a living, has to cater to a number of clients in most cases. One should not expect the same degree of personal attention on a $3,000 caribou hunt, for example, on which the outfitter must host a hundred clients a year to make a living, as one would receive on a $60,000 personally guided safari for elephant.

Most hunts are a year or more in the planning, meaning that much of a client's time is spent concentrating on the dream. He has put aside the money for the hunt, he has read about and studied every angle, he has questioned outfitters and references and consulted the record book. In some cases, regrettably all too few, he has spent time and effort to get in shape. He has for certain purchased, pampered, and played with the weapon of his choice. He is ready to live the dream.

The outfitter, on the other hand, has gone through a year of answering letters and phone calls, attending sports shows and conventions, and doing the dreaded "marketing" that eats up a major portion of his gross earnings. He has long since passed the point at which he wonders if there will be enough left over to run the camps. During this period he has also spent money on his camps, airplanes, horses, boats, and an endless array of gear.

In the case of our caribou camps in the Barren Lands, the plane arriving to take out the last of this season's hunters also carries in the first of the gasoline for next year's hunts. Throughout the winter months, more gasoline, stove oil, diesel fuel, and airplane gas is ferried up at great expense. Camps exist at the mercy of the weather and the ever-present threat of grizzly bear depredation, under an expensive but insufficient insurance policy.

Plans for hunts, of necessity set far in advance, are based upon full camps and full airplanes, and supplies, equipment, and staff are figured accordingly. Adding to the uncertainty are the threat of falling international exchange rates, rising local taxes and red tape, and changing political situations, weather patterns, and game populations. It is hard to imagine any business subject to so many things that are beyond the control of the individual trying to run the operation. This is reality.

When the hunt dates roll around at last, the client is full of anticipation, probably having spent a sleepless night or two en route in airplanes and strange hotel rooms. In the case of our caribou camps, he alights on the beach of a lake two hundred miles out in the middle of the Barrens, to greet the outfitter and the departing guests. He has arrived; the dream is in progress and the long-anticipated hunt is about to begin. His personal week in camp is the only week of the season that concerns him.

The outfitter, guides, cooks, skinner, and camp manager are in a slightly different position. They are nearing the end of an eight-week season. They have been on stage, nose to the buzzsaw, seven days a week, and in their fiftieth day might be forgiven if they are not in quite the same frame of mind as the client on day one. However, like any good professional hunting crew, they will paste the smiles back on their faces, pitch in, and give 100 percent of their effort to make the dream come true for the client.

That effort includes trying their utmost to take good trophies. We assume that every client would be pleased to take a world record, and we hunt accordingly. The guides are experienced in judging caribou, and they will try to dissuade the client from taking inferior trophies. However, as anyone who hunts antlered game knows, some seasons produce better-than-average heads, and in the other seasons one must be happy with whatever hard work and fate decree. Although we are record-book-oriented, our bottom line is that we are abundantly happy with any trophy that makes the client happy. He or she is the person who has paid the bill and who will live with the result in the trophy room. In most cases, the dream coincides with the reality.

The outfitter, of course, has his own set of dreams. For instance, he dreams of a season in which the bookings come easy and the clients arrive at the right time, with the right gear, and in shape to hunt. He dreams of the day all the camps are paid for, all the boats and motors work, the game is plentiful, the clients are happy and successful, and after it is all over with, the bottom line shows a modest profit.

Reality is often something different, despite years of experience and months of planning. Just when it appears that everything is covered, a couple of outboard motors fail, there's an airplane mishap, a generator packs up, and the whole bottom line changes.

In a ten-man caribou camp two hundred miles out, on the end of a charter costing nearly $3,000, there is a very slim margin for mishap. When one is confronted with running a ten-man camp for a week with only five people, for instance, he knows any profit for the next two weeks is taken care of. When a client's check bounces, that is one week out of the season down the drain. When you have two such losses in a two-month season, you may as well have stayed home.

In the high Arctic, the margin is even more critical. One spends an entire year getting ready to run thirty hunts over five weeks. It is expensive to train guides and get gear and communications in place. Everything you touch in the Arctic costs approximately four times what it does in the southern part of the continent. If one booking agent comes through with only half as many clients as promised, while you have booked around the dates and declined other deals, then it does not matter what you do with the rest of the season. Certainly, the hunts must be carried out and the commitments honored. Financially, you should have stayed home and tried to figure out some other line of work.

Certainly, dreams are what keep both the client and the outfitter coming back for more, but reality is what determines whether or not the outfitter is going to be there next season.

DEALING WITH THE DRONES

Tom Hennessey —

The hunting profession must certainly rank among the most difficult in which to make a living. Some may pity the poor farmer or fisherman, whose lives are dependent upon uncertain markets, weather, and other uncontrollable forces. The business of guiding hunters and anglers shares these difficulties and goes far beyond to such intangibles as game resources, varied clientele, and, worst of all by far, determined and unending interference by the forces of government.

If this one major impediment were modified or, better yet, removed, one could almost enjoy dealing with all the other problems combined.

We have never resented or regretted our total compliance with game laws and our support and assistance to those who do their best to enforce them. Indeed, we feel a kinship with the hard-working and dedicated "troops in the field," who exist, as do we, at the whim of the Drones in High Places.

Dealing with the Drones

Nowhere was this problem more apparent to me than in our home province in eastern Canada. For years the outfitting industry had existed as a model of self-reliance and capitalism. Under this system, as a farmer friend of mine put it, "Just like a pail of new milk, the cream rises to the top and the cowshit settles to the bottom." Then the government, in all its forms and manifestations, discovered us. From there it was all downhill.

We had always had a Department of Natural Resources, and had managed to get along with them because of our shared concerns about wildlife management. Sometime around 1970, someone needed jobs for his friends, so a Department of Tourism was established. Then our troubles really began.

First of all, Tourism held public meetings, including one in the nearby village of Riley Brook. We were told in no uncertain terms that the days of guiding and outfitting sport hunters were over and done with. From now on we would all make a living catering to recreational canoeists, cross-country skiers, birdwatchers, and naturalists.

Going along with their advice (after all, one must listen to the highly paid experts), our little family company invested about three seasons worth of time and money we could ill afford. We bought canoes and gear, set up campsites along the lakes and rivers, and sat back to await the promised horde of people who would appear and pay for our services.

On one occasion that I remember well, we traveled to the capital for a meeting with the new minister of tourism. When asked how many clients we could service, I modestly replied that we could probably handle ten a week all summer.

The minister, recently back from a junket to Louisiana to suck up to the cousins of his Acadian constituents, reared back in his chair, almost upsetting his lobster and wine. "Boys," he proclaimed, "I will be terribly disappointed if you can't handle ten times that number a year from now!"

Pretty heady stuff to us country boys. Turned out, of course, to be absolute and total bullshit and the biggest disaster our small company ever survived. After five years and literally millions of dollars down the drain by government, they looked around and discovered that the poor old outfitting business, catering to sport hunters and anglers, was the only remotely successful "tourism" in the province. What to do?

"Obviously," said the paper shufflers and tourism experts, "the outfitters are all millionaires, rubbing shoulders with the rich Yankees, so the thing to do is spend more of the taxpayers' money to create more outfitters to compete with the ones who have somehow managed to make it on their own."

This they did in good measure. New Brunswick went from about a dozen financially viable, family owned operations to what I counted as over 280 the last time I had the stomach to look at the list. For all practical purposes, the "experts" destroyed the outfitting industry in New Brunswick.

Not to be outdone, following that successful example, every other province and two territories have carried on the same policies. Tax the successful businessmen to support and increase the number of dreamers and incompetents, encourage them to cut prices to compete with the professionals, and within a few years it will all be successful if the goal is closing down the industry.

Dealing with the Drones

This is the way to increase the empires within the government service. Who cares about a few guides and outfitters anyway? They are just another raw resource, necessary for a while to expand the bureaucracy but ultimately—like the wildlife and the forest—expendable!

As if this wasn't enough to bear, we were also "discovered" by both the provincial and the federal Revenue Departments with their armies of accountants and lawyers. Nearly overnight, a little seasonal business that had supplied greatly needed employment to rural and native people was required to comply with the same amount of government harassment as General Motors.

In addition to income tax assessed on two levels, all of a sudden it became mandatory to collect, administer, and submit to the government reports on: employee income tax; a pension tax requiring the employer to match every dollar; unemployment insurance requiring the employer to cough up a dollar and a half for every dollar the employee puts in; and now, in the NWT, an additional payroll tax.

The days of paying a man a "day's pay for a day's work" are long gone indeed. For every dollar you pay someone, it costs you another dollar in contributions, bookkeepers, and accountants just to stay out of jail.

Then, to add insult to injury, first a provincial sales tax, and then the despised GST were added to the burden. Now the outfitter was put in the miserable position of being an unwilling and unpaid tax collector for the government. Otherwise, where would they get the money to support the Drones and Snivel Servants who harass your every move from cradle to grave?

The sales tax brought many of us into direct confrontation with the bean counters of the Department of Revenue. Eventually, we ended up in court, where the magistrate was to decide how this new tax should be applied to our particular industry. The government lawyers, accountants, and other lackeys presented their case declaring that everything else in the country was taxed, so therefore the services of a hunting guide should not be exempt. They made a very lengthy and impressive presentation.

When it came my turn to testify on behalf of the outfitters and guides, the magistrate had only one question. "Mr. Webb, what, in your opinion, are you selling to these visitors?"

"Your Honor," I replied after a moment's thought, "what we are really selling here is fresh air, dreams, and bullshit, none of which, to the best of my knowledge, is taxable."

BANG! went the gavel, to quiet the room. "I agree. Case dismissed!" I had won. Standing up for principle had paid off, albeit temporarily.

Five years later, the Drones, who always win in the end, came back from another angle and we were saddled with an 11 percent tax. This had to be added to our fees, just when inflation was already pushing our prices beyond the reach of most prospective clients. Many of the old-time outfitters were driven out of business because they couldn't handle the bookkeeping required. We hung on and swallowed it.

So where does the industry stand today, coming up to the end of the century?

For years now our family owned enterprise has gradually moved our operations out of New Brunswick, Newfoundland,

and Quebec and become totally based in the Northwest Territories. We have had to become migrants, as surely as the people crossing the Rio Grande. We are now working out of Yellowknife and living a large portion of the year on the Arctic coast at Coppermine.

But you're never free for sure. The federal government's red tape and taxes follow you to the ends of the earth. However, the majority of the people we work with are down-to-earth troops. Some are native northerners; the rest, like ourselves, are economic refugees from elsewhere in Canada.

Our hopes and future, we believe, lie even farther north. In Coppermine we are building a new home for our business. Working in a partnership with the local Hunters and Trappers Association, we carry on the finest sport hunts in the North and plan to expand into other forms of tourism.

With the implementation of self-government by the Inuit, we feel we are once again embarked on a new and exciting period in our business. People have been expressing doubts about the ability of the local people to govern this new territory. I can only reply, "They could hardly screw it up any worse than has already been done to the rest of Canada by politicians and bureaucrats over the past fifty years."

"Nunavut" in the native language means "our land." It has become our home as well, and here lies our future.

Having survived open-heart surgery, the bypassing of five coronary arteries, and the passing of my sixtieth winter, I now attempt to evaluate whether it has all been worth it. As my wife reminded me recently while we were reminiscing, there was never a season in which we could simply devote our energy to marketing and running our operation. There was always something dreadful on the horizon.

By counting the gray hairs on my head, I can tally the number of struggles that we have had to face. To the best of my recollection, the majority of bad decisions were made at the top. They had nothing whatever to do with game management, advice from the staff in the field, common sense, or economics. Nearly 100 percent were based simply upon political expediency, or the whims of the current minister in charge.

Bitter? Yes, more than somewhat! I resent every single second I've spent worrying and fighting these supposed servants of the people—time that could have been spent making a better living for my family.

On the other hand, I am thankful, and proud as well, that we won enough times to keep our business alive, ourselves and our guides employed, and our spirit unbroken so we can start anew in Nunavut.

SOMETHING LOST IN TRANSLATION

Tom Hennessey —

Except for the naturally talented multilingual individual or the highly trained translator, most of us stumble through life knowing just one language, and perhaps a few foreign phrases picked up as one travels. Years ago I was known, in the right circumstances, to become fairly fluent in a number of tongues, usually helped along by a few belts of rum and a judicious use of international sign language and baby talk. It has been said that if you know the equivalent of *"Oui,"* *"Non,"* and *"Faire l'amour"* in every language, you could never go too far wrong.

Despite the best of intentions, however, sometimes something is lost in translation. The following are personal observations.

CREATIVE OBSCENITY

In deference to the sensibilities of those who have never recently read a book, been to a movie, or watched television; who have been locked away in a convent for the past forty years; or who have just arrived from Mars, I will not employ the most commonly used four-letter adjective/adverb/noun/verb in the English language. I will instead attempt to tell this story in a more refined manner by using in its place the more obscure term "flipping."

I was guiding a lady angler, member of a party from one of the old-time salmon clubs. On this day it was decided that I should haul a canoe out to Britt Brook Crossing and sail the lady down to the mouth of the Serpentine. Here we would meet up with her husband and another guide, drop down to Strathcona for the night, and sail on out in the morning.

In those days it was quite a rough old trail out through the Black Peaks, past Haystack and the Everett Brook Lakes, then down over the hill to the crossing on the Campbell Branch. We left at daylight, and it was still early as we came down toward the river. Rounding a turn, I was surprised to meet a half-ton truck driven by a sometimes guide of mine. Beatle Joe, besides being a good river guide, was one of the slickest poachers in the country, so I knew he would have a report on the river for me.

Beatle was also known for his highly colorful vocabulary, but since I rolled the window down only halfway and kept the motor running, I figured perhaps my lady passenger would not hear much of what was said.

"What's the water like? I hope you haven't poached out all the fish overnight!" was my first concern.

"Well, flip me with a rubber duck, if it isn't the old Boss! For flippin' sure you didn't haul clear the flip out here just to sail down the flippin' Branch, did you?"

I sort of mumbled a reply, and he went on.

"Not a flippin' chance to catch flip-all in that flippin' river. Flippinest thunderstorm last night: flippin' near blew my flippin' tent all to flip, poured down enough flippin' rain to put the flippin' fish clear the flip up into the bushes. Wouldn't give a flip for your chances of fishin', but lots of flippin' water for good sailin'."

Pulling away somewhat embarrassed and not knowing how much my guest had heard, I ventured the observation, "Sounds to me like we might be in for a rough day."

"Oh, no!" declared the lady. "Can't be too bad a day with all that flipping going on. I'm sure we'll have a delightful journey!" And we did.

STUCK ON A TECHNICALITY

It was sometime in the '70s when we produced an excellent film on shooting ruffed grouse and woodcock in northern New Brunswick.

George Klucky from New Hampshire was the cameraman; Jim Rikhoff and Russ Carpenter were the gunners. Given superb autumn scenery, good dog work, and excellent shooting, we produced in just three days an exceptionally good film. It remains a classic today. However, when premiered before an august audience in New Hampshire, a small technicality almost brought us to grief.

The highly prestigious and exclusive New England Ruffed Grouse Society honored us by inviting us to present the first showing of the film at its annual general meeting. Unfortunately, production problems at the lab in Boston delayed the final sound mix, and the film was not complete when the date was upon us.

I was all for backing out and trying to reschedule the event but was overruled by the others involved, especially George the cameraman. To present this film to such a high-class audience, especially in his home state, would indeed boost his fame and fortune. Besides, he was in the habit of running his films without a soundtrack, supplying music and narration himself through an amplifier to most audiences.

We set up the screen and projector in one of the largest and most elegant club meeting rooms I had ever seen. The paneled walls, the huge stone fireplace, and the high ceilings reminded me of a Scottish highland castle. We were wondering if our sound system would be adequate in such an immense area.

As the club members and wives arrived, we could see that they really took this ruffed grouse business seriously. Middle-aged and older, affluent without a doubt. No blue jeans or rubber boots in this outfit. Most of the men wore their shooting costumes: corduroy jackets with leather patches, breeches, and long stockings with red tabs on them. Most also wore their favorite shooting hats with the little red dingus and the ruffed grouse feather. Some carried knobby canes or various fancy shooting sticks, and a dog whistle hung by a thong from every neck.

This was definitely not the type of crowd we usually entertained around the sports-show circuit. I was a bit nervous about it all, but George, full of self-confidence, was all prepared to go. The lights went down, and the opening credits began to roll against the background of red, yellow, and gold autumn leaves. Then George faded back on the music and began the narration.

He introduced Russ and Jim, the well-known outdoor writers, and Fred, the celebrated northern guide, then launched into a description of how one went gunning for the fabled *ruffled* grouse. My heart nearly stopped!

Sidling over to him at the microphone, I whispered in his ear, "George, it is NOT pronounced *ruffled* grouse, it is *RUFFED* grouse!"

George recovered nicely and went on. On woodcock he was fine, but whether it was confusion or a mental block or what, he persisted in calling Old Thunderbird by its dreaded misnomer, ruffled grouse. And this in the presence of the purest of the elite in the ruffed grouse world.

Finally it became too much. There was a crash, and all eyes swiveled to a red-faced old gentleman in kilts, who again smashed his cane on the floor. Despite the near darkness, I imagined I saw the veins struggling to burst in his neck. He was outraged!

"*RUFFLED* GROUSE, *RUFFLED* GROUSE INDEED! RUFFLES ARE ON THE OLD WOMAN'S DRAWERS! FOR CHRIST'S SWEET SAKE, MON, DO YE NOT KNOW THE NAME OF THE FOOKIN' BIRD?"

I could have crawled out the crack under the door. George, however, went blithely on, perhaps a bit subdued but certainly not defeated.

After all, what's a small error in translation?

BUT WE ALL SPEAK ENGLISH, DON'T WE?

As a young man, I was guiding for the Nictau Fish & Game Club up in the woods of northern New Brunswick. This club, composed mainly of wealthy sportsmen from the U.S., was an

institution in our part of the world. For many years it provided
employment for many people of the surrounding area as guides,
cooks, wardens, and managers. I have pictures of my uncle
there a couple of years before I was born. We thought it would
be there forever, but "progress" and politics brought it all to an
end in the early 1970s.

On one occasion, one of the club's oldest members had
brought a group of around a dozen people to spend two weeks
trout fishing and enjoying the solitude. Among the guests were
a lord and lady from the British aristocracy—business friends, I
believe. It fell to my lot to guide the lady, while Phil Howard,
one of the senior guides, took care of the gentleman.

The regular routine was for each guide and guest to go
out by canoe for a couple hours of fishing in the morning,
return for a leisurely lunch and an afternoon nap, then after
dinner disperse again by canoe for the evening's fishing. It
was totally fly fishing and mainly catch-and-release, ideas at
least a half-century ahead of their time as far as the local resi-
dents were concerned.

When you sit alone with a guest, anchored out for hours
at a time, you must be prepared for conversation on a variety
of topics, aside from the blackflies and the fishing. We used
to have a saying that if the guest wanted to talk, we would
oblige, and if he or she wanted to stay quiet, we appreciated
not being on stage.

Camp manager Alfred Fergeson and chief guide Gordon
Black had both impressed upon the crew that good tips would
result if we agreed with everything the guest said and fulfilled
all requests within reason. Despite the fact that the lord and

lady spoke what I assumed was the proper version of English, and we all spoke our local variation of the same, there were times when I was unsure whether my responses to questions were appropriate. After a few days with the lady, my ears became tuned to her conversation, but I never quite got the hang of half what the lord was saying.

One fine morning it all became extremely confusing. The guides and cooks always arose about five o'clock. Guides were at the breakfast table by six, and guests came in precisely at seven. While the clients were eating, it was the guide's job to tidy up and sweep out the cabins, make sure there was ample firewood, empty the chamber pots, and bring in fresh water. Then we were free to rig our canoes and await the pleasure of the visitors.

This morning the lord appeared at breakfast alone. I hung back awaiting the arrival of the lady, my signal to go clean up their cabin. Half an hour later I was still dangling when His Lordship appeared in the dining-room door, napkin in hand, and addressed me thus: "My word, Webb, I fear your fishing partner is still abed. Run down like a good chap and knock the lazy old thing up for me, will you?"

I was left standing with my mouth hanging open, wondering if I had heard him correctly or not. Her Ladyship and I had become fairly friendly, but not to *that* point.

As I stood outside, undecided as to what to do but remembering the chief guide's orders to perform any task our guests desired, I had about decided to go down to the cabin and try to carry out his orders when I saw our cook, Rachael, beckoning from the kitchen door. I knew that Rachael could be trusted to give me sound advice.

"Jesus, Rachael, did you hear what he wants me to do? She isn't all that bad looking, but I don't know how I would ever explain it to the wife when I go home."

She was trying to contain her mirth. "You've got to be around Englishmen more to understand some of the things they say. He doesn't want you to perform his husbandly duties for him, he just wants you to go knock on the door and wake her up!"

Half-relieved and half-disappointed, I ran down to the cabin and performed the required service.

Sometimes it takes some translation.

PARDON ME!

In the good old days, before hydropower was developed and mechanical logging ruined the country, almost everyone along the Tobique River worked for one or another of the salmon fishing clubs or outfitters. The Ogilivie brothers ran a famous camp, located on the Oxbow portion of the river. Here they employed many locals as guides and camp staff. Catering to rich and prominent persons, the camp operated during the decades between the two World Wars and up into the late 1950s.

One of the guides was named Garfield. Like all Tobique guides in those days, Garfield was an expert canoe handler who knew the water at all times and seasons. His only problem came in dealing with the visiting sports—the unfortunate result of his having been born with a cleft palate, causing a fairly serious speech impediment. However, he got along very well most of the time and was in fact requested by many of the returning clients.

Something Lost in Translation

On this occasion a party had arrived that included a wealthy New York businessman and his spouse. When the guides were assigned, the lady was to go with Garfield. After lunch the head guide explained that there was time for a few hours of fishing before dinner, and the guides were all ready to go. Fishing had been fairly good for the last day or two, and whoever was ready to go first would have the choice of the pools.

Being the first to put her rod together, and carrying her tackle bag, the lady proceeded down the steps to the beach and introduced herself to Garfield. Unfortunately, the head guide neglected to go along to make formal introductions, and the conversation went something like this:

"Hello, Garfield, my name is Susan. I am sure I will enjoy fishing with you. I guess we are ready first, so as you are the expert, what is your advice for the afternoon?"

Garfield, straining to make a good first impression, blurted out something that sounded like "Fuh fuh fup freamerown!"

"What did you say?" asked the startled lady.

"Fuh fup freamerown, fup freamerown!"

"Well! We shall see about this, my good man!" she said, tossing her rod and bag to the ground and storming up to confront the head guide on the steps of the Lodge.

"I want you to discharge that man immediately. I have never been so insulted in all of my life!" she cried.

"My goodness, Missus, what happened? Old Garfield is a born-again Christian and one of the best guides we have here."

"Well, he must be drunk or something," she insisted. "When I asked him very politely what my choices were, he informed me very rudely that I could go *f---*, *scream,* or *drown*! No one has ever spoken to me like that before!"

"Oh, my goodness gracious, Madam. Garfield would never say anything like that. He was just asking you if you wanted to go *upstream or down.*"

Sometimes the details get lost in translation.

POLITICAL CORRECTNESS HAS ITS REWARDS

(Minutes from a meeting of a northern Canadian tourism association)

The meeting was addressed by Ms. Naturalist, representing the eco-tourism segment, regarding funding for advertising.

"Ms. Chairperson, executive and fellow members. As one who wishes to bring naturalists, birders, whale watchers, and other non-consumers of wildlife to enjoy the beauty of our country, I propose the following motion: That the association cease its support and promotion of the blood sports of hunting and fishing and dedicate its efforts toward promoting more wholesome activities."

Chairperson: "Do any of the members present wish to speak regarding this motion before it is put to the vote?"

Old Outfitter: "Yes, Ms. Chairperson, I wish to direct the following to Ms. Naturalist. We all appreciate the beauty of our environment, and we all strive toward conserving our natural resources. Thirty years ago, before you were born, we found out that the only people willing to pay enough money to support employment in our isolated communities were the hunters and the fishermen. Twenty years ago, while you were still in grade school, we tried catering to canoeists and cross-country skiers, and we went broke. Five years ago, when you were still attending college in the city, we attempted once more to gain a livelihood for our guides in what you term the 'non-consumptive market.' It was once again a failure. Now, in speaking to your motion, I would suggest that you roll it up and stick it where the sun does not shine! Thank you."

Laughter from some and cries of indignation from others were finally quelled by gavel-pounding, and order was restored.

Chairperson: "Mr. Outfitter, on behalf of Ms. Naturalist and this association, I must ask you to apologize for your impolite remarks before this meeting proceeds further."

Old Outfitter: "Ms. Chairperson, Ms. Naturalist, fellow members. I must apologize if my remarks are out of order. In my desire to rid my speech of anything that might be construed as being sexist or politically incorrect, I made reference to an orifice universally possessed by male and female alike. If the Chair so wishes, I can rephrase my comment to something more gender-specific!"

Meeting adjourned.

INSIDE INFO ON PICKING AN OUTFITTER

Tom Hennessey —

I recently came across yet another magazine article on the subject of picking an outfitter. Having been the target of "picking" for most of my life, it got me thinking about how and where we may have gone wrong. I started by looking in my dictionary. Definitions of "picking" include the following, all of which—alas—I have been subjected to at one time or another:

1. To harvest
2. To pluck
3. To rip off, bit by bit
4. To poke at with the fingers
5. To break up with a pointed instrument
6. To steal the contents of

7. To open without a key
8. To provoke
9. To unravel
10. To select from a group

Thank God for the last one, at least, although even this one leaves the "pickee" somewhat at the mercy of the "picker."

Let's suppose a prospective client is cruising a sports show in hopes of picking the outfitter who will make all his dreams come true. His success will depend to some extent upon what type of outfitter he wants to pick. Keep in mind that these are general observations gleaned over forty years, and there are always exceptions to any rule.

Do you want to book with an outfitter who started out as a guide and later struck out on his own? Or do you want to book with a city businessman who woke up one morning and decided that hunting was neat stuff, so he cashed in his pension fund and purchased an outfitting business?

There is a difference!

Do you realize that in some areas the cost of travel and logistics bears no relationship to what you are used to in the civilized areas of the planet, and despite the outfitter's healthy outdoor lifestyle, he's in this to make a living? Or is the price of the hunt your first consideration in picking an outfitter; are you always looking for a deal?

There is a difference!

Do you want to book with the guy in blue jeans who shuffles his feet, looks sometimes at the ceiling and sometimes at the floor, does not guarantee anything except to tell the truth about what has happened in his area to date, admits he is not always right, cannot forecast the weather or game migrations, and can only give a vague promise to do his damnedest for you? Or do you want to book with the guy in the suit and shiny shoes whose handshake is dry and firm and who looks you directly in the eye and tells you exactly what you want to hear?

There is a difference!

Do you want to book with the guy you've seen for twenty years who has paid for a booth and donated to your club, who will answer your questions in the booth, who offers you hunts at a rate it takes to produce quality, and who will not try to tree you like a bobcat in the bar at 3 A.M.? Or do you want to book with the guy in the big hat, high-heeled lizard boots, and nifty designer safari suit—the guy with the gigantic photo album who trolls the hallways, banquet tables, men's room, and convention bus—the guy who rudely butts into the conversation and tries to cut you out of someone else's booth like a calf at a rodeo?

There is a difference!

Do you want to book with the guy with the broken nose, busted knuckles, heart-bypass scars, and Maalox stains in the corner of his mouth? Or do you want to book with the guy with the movie-star suntan, the pearly white teeth, and the $100 haircut?

There is a difference!

Do you want to book with the hard-nosed, sober manager who will have the crew up and ready to go on time, turn out safe and successful hunts year after year in an unspectacular manner, and not let the inmates run the asylum? Or do you want to book with the jolly "hail fellow well met" host and gifted raconteur who will drink your Scotch, kiss your ass, and pat you on the head after missed shots and blunders?

There is a difference!

Your answers to these questions will determine to a great extent whether you get back alive and happy after an experience you will treasure forever.

Should the process ever be reversed and the "pickee" put in charge of picking, I would only pray for a few basic blessings: That people read my literature, send back the signed contracts, submit the money on schedule without any bounced checks, and arrive as scheduled and equipped as instructed with the required physical ability and mental attitude. And, oh, yes, the single most important requirement—determination to enjoy the experience regardless of killing something that will qualify for the record book.

It most certainly does make a difference!

SEE YOU AT THE CONVENTION

Tom Hennessey

Because part of the life of any professional guide is the marketing of his services, many of us have become trapped in the exotic world of the sports-show-and-convention circuit. Shows and conventions, like everything else in the business, have gone through some shocking changes. The log-cabin booths and the wood-chopping and tea-boiling competitions of our youth are pretty well gone. Now it is mostly sophisticated, slick marketing, and you are just as likely to hear outfitters talking about their newest computer program for direct mail as about their airplanes or horses.

Basically, they are still opportunities for prospective clients to get a firsthand look at the guy into whose hands they may consign their lives and deposit checks. Public relations and marketing, even after all these years, remain a total mystery to me. How come we used to be able to attend a sports show, stay drunk for ten days, and go home having booked upwards of two hundred hunters from clear across the USA? Nowadays we stay sober and serious, change our shirts every day, talk our guts out, and are not nearly as successful. I guess I will never figure out what turns on the public.

Like most of my contemporaries, when I'm up to my ass in snow, wallowing in the blood, sweat, and mud of the hunting seasons, I eagerly look forward to the marketing season. The big hotels and convention halls, the banquets, the camaraderie of genial dudes gathering to discuss the triumphs of past hunts and plan future ones all look attractive from a distance.

Sure as hell, halfway through the first show, with two more months to go, most of us older hands are footsore, hung over, claustrophobic, choked to death, and fed up to the gills with civilization. At such times, you might find me outside the hotel taking a few breaths of smog and searching frantically for the sun or a familiar star to orient myself.

Perhaps I am simply getting old. I always half-envy certain outfitters and booking agents who do a much better job at selling than they ever do at hunting. They're still bellied up to the bar at three in the morning, arm around some dude they're buttering up for the kill, or horning in on a table full of strangers at the banquet with their immense photo albums.

I am ashamed to admit that as a social animal, I am a total disaster. No matter how many years I have tried, I am about as comfortable as the town whore at a church picnic in these surroundings. Being used to the wide-open spaces of the North, I cannot abide crowds and noise, and any gathering of more than three people puts me on the defensive.

Fifty years of guns going off in my ears has left me deaf to the point of confusion. I find it simply impossible to engage in polite conversation around a twenty-person table—especially while two thousand people are clattering and screaming, drowning out some speaker or performer at the far end of a room as big as a hangar.

While I appreciate the fact that some people view these gatherings as very important social occasions, to me they are a nightmare. I cannot even estimate the number of times kind and well-meaning friends have insisted that I join their table at a banquet. Everyone except me appears relaxed and elegant in their evening clothes, enjoying the occasion immensely. I sit there sweating like a pig, scrunched up in a too-small space, feeling bloated in my ten-year-old suit. I'm trying to catch phrases and read the lips of people across the table who insist upon interrogating me about Christ knows what above the uproar.

Trying to select the right fork and choke down what to me has all the appeal of broken glass; I am doing my damnedest to will my nose not to drip on the tablecloth. Sitting cross-legged, attempting to hold back the bubble of gas that is lodged up under my rib cage where it threatens to stop my heart, I must look as if I am having a wonderful time.

My friends, I hope that you will sympathize with my phobias as they apply to urban climes. I pray that you will understand when you see me at a cocktail party with my back in a corner and my eyes on the exit while I nurse a warm Lone Star. Please forgive me for not joining in your social life and entertaining you with scintillating conversation.

I love you one and all, and if you will please just send me the deposit check, then come up and see what we do in my part of the world, we will all be buddies forever.

ENDANGERED SPECIES

Tom Hennessey —

Am I becoming more paranoid and pessimistic in my old age, or have we already lost the war against the antihunters, antigunners, and various other idiot organizations? If you are in my business you can't pick up the paper, read a magazine, or turn on the television nowadays without running across something guaranteed to raise your blood pressure and lower your hopes of survival. I am beginning to believe that the hunter, and those of us whose lives are tied to guiding hunters, are the true endangered species. As far as I can see, we are surely headed for extinction.

Think it can't happen, that good sense, scientific fact, or even economic considerations have anything to do with it? Think again. Take a good look at the public's intelligence level regarding any natural resource issue. Good sense has nothing to do with it. We are dealing with ignorance, emotion, and the cynical exploitation of the uninformed by skilled manipulators. I find it ironic that they have jailed a TV actor/evangelist whose only crime was accepting the money that stupid people insisted on giving him. Much worse examples of ripoff occur in the Anti-Everything Industry, where dumb people are fleeced for various "causes" for the enrichment of a few at the top—just what the evangelist was accused of. The difference is that in addition to being crooks, the anti-everythings are in most cases destroying wildlife and the environment while wiping out the livelihoods of people involved in the harvest of these renewable natural resources.

Every day we see more battles lost as the rural aspect of our society changes. Generation by generation, traditional land-based values are disappearing into the urban swamp. This is not a one-way highway. City people move to the country for the rural lifestyle, but soon can't stand the odor caused by the picturesque farm animals that looked so cute on television. Pretty soon the petitions start, and the fourth-generation pig farmer is driven out to make room for the continuing expansion of the human animal.

Everywhere things are changing. How many honest kill shots have you seen in any of the big-game hunting publications lately? Now they all seem to have art directors who prefer to purchase cutesy critter pictures taken in parks and preserves. The fact that a lot of the photos don't bear any connection to the article being illustrated seems to escape most of them.

The constant antigun and antihunting slant in all forms of media is growing daily. I was amused to see the reaction when then-President Bush took his annual hunting and fishing trip to Texas. As would be expected, the hyenas were baying at his heels as he tried to justify his choice of vacation. You may have noticed that no one asked many questions about the fishing he did. The jerking of a bass out of its natural environment to flop around suffocating to death doesn't seem to upset anyone. After all, it is a smelly, scaly thing, and with the possible exception of Flipper, there has never been a TV personality based on a critter with no legs. When it came to shooting quail, though, that was something else. We will never know what would have happened if Bush had chosen to go deer hunting. Some of the press questioned his right to shoot the darling birds and were appalled that it might be for "sport." However, once they were assured that he really hated to do it but times were tough in D.C. and he had a big family to feed, it was accepted somewhat reluctantly as justifiable homicide.

The right to own firearms continues to be a horrendous battle, part of which we are losing daily in both Canada and the U.S., despite the fact that every scrap of reason resides on one side of the issue. But reason is never enough. The same people who want to take guns away from the populace insist on forgiving and releasing criminals who murder with guns. Anyone from another planet would see no logic in their argument, but that doesn't stop them from winning.

Some of the battles are lost by default. No one in the progun organizations that I am aware of raised even a whimper in defense of trapping or the ownership of three-wheel ATVs, despite the fact that they are closely related to the gun issue. If the three-wheeler can be outlawed because stupid people hurt themselves while misusing it, what is the future for guns?

It is difficult to win a war armed only with facts and reason while the other side has access to hype and emotion. At least three of the top big-money protest organizations got their start and made their first fortune by exploiting the seal hunt in eastern Canada. It is interesting to note that once it was all over, one of them felt obliged to admit that it had been lying, grossly misrepresenting both the ecological and biological facts of the situation. However, the group stated it had been justified in destroying the livelihood of several thousand Canadians, including the northern natives, because "The public found the method of harvest to be repugnant." This after the group raised millions of dollars to make sure that every person on the planet had the opportunity to view the blood on the ice.

This surely illustrates that any unscrupulous group, by appealing solely to raw emotion, can raise money for a phony cause while enjoying tax-exempt status with the government. Of course, this concept works best if the object you happen to be misrepresenting is like the baby seal: cute, cuddly, white, and with big blue eyes.

When I witness the genuinely worthwhile efforts of Game Conservation International (Game Coin) to save the rhinoceros, for example, I am tempted to write my friend Mr. Tennison and say, "Gee, Uncle Harry, you are trying to save a critter that is big and ugly. Why couldn't we pull an Iran-Contra type of hustle, raise the money to save the koala or the panda, then divert it to save the rhino?" I am sure we would be inundated with donations immediately. Alas, the people who know what really needs saving are reluctant to lower themselves to the methods of the self-appointed animal rightists.

Endangered Species

Sitting around various campfires, some of us in the hunting business have tried to come up with ideas for our own survival in the coming decades. Fortunately, perhaps, most of us currently worrying won't be around all that much longer, but the end is coming faster every day. I have some personal thoughts on the matter:

The only salvation I can see for myself is to obey the adage, "If you can't beat them, join them." With this in mind, I plan to become "The Born-Again Outfitter," jump on the "anti" bandwagon, and in a very short time make more money than I have in a lifetime of guiding hunters. Just think of the advantages. I wouldn't have to try to supply honest answers to the million questions anymore; I could just ad-lib them. We all know people will believe anything—the more ridiculous the better. For my TV appearances, I might have to do without the porcupine-quill band on my cowboy hat, wear plastic shoes, and replace the skinning knife in my belt pouch with a blow-dryer or something. I realize I would also have to make some adjustments in my personal life. I would probably have to retire my wife of over forty years. Having aided and abetted me and cooked in hunting camps all her life, she probably wouldn't fit in with my new image. Not to worry, though. I would have lots of young college stuff and movie starlets hanging off my neck like the other anti-hunting millionaires.

Some added benefits: I wouldn't have to risk my life dozens of times a year in airplanes and boats, freeze to death on muskox hunts in the Arctic, sleep in flapping tents on the Barren Lands, drown in the tuckamore thickets of Newfoundland, battle the tide in Ungava Bay, or haul barrels of guts for bear bait in New Brunswick. Everyone has met at least a few examples of the type of hunter that the anti-s claim represents all of us, so I could drag up stories about some of those. I could dig up all the "outs" from the hunting films we have made over the years, including the less-than-perfect kill shots that the public has never seen. I could even buy the rights to some of the amateur bowhunting videos currently being used to gross out people at sports shows. After all, it doesn't take too much intelligence to misrepresent our sport, or these people wouldn't be so successful at it.

Come to think of it, if I could stand being a cynical, hypocritical, traitorous son of a bit-- of great enough proportions, I could be rolling in clover in six months.

If I became bored with how easy it all was, it would be possible to branch out in new directions. After all, the present groups of idiots have barely scratched the surface. I would avoid the highly competitive areas such as saving the seal, whale, dolphin, monkey, sea otter, and other easy picks. There is no need to further enhance the civil rights enjoyed by the pet community, for example, but if we are to take their arguments about all living things to their logical conclusion, the sky is the limit.

One would want to avoid the already overdone causes such as wearing fur coats. For a while there, it seemed that fur was okay if the skin was taken from an animal that was bred, raised, and killed for that purpose, as opposed to the wild animal, less than 1 percent of which ever encountered a trapper. Now, since farm fur is out, we are supposed to believe that phony fur made from petrochemical derivatives is somehow environmentally more acceptable than the natural product. Some other cretins also wish to wear various other types of plastic, all of which contribute to environmental destruction, so we can forget taking on leather as our "cause."

Perhaps I could start a protest against wool. Can you imagine the various avenues of animal civil liberties we could get into here? What atrocities are committed within the sheep-raising industry? How horrid the shock to the poor animal's system when its fleece is removed, and imagine the traumatic impact upon the sensitivities of the poor little ewe as some fearsome ogre with clippers lays bare her most private anatomy. I have heard that some people even eat the young of the species. Too terrible to contemplate, a natural to expose. Sheep are cute, too.

The array of causes is endless. Let's end exploitation of all animals. To begin with, consider the plight of the pets that the antihunters adore. Can you imagine worse exploitation than to be born to slavery—a fish in a bowl, a bird in a cage, or a hamster destined to run around a wheel all its life? With the exception of sled dogs and hunting dogs, most pets exist only at the whim of a human master and are reduced to begging and sucking up for a living. Some would advocate giving up the consumption of all forms of animal protein and becoming vegetarians. But what about the genocide inflicted upon our insect friends in the pursuit of successful agriculture? True, you could banish all chemical pesticides and nonorganic fertilizers. When I was a kid on the farm, we fertilized with animal manure. But if we quit eating meat, are we going to keep animals just to produce fertilizer? Before DDT, we walked down the rows in potato fields picking off potato bugs and drowning them in a can of kerosene. You couldn't do that in our ideal world because you would be violating the bugs' rights and ripping off the environment to provide the kerosene.

I guess you can assume that the ultimate "cause," taken to its logical conclusion, would be to remove all human presence from the planet. And here the anti-s have already started. Whether they realize it or not, they are engaged in the business of extinguishing the rights of the human animal to exist, starting with outfitters and hunters.

How much easier it would be to save the environment and solve the world's real problems if these people would only face reality, join the sportsmen, and put their money and energy to some genuine use.

Maybe we should just quit worrying about it, have another beer, and pretend that we are winning—that we are *not* the real endangered species.

WHAT IS BETTER, LUCK OR SKILL?

Tom HENNESSEY —

(This account first appeared in the Victoria County Record, *November 1976)*

How many times have you pondered the relative importance of luck as opposed to skill in the successful pursuit of fish and game? In the guiding business we have seen both sides of the coin and have begun to form some pretty definite opinions.

A number of years ago, we were honored to host a gentleman who was undoubtedly one of the ten best-known sportsmen alive at that time. Executive Editor of one of the "Big Three" sporting magazines, author of several books on fishing and hunting, and experienced on every major salmon river in the world, he arrived early in July with his attractive wife to try the fishing on the Tobique.

The gentleman was armed with the best of gear—rods by Leonard, Hardy, and Orvis and flies of every pattern and size. With Coleman McDougall guiding the lady and I the gentleman, we expected to take a fish or two.

At the end of a week of beating the water, all agreed we'd had a fine time and seen some pretty water, but the fact remained that we couldn't kill a salmon. Having at least hooked a couple of fish should have made us feel a bit better, but you can't take pictures for a magazine of the one that got away, much less eat him. So much for equipment and experience.

The following week, one of our oldest friends in the business arrived from Indiana—a far piece from salmon water. John had never seen salmon outside a can and had never fly fished in his life, but he considered this no great drawback. John is what you might call one of the more relaxed type of sportsmen.

Although serious when actually engaged in hunting and an excellent shot, John had always considered the fun aspects of any trip to be more important than the amount of game bagged. One result, incidentally, is that on two bear hunting trips he had taken two trophies, as he had done on two bobcat hunting ventures.

When I endeavored to explain that Atlantic salmon fishing was an art in itself, his reaction was, "We'll just take a crack at her and see what happens."

He had been absent from the country for some time, so the first couple of days were taken up with visiting and treating the considerable number of friends he had among the guides in the valley. During this time, a fly-casting lesson and a taste of salmon were donated by a thoughtful friend so when John sobered up he would know what he was after.

The preparations paid off handsomely. Coleman and I were busy with other guests, so my sons, Rick and Martin, volunteered to take John on his first salmon fishing adventure. With a fly rod of no particular brand, picked up at the Canadian Tire

Store in Grand Falls—which happened to be next to the New Brunswick Liquor Commission outlet—and two flies tied locally, he was not long in proving that there isn't much to this salmon fishing racket.

Within the first hour on the Serpentine, one fish was hooked, played, and lost while another, a sixteen-pounder, was landed. Proceedings were immediately adjourned and a return made to camp, where suitable celebrations lasted well into the evening.

The next two trips with the boys to the river resulted in the taking of a nice grilse, and another salmon going thirteen pounds. As John is never game-greedy, the remainder of the week was spent making farewell calls around the country.

So who can say which is more important—luck, skill, equipment, or experience? The only thing I know for sure is that if I am ever lost on the Barrens, starving, and with one shell for the .30-30, I sure hope old John turns up, especially if he brings along his good luck and that jug.

HUNTERS OR SHOPPERS?

Tom Hennessey —

In a recent September, in the middle of another Arctic hunting season, I passed my fifty-fifth birthday. I can now officially term myself "middle-aged," assuming that I am going to live to be 110. Having spent about forty of those birthdays in camps in one place or another, I guess you might say that hunting is both a lifestyle and a livelihood for my family. Now, however, as we march through the last decade of the century, it seems to me that we are losing ground in the fight to retain our hunting heritage, and some of the fault may be our own.

We are engaged in a fight, the outcome of which will determine the course, if any, that hunting will take in years to come. The days of the free-ranging professional hunter, on this continent or any other, have just about come to an end. Various influences have crept into the picture. Rising human populations, rapid urbanization, loss of wilderness, and the rise of various animal-rights industries have all brought about negative change. Many of these factors seem to be beyond our control, although we must keep trying. The hunting and conservation organizations—especially Safari Club International—continue to fight the good fight to educate the undecided and to present our case to the world. There is, however, a disturbing trend in our sport of which we are all aware, for which we are all responsible, and which only we can address. A recent article by Warren Parker entitled "It's Time to Clean up Our Act" puts it very clearly.

I am fully aware that it has always been in my interest as a professional hunter to produce high success rates and to fill the record books with trophies taken by our clients. I am equally aware that as a businessman who depends upon guiding hunters for a living, I probably should not be writing preachy articles that might be read by potential clients. However, as all of my friends know, I do not make a habit of avoiding issues.

It is easy enough for the retired professionals to be critical of today's situation; their family's livelihood no longer depends upon hunting. It also seems mandatory for those "born-again bandits" who go belly-up to the antihunting movement to spill their guts about our profession. If some of us who still make a living out of hunting don't start speaking up, I think hunting could go down the drain within our generation.

All of us sportsmen—hunters and professionals alike— had better give some thought to getting back to the days when a hunt meant a hunt, and the killing of an animal was the attainment of the dream rather than the entire point of the operation. It is fine to defend hunting based upon arguable management considerations or sustenance-based food harvesting; but if we are going to defend what the anti-s call "killing for sport," we had better put it back on the basis of hunting rather than guaranteed harvesting. The hunting of game is as old as mankind itself. Among the most primitive

Campfire Lies of a Canadian Guide

societies, in which hunting for food was or is of paramount importance, the taking of exceptional animals has always added excitement to the chase. Many cave drawings depict trophy-sized critters, while not much time was spent bragging on the walls about the better-tasting but smaller ones taken for eating. There is no question that trophy hunting, done ethically, is an honorable pursuit. The utilization of an animal to create employment, in areas where not much else exists, is usually of greater benefit than killing solely for the table. In many areas, it is the only remaining link to a traditional hunting lifestyle, allowing native people to both retain their heritage and earn the money we all need to exist in the modern world.

When a northern Canadian resident wants to eat a muskox, for example, a tag is drawn from the community quota. The man uses his snowmobile, burns his own gas, kills a muskox, and brings it home to share with his neighbors.

When one of our down-south sport hunters kills a muskox, employment is created for many people right down the line. The professional hunter, the staff of the local hunters' and trappers' association, the guides, the hotel, and the airline all benefit. The people who sell gas and gear, rent snowmobiles, operate the community taxi, and sew the skin clothing right on down to the taxidermist, all see part of the economic benefit. The client takes home the inedible hide and horns; the meat is shared in the community. That muskox is not any deader than the one killed by the local resident, so I know that truth and justice are on the side of properly regulated trophy hunting.

I will argue any day with the Bambi Bunch, who give lip service to preserving the environment and protecting primitive peoples while destroying the livelihoods of those people by ending trapping and seal hunting and trying to end sport hunting. I guess you can gather that I believe in trophy hunting. So what am I worried about?

I am one of the persons who have made a living partly because of the existence of the various record books. Have I suddenly had second thoughts about the matter? One might wonder why I feel the need to express a feeling so elusive; it is hard to put a finger on my belief that if hunting declines, we ourselves will have been part of the reason.

The word hunting, as has been pointed out by people smarter than I, is defined as "searching, seeking, looking for." Nowhere in my small dictionary does it say "shooting, arrowing, stuffing, and hanging on the wall."

As professionals in the business of hunting, we are supposed to be selling an opportunity to "seek, search, look for," and ultimately to kill cleanly and with respect, and to harvest both the meat and the memories. Nowhere can I find a definition that says the hunting professional is selling animal carcasses.

The record systems, the various "slams," have all been supported by people like myself, who are in the business of helping to fulfill these objectives. Those systems have been of tremendous value to us, and have helped us meet some of the finest people and best hunters in the world. They have also, unfortunately, brought about an increasing number of unrealistic expectations, and in some cases, demands that the objective be met by any means and at any price. Blessed is the experienced hunter who arrives with the attitude and the ability to give it an honest, enjoyable effort and to be happy with the result—whatever fate decrees. These are the same people who ultimately seem to take the best trophies anyway, and to have a lot more fun doing it, as I once pointed out at an awards ceremony at which we received very high recognition. Probably 90 percent of the records are taken by accident, and the remaining 10 percent are crooked deals. So let's quit worrying about the measuring tape and get back to having some fun hunting.

You may well wonder what has caused me to worry about where we are going. I am still thinking about that birthday last September in a Barren Lands caribou camp, up to which time we'd been having a pretty standard season. In all of our years operating caribou camps in Newfoundland, Ungava, and the Northwest Territories, we have legitimately maintained a 100 percent rate of success, taking big trophy-class caribou and showing up at the top of the record books all along. Throughout this time, when booking clients and again when welcoming them to our camps, we have always stressed that, like anything else in life, we can strive for 100 percent success but must at some point face the day when it is something less than 100 percent. I have also stressed that we would always strive for perfection, but I did not intend to listen to any whining when that goal was not achieved. We take pains to explain to anyone who will listen that we are in the hunting business, not the killing business, and if I was in the critter-selling business I would probably do it by mail order and save us all a lot of inconvenience.

Now at last, on this September Barren Lands hunt, I had the suspicion that despite all my advance explanations, we might have hit a week in which caribou density was not as great as usual while the density of "hunters" might have been slightly greater.

Hunters or Shoppers?

Up until the third day, enough animals had been seen to make the hunting interesting. One book bull had been taken, and several decent representative heads had been turned down. The fact that for three days the weather had been absolutely beautiful for this part of the world hadn't helped matters. Great weather for picnicking isn't always the best for hunting.

When you are in the heart of the Barren Lands, you are for sure in the middle of caribou country, but as some old guide once said, "There ain't nothin' as empty as caribou country when there ain't no caribou!" My son's camp, fifty miles north of us, and another camp seventy-five miles beyond both reported that herds still were filtering through, so I knew that we would still see plenty of animals.

However, by the end of the third day, despite the protestations on Day One that "we are just here for the good time," I began to pick up subtle hints of what was to come. "We always thought caribou hunting was 100 percent guaranteed," and "We only saw about thirty bulls all day long" were a couple of the comments. Others included: "Does it usually get better later in the season?" "How are they making out at the other camp? Maybe we should have gone there." And "We're not complaining, but we thought we would see more caribou."

"Well, boys," I told them, "running short of caribou is like losing your grandmother. You know the old girl is going to croak someday, but for Christ's sake, don't bury her until she quits breathing!"

As things turned out, the weather changed, more caribou moved through, and everyone took his bull. Once more I was transformed from Ol' Fred the Crooked Outfitter to Good Ol'

Fred, Guide Extraordinaire. Looking back over forty years of guiding, I find it remarkable how many times a change in the weather not only brought aches and pains to my abused carcass but also changed me totally in the eyes of the client. Miraculous beyond a doubt!

Autumn of 1990 was not one of the best in history for hunting central Canada barren ground caribou. In fact, two competitor outfits had very slim hunting, even though at least one continues to lie about it. I definitely do not take satisfaction in anyone's misfortune. Indeed, it must ultimately happen to all of us. After all, the animals do not read the script, and they do not care how famous old Fred is or how much money it cost the client to get there. They just go about their own business, as they have done forever, making their annual journeys unconfined by fences and controlled only by natural forces. We and our Inuit friends will still be there, hoping that if we work hard enough and the God of Hunters smiles on us, we may save a few big old bulls from a less worthy end.

We hope that hunting as a sport remains alive and well for many years, and that on the day when we are no longer 100 percent successful, we will still have a camp full of companions who are hunters and not just shoppers.

SALUTE TO MODERN-DAY DIANAS

Tom Hennessey—

My dictionary identifies Diana as the mythical Roman goddess of hunting, chastity, and the moon. While the last two are outside my area of expertise, I can certainly attest to the skill and dedication shown by the many ladies who have hunted with us over the years.

Historically, it seems to me, the female has been stuck with a supporting role when it comes to outdoor adventures, limited to packing and paddling and propping up the ego of the lord and master. Only once in a while, by a slip of the pen, have we males acknowledged women's help, and then reluctantly. For example, everyone knows that Lewis and Clark crossed the mountains to the Pacific, thus ensuring themselves a place in history. What they barely hinted at in their journals is the fact that without the help of a native woman by the name of Sacajawea, acting as a guide and interpreter, they probably would never have made it. In another case, at the beginning of the century, Mina Hubbard successfully organized and carried out a tremendous wilderness journey from the coast of Labrador to Ungava Bay. This was a year after her husband messed up and starved to death trying to do the same thing.

Occasionally, credit must be given where it is due. So here, at the risk of alienating all of my male clients, I will tell you why we welcome ladies on all of our hunting trips.

When I began guiding in the East nearly forty years ago, most female guests came with their husbands to dabble in the gentle sports of salmon angling and woodcock gunning. Usually, either the youngest guides, like myself, or the over-the-hill old-timers were assigned to take care of them. I could never quite see the logic behind this arrangement, but that's the way it was.

Ladies in pursuit of big game were not common, but there were a few, one of whom I recall fondly. She was a young lady of Eurasian extraction, her name quite unpronounceable by anyone in our part of the country. We simply called her "Honey." Her husband, a man of advanced years, started out the trip by promising me great rewards if his new spouse could kill a bear, a deer, and various other critters. By the end of two weeks, he and his veteran guide had scored zero while Honey and I had fared much better, and his attitude had deteriorated noticeably.

Throughout the 1960s and 1970s, we began to encounter more women interested in the sport, and those content to read a book in camp were becoming the minority. While the gals had previously put up with making do with their husbands' cast-off guns and gear, now they began showing up wearing their own L. L. Bean boots and toting rods and rifles fit for some serious business. This change seemed to have nothing to do with the emerging women's lib sentiment. On the contrary, all I met were greatly at home in their femininity, with no desire whatever to be "just one of the boys." They only wanted an equal crack at the action.

I am occasionally asked whether or not a particular hunt is "suitable for a woman." The reply has always been that if a person is a hunter, he or she is a hunter, regardless of whether they button their pants on the side or up the middle. There are plenty of people of both sexes who have no desire to experience life in a wilderness setting. Those people take up activities that keep them within the confines of civilization. If they don't, they should. There are, after all, some trade-offs to be considered.

A couple of experiences have proven to me that the lack of fancy washroom facilities is not necessarily a matter of life or death to those who enjoy wilderness adventure. One fall ten years ago, we were opening a brand-new caribou camp on the shores of Ungava Bay with a group of Eskimos from the area. We had gone up the coast, located the site, paced out a "runway," and against a tight deadline, proceeded to build a camp capable of hosting eight soon-to-arrive guests. On the fateful opening day, while the Twin Otter was buzzing the area to push caribou off the strip, we were still putting the finishing touches on the setup. As I raced up the hill to welcome the party, which included a lady hunter from Long Island, it struck me that the camp wasn't quite complete.

"Mary Jane," I blurted, "I hope you went to the bathroom in Montreal or Fort Chimo because we haven't had time to build one here yet."

"Don't worry," she assured me. "Whatever suits you guys will do for me."

The problem was rectified within a couple of hours, and the camp was opened with one of the best weeks I have ever spent hunting.

On another occasion, we were hosting a lady on a hunt for muskox in the western Arctic. Muskox hunts in late winter can be honestly described as a genuine Arctic adventure. You travel by snowmobile with an Inuit guide and tent-camp at night in temperatures sometimes sinking to forty below zero. With expert guides and good equipment it is not exactly life-threatening, but it certainly is not to be compared to a vacation in Florida. Bathroom facilities, of course, are in most cases nonexistent. Back in town after that hunt, while we were talking over the trip and admiring the exceptionally fine trophy she had taken, I asked her if she had learned much about Arctic survival.

"Well," she told me seriously, "I have learned that you have to be careful not to pee on your *mukluks*, or your feet will freeze solid in no time."

That's the kind of gal I don't mind hunting with anywhere.

When it comes to the physical demands of hunting, a person's condition, of course, is the most vital factor, and sex is about the least important consideration. In my years in the wild places, I have seen enough examples of the female as a combination pack animal and companion to dispel any ideas that they can't handle hard going.

I have heard the concern that the vocabulary of the guides might contain colorful adjectives that could traumatize the delicate ears of lady guests, and this has mystified me somewhat.

Salute to Modern-Day Dianas

Some of us may indeed be guilty of an occasional slip of the tongue during times of extreme stress—even myself, I blushingly confess. However, every backcountry guide I know would be horrified to see what passes for entertainment in some of the currently popular movies, not to mention what your four-year-old kid watches on daytime soap operas.

Gun-handling is another area of concern, and here I will generalize a little, but it has become almost a camp cliché that the lady in the lineup will be the one who hits the sighting-in target dead center. I don't know whether this next factor has anything to do with it or not, but usually the girls seem to have the good sense to be shooting something that doesn't break their collarbone or open up a gash between their eyes every time they touch the trigger.

When it comes to hunting from stands, we have found that the ladies seem to excel. Coleman McDougall is a guide in his mid-seventies working in our eastern Canada bear camps. He started guiding when I was a kid, and that's a while ago. I rely upon Coleman to take care of the female hunters, and he can tell you plenty of success stories that can't all be written off as good luck. He works some bear stands that he considers to be almost guaranteed successful with a woman occupant but never successful with a man. We have tried over the years to figure out why that seems to be so. We know that the girls we have been with have been good shots and seem to have plenty of patience, but most of all, Coleman claims that the ladies listen to their guide. They do what they are told, don't spend all week trying to prove they are smarter than the guide, and mostly this pays off.

So, do we have nothing but pleasant memories of days afield with these Dianas? Well, almost. There are, after all, three distinct types of women that have shown up in my camps. One comes to hunt, and she is a joy to all concerned. One comes to relax in the fresh air, and if there is a spare seat on the airplane, we are happy to see her. The third type comes to make damn sure the old man doesn't have any fun. Fortunately for us all, this third type is extremely rare. I haven't seen one since 18 June 1963.

Although women do not make up a very large percentage of our clientele, their numbers are increasing every year and we are mighty pleased to welcome them. Many years ago a lady client, older and wiser than I at the time, left me with a bit of advice that stuck with me for years. She told me that there are really only two things that make the world go around. One of them is money, and women control at least half of it. I forget now what she told me the other thing was, but I suspect they probably control all of that.

POLARIS

Tom Hennessey

(First appeared in the *Victoria County Record*, 1976)

I stepped out of the guide shack the other night to check the weather, among other things, before turning in. I was glad to see the clouds blowing away, leaving the Big Dipper and the North Star shining bright and clear. Later, in the sleeping bag, dozing off as I listened to the boys cough and snore and the camp mouse make his nightly rounds, I was reminded of other nights and other companions, but the same old North Star always sat up there. I dreamed:

. . . Of a nighttime parachute jump when, after the cold knot formed in my stomach, after the frenzy of Go-Go-Go, after the wind-whipped exit and the gut-jerking opening load, I swung beneath the welcome canopy and had time to line up on that old North Star. Then a poorly executed rollout brought my knees up to my chin, and other stars appeared before my eyes.

. . . Of a night in Labrador when we got turned around after snowshoeing behind a band of caribou all day in a blizzard. Trapline partner, Emil, who couldn't speak a word of English, managed to let me know that he intended to walk to the north shore of the St. Lawrence River, three hundred miles away. Finally a break in the storm clouds settled the argument. The North Star was located, showing the direction to camp, only a few hours away.

. . . Of a March night in the North Atlantic when—with the first break in twenty-eight days of rolling, pitching, and nearly swamping—Raymond Ross from Riley Brook and I watched the star appear and disappear as the ship surfboarded over seventy-foot seas, and he said: "Boy, the biggest liars back home will never believe this!"

. . . Of a night on the bridge of a 50,000-tonner threading its way up the Schelde Estuary to Antwerp, thinking of the many Canadians who had given their lives to cover this same route a few years before. Now that we had all the modern aids to electronic navigation, I was still marking time checks for the navigator taking sextant shots on the North Star.

. . . Of a night spent on a barge aground on a reef in Ungava Bay, trying to maintain communications with a would-be rescuer while two Newfoundland seamen stood waist-deep in the seas sweeping us, holding aloft the emergency antenna. The mate plotted our position with shots on the headland of Diana Bay and the North Star.

. . . Of a night in a Central American town when, as I came out of a bar and walked down the wrong street, I found myself flung up against a wall with the front sight of a submachine gun digging into my kidneys. Somehow I managed to convince the police in nonexistent Spanish that I was a harmless Canadian tourist when they fished the passport out of my pocket. Later, walking down the beach and looking toward the northern horizon, I remember saying to myself, "If I ever get home this time. . . ."

. . . Of a night spent poling a canoe down the Northwest Gander with Jimmy John, a Micmac guide, and a moose hunter from Pennsylvania. Guided only by the North Star, we paddled across the corner of a great big lake to Glennwood for the sport's luggage and a quart of rum. The luggage was there, but the rum wasn't, and we had to turn around and paddle and pole back up to camp without the comfort of refreshment.

I remembered traveling with Marcousee on Ellesmere Island; Paulusee and Kopenwaak; Fred Earle of Black Tickle, Labrador; Roberto in Ponta Delgada; the third engineer who went crazy in Gothaab, Greenland; Ollifur Bjornson in Reykjavik; and the many, many other companions of other nights and other places.

Seasons and companions change, time passes, and we have all grown older. But that old North Star stays right up there and guides it all. Maybe not quite perfect True North, but close enough to suit me.

LEROY AND THE PERVERTED BEAR

Tom Hennessey —

Only once in a while is a man lucky enough to witness the birth of a legend. I was so blessed in the case of LeRoy and the Perverted Bear.

LeRoy Johnson, longtime Tobique River guide, worked for me during the 1960s and 1970s guiding bear hunters. Now retired, LeRoy remains a local landmark in northern New Brunswick. In a business in which the ability to be a bit creative is not viewed as a handicap, I would judge LeRoy as being at the top of the profession.

It was a May morning in 1968 or so, and we were having breakfast in the bear-hunting camp when someone arrived with the news that a man had been badly mauled by a bear and was being treated in the hospital downriver.

The facts seemed to be fairly straightforward, but any story of a bear attack is bound to raise some excitement among a bunch of first-time bear hunters. It seemed that a prospector was running claim lines when he crossed a brook by walking on top of a blowdown. Jumping off into the brush, he landed square on top of a sleeping bear. The chances of this happening are somewhat less than those of being hit by lightning, but probably the wind was in the right direction and the noise of the brook masked any noise he made crossing the log.

Naturally enough, the bear, being most rudely awakened, had sprung up, swatted the guy and broke his shoulder, then tramped all over him while departing in haste for parts unknown. Accident or not, the result was a badly damaged shoulder, a few broken ribs, many lacerations to both hide and clothing, and, I presume, a good lesson in not jumping into brushpiles unannounced.

At this point we did not have all the facts, but you can be sure that speculation was rife among the uninitiated hunters as to the danger involved in hunting the ferocious black bear. LeRoy's arrival did little to dispel their fears. As they clamored for the guide's expert opinion, LeRoy, never at a loss for words, had just what they wanted. "By God, boys, we're in for it now. I thought we had killed him or driven him from the country, but he must be back. Just as sure as there's shit in a pup, it's that damn old Perverted Bear."

Tom, the other guide, and I had to look away. I did notice that although some of the guests appeared a bit skeptical, a few of the younger ones were taking it all in as Gospel.

"Oh, my, yes," LeRoy continued, "all that scratchin' and the clothes all torn off is just like what happened to that guy we had up on Reardon Mountain. That dirty old boar just grabbed him from behind and roused him out through an old dry top, tore him all to hell. Started the rivets right out of his brand-new overalls. You remember, boys" (looking at the other guide and me), "he didn't know whether to sue the outfit for pain and suffering or for sexual abuse."

I had to escape the table. We had plenty to do getting geared up for the trip to Nictau Lake to set up stands for the evening hunt. I knew we didn't have to entertain the sports with LeRoy around, although I did take him aside and warn him not to get them too worked up or we would have to sit and hold their hands on the stands.

With three of us looking after five hunters, the practical method was to put them in blinds overlooking where the bear had been feeding and then retire to a position from which we could hear if someone shot. This way there was less human scent around, less noise, and it was really a matter between the hunter and the bear.

By the time we got up into the area late in the afternoon, I could see that at least a couple of the guys were apprehensive. Although they didn't want to believe that any danger existed—especially the kind LeRoy was talking about—they were beginning to wonder if there might just possibly be a grain of truth in his stories.

When you put people out on stands where they will be all alone for about eight hours leading up to pitch-dark, you try to anticipate and answer all of their questions. Rifles had been sighted-in, they had a lunch and a Thermos, and each was in a blind facing the bait at distances varying from thirty to a hundred yards. They were well concealed, had a rest to

LeRoy and the Perverted Bear

lay their rifle across, and everything possible had been done to ensure that if a bear came, they would be able to make a clean shot. They were told that we had placed them according to wind direction but that most sites had two stands so if the wind shifted drastically, they could move to the alternate location.

Having told them all of this, LeRoy had to add one more admonition: "Now, boys, you sit still as a mouse—no reading those old skin books. Keep awake, stay on the ball, but once in a while sneak a peek around behind you. If you feel those big furry paws go over your eyes and his hot breath on the back of your neck, you are surely in for a hell of a time. I'll give anyone my season's tips if you'll just kill that goddamned old Perverted Bear so I dare to bend over when I need to get a drink from the brook."

At about eight o'clock in the evening, LeRoy and I were camped only a half-mile from the last man we had put out. Tom was twenty miles back down the road, strategically placed to take care of the first three hunters. I had intentionally stayed close to the youngest guy in the party, a nice kid from Long Island on his first bear hunt, probably the most nervous in the gang. I always figure that first-time city boys out there on their own in the woods probably feel about like we guides would if we were left alone in New York. Terrified to hell, no doubt.

On this particular site, a long stretch of old half-grown-in logging road, we had made a blind of small fir trees right out in the road. The hunter had an unimpeded view straight down to the bait, but as it gets dusky, the lane certainly "narrows in." He had been told that come full dark, he should unload and case his rifle, take out his flashlight, and stroll down to where we'd be waiting for him.

About 8:30, a full hour before dark, *Ka-Bloom!*—the silence was shattered, seemingly almost on top of us—the sound all bear guides love to hear. Then we always wait to hear the follow-up insurance shot. Nothing. Did he get him, did he miss him, or did his rifle go off while he was playing with the safety? All were definite possibilities in our experience. "Good for you, boy!" cried LeRoy. "Shoot the bastard again. A Monday night bear is better than ten Saturday night bears." The guides are usually as shook up and excited as the hunters. After weeks of preparation and all the time spent waiting to hear a shot, it all seems to fall in place at last.

Always the pessimist myself, believing the worst in hopes of being pleasantly surprised, I said, "Come on, LeRoy, we'll stroll up, see if he missed a bear or shot at a raven. Be sure and whistle and wave your hat around. Try not to look too much like a bear walking up that road." We had hardly started up the trail when around a bend came the kid at a dead gallop. Coat off, hat in one hand, eyeglasses in the other, red in the face, he pounced on LeRoy. "Oh, my God, you were right. He came there to get me, that bastard of a Perverted Bear!"

LeRoy, for once, had nothing to say; as flabbergasted as I was, I recovered the powers of speech first: "What in hell happened, where is your rifle, did you hit him, is he dead, how big is he, is he right on the road?" For once I was bombarding the client with questions instead of the other way around.

Between gasps, the story unfolded. Sitting in the blind, peering straight down the road at the bait, the rifle's safety off, he felt a presence or heard a scuffle in the gravel behind him. Hair standing up on the back of his neck, heart in his throat, he sneaked a glance over his shoulder. "Holy Moses, there he stood, up on his hind legs," he puffed out. "Looking right down into the blind at me, just ready to pounce."

"Jesus, man, did you hit him?" blurted LeRoy.

"Hell, no!" the kid cried, "I just pulled the trigger right straight ahead, dropped the rifle, and took off down the road for help. That sonofabitch was just about to grab me, sure as shootin'. I could hear him pantin', and you could've stuck oranges in his nose holes, he was that big. You told me that he'd come from behind."

Up at the stand, it was immediately apparent just what had happened. Examining the scene of the crime, I could see where the young man's bullet had struck the road about ten feet ahead of where he had dropped the rifle. In the gravel a few feet behind the blind, the sign was plain enough. A large bear had whirled around and taken off up the road in twenty-foot leaps, spinning up the gravel from his pads. There at the top of the ridge, the wind must have shifted with the coming dusk so he couldn't smell the hunter. With his less-than-keen eyesight he must have decided to creep up closer to identify the funny-looking thing sitting in the middle of the trail. When that magnum went off, his only aim in life was getting the hell out of there. He'd have a great story to tell his buddies wherever the bears get together.

Whatever tale that bear may tell, it will have to be something to top LeRoy's version of what happened. A legend was born right there that persists until today in bear camps all over northern New Brunswick. The kid from New York would never go back on a stand again. He contented himself with trout fishing the rest of the week, but only in a boat anchored well away from the bushes.

If you don't believe what I have told you, the next time you go up the Tobique River to Nictau, just drop in and see LeRoy. I'm pretty sure he could be convinced to tell you the story about the Perverted Bear.

GAME-LAW ENFORCEMENT

Tom Hennessey —

To those engaged in legitimate professional hunting, there is no one more deserving of contempt than the commercial poacher. This term does not include the person who has found it necessary to kill an occasional deer or moose outside the government-imposed season to feed his family. Indeed, many of us who are old enough to have experienced that kind of hardscrabble living and honest enough to admit it can tell a few tales from those so-called "good old days." Most animals taken in such circumstances, regardless of the month of the year, were carefully selected, inevitably shared, and totally utilized.

What has made the term "poaching" a dirty word are the big-volume, commercial poachers who have absolutely no regard for the damage they inflict on wildlife resources. These are the criminals on whom the people being paid to enforce the fish and wildlife regulations should focus.

In my lifetime I have encountered three types of game wardens:

1. The office-bound bureaucrat who does not acknowledge that poaching is rife in his area and is unlikely to get his highly polished shoes muddy finding out.

2. The unimaginative drone who is proud of "going by the book" and spends his time harassing the honest guide or hunter while the real poachers carry the country away.

3. The *real* game warden, hard-working and dedicated, woodwise and capable of commonsense initiative, who is willing to put in plenty of unpaid overtime in adverse conditions. Usually this individual was in the past a guide, a trapper, and quite possibly an occasional poacher himself. This is the warden who will do more to protect fish and wildlife than the rest of the office gang combined. Unfortunately, due to limited formal education, politics, and interdepartmental jealousy, he will rarely be promoted very far up the ladder.

I have known all three types of wardens clear across Canada, and have had the pleasure and honor of working closely with several of the third classification.

Here I will relate a few experiences gained over years of contact with the guardians of our wildlife resources, in numerical order of the categories presented above.

The Bureaucrat

In the middle 1970s we ran spike-camp bear hunts in a new area of southern New Brunswick. Having moved down there temporarily from the northern zone, where we assisted extensively in poaching control, we were totally amazed at what we encountered. This was in the month of May, when we were not accustomed to finding anyone else in the woods.

Here we were continually seeing tire tracks on roads that went nowhere, and encountering strange vehicles at all times of the day and night.

Our hunters, sitting on widely scattered bear stands, came in nearly every night with reports of "mystery shots," for which none of us could account. Finally, with very little effort, we searched out the kill sites of three deer and two moose. Now we had enough evidence to report to the District Ranger in Canterbury.

It did not take us very long to discover that our efforts at cooperation were not only not wanted but were actually resented.

"Oh, yes," said the impeccably pressed and shined Guardian of the Forest as he reluctantly removed his feet from the desk, "I have heard about how you guys up north hold the record for the most convictions. I am proud to say that in contrast, there are simply no poaching problems in my area."

Not wishing to bring a bunch of petty harassment down upon our own heads, which would have been the result had we pressed matters, we thanked him for his time and took our leave.

Going by the Book

Quite a few years ago, before everyone became educated to the fact that it is not in the interest of working outfitters to do anything outside the regulations, we had an amusing incident at one of our caribou camps in the Northwest Territories.

On change-over day the incoming hunters are not allowed to hunt, so everyone was in camp. Out of the sky swooped a Jet Ranger helicopter, as in a scene from *Apocalypse Now*. It deposited two Rangers from Yellowknife right in front of our kitchen. We welcomed them in for a cup of coffee and offered a tour of the camp. One of them accepted graciously. The other opened his enormous briefcase and started acting like J. Edgar Hoover, to the vast amusement of our guests and the native guides, who knew the guy from town.

He had to check everyone's license. This I certainly did not mind; after all, as a taxpayer I was helping to pay the $1,200 an hour for the Jet Ranger, plus his wages. Then disaster struck. One of the guests from New York could not produce his paper hunting license. He had the tags but not the piece of paper. Since our expediter takes everyone to the Game Office and holds his or her hand, and because the New Yorker had the tags, it was apparent that he had indeed purchased the license. In fact, our interrogator himself had personally issued the license before boarding the chopper to "drop in" a few hours later.

"Big problem!" said the guy who went by the book.

"Bullshit!" said I. "You know the guy bought a license, he has the tags, and at the end of the hunt he has to go back to the office to obtain his export permits. At that time he can sign the proper form for people who lose a license, pay $10, and all is taken care of."

"Oh, no," said the Uniform. "He does not have the piece of paper; therefore he cannot go out in the boat tomorrow."

"Bullshit!" said I. "There is no requirement for a piece of paper to take a boat ride, not even here in the NWT, home of all the failed bureaucrats who couldn't get a job down south."

We decided to call it a draw. Instead of attempting to impose the death penalty, he would take his $1,200-an-hour helicopter and fly back to headquarters to pursue the matter further. Ten minutes after somewhat strained "Good-byes," the New Yorker knocked on the door of my shack.

"Guess what?" he said brightly.

"Don't tell me you've found the goddam piece of paper or I will shoot your ass!"

"Yes, I had hidden it under the lining of my camera case," was the embarrassed reply.

Radio conditions were snafu; I couldn't contact Yellowknife. Next morning all the hunters departed the beach to commence the hunt. About noon a Twin Otter arrived. This was a $2,800 charter. Out of it got a young lady with a large briefcase. Turned out she was a departmental employee, and a Justice of the Peace to boot. She had brought the proper forms to apply for a replacement license, the receipt book for the $10 lost-license fee, the official stamp, and a large Bible on which to swear an oath that the license had been lost.

"Guess what?" I greeted her. "Come on in and have a cup of coffee. Your visit has only cost the taxpayers about $10,000."

Real Game Wardens

Fortunately, there are many of what I term *real* game wardens at the field level. We have worked closely with them in New Brunswick; Newfoundland and Labrador; Ungava, Quebec; and the Northwest Territories. The ones we work with now, mainly in Coppermine and in Yellowknife, are true professionals dedicated to doing a commonsense job of wildlife management.

Along the line some amusing incidents have occurred. The following ones in New Brunswick are good examples:

Adventures with Junior

In order to save anyone any official embarrassment, I will disguise the officer's identity by calling him Junior. Junior, when I first met him, was a guide, a hunter, a trapper, and one of the slickest poachers in our part of the country. When hired by the game department, which had been unsuccessful in apprehending him, he went away to Ranger School and managed a 180-degree change in his attitudes toward fish and game regulations; but fortunately he retained all the ambition and competitiveness that had made him so successful before the transformation.

Whereas most of the rangering had previously been done from the office and by vehicle without anyone actually getting his feet wet, all of a sudden things started to happen for the better. Junior brought to the job not only a sense of dedication but a sense of humor as well, so even the hardest-bitten Acadian poachers soon respected him.

Awakened one night by shots nearby, I phoned Junior. In a few minutes we were roaring up the road. With us was Ace, his highly trained German shepherd, which loved nothing more than a midnight romp to run down poachers. About a mile above our house, coming around a turn in the road, we almost collided with a speeding automobile. Junior immediately switched off the lights, did a quick about-face, and took off in pursuit. Rounding the bend again, we were surprised to see the same car parked with the lights off.

Upon approaching the vehicle and shining a light in, we discovered the driver, pretending to be asleep on the front seat. In the back seat was an empty rifle case, among other things. We knew immediately that this guy and at least one, probably two, accomplices had shot a deer and someone had bailed out to take care of it while the driver took off with the vehicle. This was standard and pretty unimaginative practice for highway poaching, something that Junior and I both were well acquainted with from the days of our untamed youth.

Our sleepy friend, who initially couldn't speak a word of English, suddenly discovered that he could handle that tongue after being dragged out and bounced off the hood a couple of times. In fact, with old Ace sniffing his legs, he became quite talkative. He said he would show us where they had shot at some deer in a field down the road a mile and his two chums had gone after them. We were soon at the scene, with the dog out looking for tracks.

Within a few minutes we heard a bark. Plunging through the wet brush, we almost fell over one of the shooters, face down and whimpering as old Ace held him to the ground. With that one cuffed and back to the road, we went back in and found two dead deer, the light, and the rifle. One matching .308 shell was found on the road, another in the back seat of the car.

"What'll we do about the other guy still on the loose?"

"To hell with him!" Junior replied. "We've got their wheels and the rifle. He won't get too far away."

Sure enough, later that day he was spotted frantically paddling a stolen canoe with a piece of board, and was driven ashore by rifle shots and captured down in the village. It turned out that these three were part of one of the worst poaching rings in the northeastern part of the province, with several prior convictions. A hefty fine and sixty days in the cooler were added to their professional resumé.

This was just one of more than sixty night-hunting cases successfully prosecuted that fall!

LENDING A HELPING HAND

It used to be that poachers were pretty good woodsmen and accomplished hunters, but through the 1970s and early 1980s our area was besieged with two new breeds of law-breaker. There was what we called the "citizen poacher," and there was the "gangster poacher." Neither was too bright.

The citizen poacher was usually your typical pillar of the community or, as the nursery rhyme goes, "butcher, baker, candlestick maker, doctor, lawyer, Indian chief." On two occasions, prominent provincial politicians were caught red-handed and tried to weasel their way out. One moose season, a parish priest and the chief of police from a neighboring community were rounded up. Another classic chase involved three members of the Quebec provincial police; just doing a little holiday poaching in New Brunswick. They were all the same to Junior and the rest of our rangers.

The gangster poachers were exactly that—involved in large-scale commercial poaching of anything that flew, walked, swam, or crawled. Invariably they were also active in biker gangs, dope dealing, and the strong-arm stuff.

In one case, three of these guys tried to force an Acadian tavern owner into some deal. They broke up his premises, threatened to burn it down, then made the grave mistake of attacking him with baseball bats. A Remington pump shotgun pulled from under the bar killed one of them and blew the arm off another. The story I liked best, though, was about the third hood, described in the paper as having suffered injuries in the midsection and genital area.

Another prominent poacher was shot dead in his living room, right through the picture window, in what was officially listed as a "business deal gone bad." These were the types who gravitated to commercial poaching.

As guides sworn to uphold the game laws, we were in fact assistant game wardens; indeed, no one had a more serious stake in good game management than did the people of our profession. We cooperated on every possible occasion, and shared information on what was going on in the woods even when we were not directly involved in a particular case. Most of us had enough of the "cowboy" in our character to enjoy it immensely.

I don't recall having heard the term "sting operation," and if we knew what "entrapment" meant, no one took it very seriously. After all, we were in a war, and as hunters and trappers we figured the use of bait was basic to the operation. If the poachers were too dumb to be successful, we would sometimes help them out a little bit.

One of the most effective methods used to combat the rampant night hunting was the development of what we called the "dummy deer." Whether or not our area was the first to do this is unknown, but surely we were among the very first.

Lending a Helping Hand

As in any war, as technology increases on one side, matching countermeasures are quickly employed by the other.

At first, the use of two green bicycle fender reflectors on a board set up in a clearing was enough to draw fire. This soon was upgraded to "eyes" made from the reflecting surface cut from a guardrail along a highway. These devices had just the right amount of sparkle. When this idea became obsolete, a deer was made out of plywood, complete with hide and horns.

After a season or two of the plywood deer, the amateur citizen poachers were still falling for it, but the real pros had developed a strategy that we called Toot and Shoot. When the eyes appeared to be too stationary, the shooter would hold them in his scope until his buddy blew the horn. If the deer didn't blink, the rifle was pulled back in through the window and they took off without shooting.

By this time, legislation had been passed and cases had gone through the courts so that "intent" was a major criterion in nailing a poacher. It was illegal to shine a light so as to harass wildlife, illegal to carry an uncased firearm in a vehicle, and illegal to discharge a firearm after sundown. For once the courts did something right, and this much-needed legal ammunition eventually slowed down the commercial poaching.

The "dummy deer" graduated from a plywood replica to a real mounted deer. The first one was donated by a taxidermist friend of mine, Dave Bower from Pennsylvania. On its first night out, our decoy was set up on a tight turn in the road where vehicle lights would fall upon the reflecting eyes.

The boys had improved the technique a bit by having a second pair of movable "eyes" controlled by a cord operated by one of the braver assistant wardens, lying down behind a log. Toot and Shoot was about to get some upgrading.

Around the bend came a brand-new Chevy Blazer. It stopped right on the mark as its headlights struck the eyes. Out came the gun barrel. With the toot of the horn, one pair of eyes danced around. *BOOM!* Dead-centered by a load of SSG from a full-choke shotgun, a big cloud of white Styrofoam blew out of the deer.

Up from the roadside ditch rose Junior to grab the barrel of the gun, nearly yanking the guy out through the window. Another ranger jerked the driver and the vehicle keys in one swoop. The third guy, who had a string of previous convictions to his credit, tried to make a run for it, but the dog soon rounded him up.

Standing around in handcuffs while the rangers did up the paperwork, the bad guys sent a lot of French flying back and forth as they tried to figure out where the "deer" had gone. It would give them something to think about while they served time in the slammer, along with how to keep making payments on the new Blazer that now belonged to the Crown.

In another area of northern New Brunswick, right up against the border with Quebec, a gang of poachers had the bad sense to move into our bear-hunting territory. These guys were using bear snares and had the nerve to put a set near one of our hunting stands. While we were creating employment through legitimate sport hunting, they were trying to kill bears to market the claws and gall bladders for a fraction of the animal's value to the country.

We were not long in finding a number of their snares, but lacking the time and manpower to watch them all, we decided that a little shortcut was in order. Although there is no law in the world against walking through the woods, and even looking at a snare on the way by, it is definitely illegal to set one up.

Gathering up a few props, Junior and I decided to give the boys a little help. At one of their snares close to the road, we carried in a couple of bear turds on a beer-box cover. These we placed in the trail, and made some very convincing bear tracks with our hands. At the snare itself, we clawed up the garbage bag of bait they had hung. Then we swung the snare around sideways to the trail and added a little tuft of bear hair to the slipknot in the wire cable. Anyone could now see that a bear had come down the trail to the bait but had somehow brushed the snare aside instead of walking into it.

That afternoon, with Martin taking care of our bear hunters in another part of the area, Junior and I and another ranger lay camouflaged, watching the setup. Sure enough, after about three hours of enduring the blackflies, we heard a vehicle approach and stop out on the road. Down the trail came two of the more notorious local Cajun poachers, brothers well known to the department.

There was great delight when they spotted the bear sign, gesturing and dismay when they saw that the snare was tripped and empty. Whispering excitedly, one of them pulled the snare back into the trail while the other tied it in place with a piece of string. "*C'est bon! Tout prêt pour l'ours noir.* Good! All is ready for the black bear."

Junior jumped out of our brushpile, gun in one hand, badge in the other. "*Arrêt! Chalice, garde de chasse*! Don't move a goddam inch—you're under arrest!"

As the old saying goes, "You could have snared their eyeballs with a strand of haywire."

They were not a very smart family of poachers. The previous year, the younger brother, Alexandre, had sold a white buck deer to an undercover Mountie. They would get some jail time for their latest caper, but would be back out again in time for the fall poaching season.

BLUE BEN

TOM HENNESSEY —

(First appeared in *Fur-Fish-Game*, February 1975)

Crossing a river at night on snowshoes is never a picnic, and even with special precautions it can be downright dangerous. While hanging onto one end of an alder pole, I was testing ahead with the ax. Tom Everett, the other guide, was backing me up.

With only a few feet to go, the ax suddenly dropped through a thin spot and a section of ice dropped out from under us. Scrambling ashore, we were lucky to be wet only to the knees. At this point the Mamozekel River runs swift and deep. As we sat by a hastily built fire, wringing out our socks and beating ice from our snowshoes, Tom summed it up pretty well when he said, "I guess you don't have to be crazy in this game, but it sure as hell helps." I could only agree.

It was mid-January 1973, and the second straight week of impossible cat-hunting conditions. The previous week, with a party from Pennsylvania, we'd had no luck, due to a crust on the snow that would carry a bobcat while allowing the dog to break through. This week we were starting out with an elderly hunter from Southbridge, Massachusetts. We had to give it a try, but the odds were against us from the start.

We had started out early that morning from our base in Nictau, first checking for tracks on the available plowed road, and when that failed, taking to snowmobiles. By leaving our vehicles with LeRoy Johnson, another of our guides, who lived at the end of the road, we were assured that in the event of trouble, help would be forthcoming.

Traveling on two snowmobiles and towing the dog box, we made good time. It was only midmorning when we picked up a fairly fresh bobcat track about eight miles down the trail.

Conditions seemed a bit better in this area, with about four inches of snow on top of the crust. I thought we were in pretty good shape until it became apparent that the dog was breaking through with every other jump. However, coming from a long line of real cat killers, our Blue Ben was always eager to go, and next to impossible to recall once he put his nose in a track.

As we worked along the Mamozekel, which is crooked and full of springs, I realized that the ice would probably be treacherous. As anyone who has tried to swim with snowshoes on will realize, I was hoping that the chase would lead us away from the river. As luck would have it, the tracks led straight up the valley parallel with the river.

Snowshoeing was difficult in the extreme; our choices were either to take our chances on the river ice or to crawl through tangled fir thickets along the steep slopes. I was soon kicking myself for letting the dog go on what was guaranteed to be an endurance test for all of us. Continually breaking through that under-crust and struggling out again, Ben was already showing signs of being cut up, and we could read by the tracks that the cat was just playing along on top. I knew that once Ben jumped the cat, given anything approaching an even chance, he would soon force it to tree. However, in this stuff the deck was surely stacked against him.

At about four o'clock we had to make a hard decision. We were soaked with snow water and sweat, a long way from home, and another subzero night was fast approaching. I had to admit to myself that we would never get up in time to kill the cat on the circle, and probably the hound just couldn't put on enough pressure to tree it after such a long, initial chase.

Instructing the client to follow my snowshoe tracks, I took a compass course back to the main trail, intending to bring up the snow machines. Tom continued on the track in the hope that perhaps we would get lucky and the chase would double back. An hour's hard traveling and I was back at my sled. Leaving a note for the client, I took off upriver, hoping to cut Tom's trail.

It was pitch-black by the time I met him coming up the ice. We stood and listened to the hound music. Now that it was too late, the cat was jumped and the dog was running hot, way over on another ridge. At a time like this you curse your luck, your stupidity for trying the impossible, and cat hunting in general. But you can't help admiring the sheer guts displayed by the dog. You wish he had brains enough to quit and come back, but you love him for staying with it.

We had broken two of my most basic rules, and now it was time to pay for it. Rule Number One is: Don't try to hunt in lousy conditions. Number Two is: Don't hunt from snowmobiles at temperatures well below zero. Hiking miles in the woods—soaked to the skin, hungry, and exhausted—to get back to the machine is not the perfect way to end your day. Chilled to the bone, we finally arrived back at LeRoy's home about 8 P.M., just in time to head off his son, Larry, who was coming to look for us in case of a breakdown.

Our first responsibility is the safety of the client. With a change of clothes and a hot supper, he was willing to go out again, but we advised him to rest up for another day. With the temperature now standing at ten below zero and forecast to go much lower, our next responsibility was to the dog. Having put him into a mess, we had to bring him in if we could.

Leaving a warm house again was hard, but we started back up the trail, looking for dog tracks and hoping that Ben had come out and started for home. No such luck. Arriving on top of a hill a couple of miles from where we had quit earlier, we shut down the machines to listen. Sure enough, we could hear old Ben a way over across the river. Sounding as if he was still running that cat, he finally went out of hearing along the side of a ridge. A half-hour later, farther up the river, we could hear him again, and this time he was barking treed. We listened, refusing to believe it, but he was staying in one place, and beyond a doubt he had that cat up.

Now we were really in a bind. It's not only illegal but also miserably inconvenient to tote a shotgun on a snowmobile at night, so we had only the ax and a flashlight. The dog at this point was about three miles away—through alder thickets, across the river, and up on top of a slope covered with second-growth poplar and small spruce. After thinking it over, we decided that we just didn't have the energy to tackle an alder tangle at this time of night, so we chose to take the long way around. Going back to where the trail came close to the river and then picking our way up the ice for an hour brought us to where we could hear the dog again.

Falling through the shell ice at this point was just about the last straw. But after a partial drying out, we were back on the snowshoes and working up the sidehill.

At long last we arrived. Half an acre of crisscrossing tracks told the story of a cat that just hated to tree but finally had to do so or fight. The blood on the snow came not from the cat so much as from the cuts and abrasions on the hound. A bit of searching with the light showed us the object of all our efforts—not a big old tomcat but, as we had suspected, a medium-sized one, probably a female by all the trouble it had given us. Anyway, we would have to find out another day when conditions were more in our favor. It was just past midnight and time for us to face the trip out.

Old Ben was pretty badly cut up, caked with ice, and trembling with exhaustion. But you couldn't mistake the triumph in his eyes and the cocky way he looked at us latecomers. Dead cat on the ground or not, there was no doubt in his mind just who had won that round.

A couple of hours later, over a good stiff drink of hot rum, Tom and I had to agree: Although we hadn't killed any bobcat that day, we had certainly taken part in a hunt that we'd remember for a while.

Cinematographer George Klucky and author, late 1970s.

Trying to spot a fish with Lee Wulff at Forks Pool on the Tobique.

Joan Wulff and veteran guide Noah Ruff, Little Nictau Pool.

Serpentine River moose and caribou camp, circa 1880. (Courtesy Wilson's Studio, New Brunswick.)

Author with Coleman McDougall, bear hunting at Red Brook, 1975.

Tom Everett in the bow, and Fred in the stern, Right Hand Branch.

Fred and Tom on the Bobcat Trail with Warrior and Belle.

Crossing Mamozekel River in flood, 1975.

Author and Coleman with client's bear, Shank's Brook country.

Author and Murray Parish on Tobique River log drive, 1968.

Martin Webb, Colin Adjun, Jack Atatahak, and Gerry Atatahak setting up on Victoria Island.

Guides and guests on Little Tobique River, circa 1900. (Courtesy Wilson's Studio, New Brunswick.)

Guide Peter Katiak, Inulik Lake, Northwest Territories.

Client with Inuk guide Gerry Atatahak, midnight in May.

Nictau to Nipisiquit Lakes portage, 1930s.

Martin Webb and author at Arctic base, Kugluktuk, Nunavut.

Author's father, Gundy Webb, Tobique River, 1920s.

Judy Keller with her first caribou, Ungava Bay.

Pete Barrett, fishing editor of Field & Stream, *and author, Northwest Territories.*

Author at Nictau Lodge, home base for many years.

Martin Webb and client, northern New Brunswick.

The author and Leigh Everett guiding the famous angler Paul Kukonen (in river), Campbell Branch, 1970s.

Guide Frank Hatheway and client at Nictau Lodge, New Brunswick.

Jorgen Bolt and Pamela Atwood, with a Boone and Crockett muskox.

Peter Katiak and Heber Simmons, with a Boone and Crockett muskox.

Ron Pavlik, barren ground grizzly, west of Coppermine, 1998.

Mac Niptanatiak and outdoor writer Grits Gresham with barren ground caribou at Lac de Gras.

Margarett Hanak, our lady guide, and Dan Herring with a Boone and Crockett muskox.

Colin Havioyak and guest Rob Shatzko, and their two nice caribou.

A great week with good company and good hunting. Last week the Webbs owned Courageous Lake Camp. From left: Marie Pavlik, Rose Pastorek, Lori Clemm, Old Fred, Kathy Camp, Kay Gilbert, and Beth Jones, September 1998.

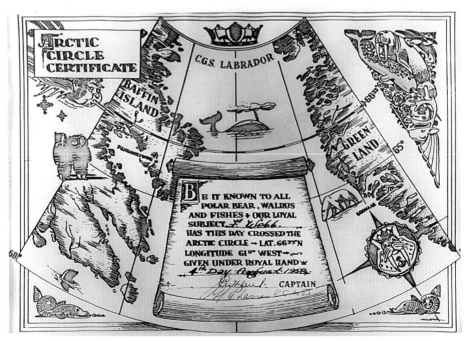

Arctic Circle Certificate, signed by Henry Larsen, first to traverse the fabled Northwest Passage in both directions.

Nictau Lake Crew. Charlie Webb (center), 1935.

Dooley with caribou that had "great bottom shovels, no tops."

The second one is even better. Judy Keller, Akuliak, 1982.

It's hard to beat the Britts! Outdoor writer Russ Carpenter and Brittany spaniel.

Looks like a fresh track . . . smells like one, too! From left: Client from New Jersey, Bobby Sussino; author; Blue Ben; and Tom Everett.

Author with gunwriter Russ Carpenter.   Russ was editor of Argosy *and writer for* NRA. *First bobcat taken with new Thompson-Center Hawken muzzleloader, 1970.*

Gordon Birgbauer from Algonac, Michigan, and the woodland stag that made No. 1 in Boone and Crockett's nineteenth awards.

LeRoy Johnson (left) and client from Virginia—the end to that perverted bear.

The way we did it in the good old days.

Bull down in the tuckamore—now the work starts!

BRITTANY JOE

Tom Hennessey

We were sitting around the lodge one evening after an enjoyable day afield with grouse and woodcock gunners. The conversation, as it often did, got around to the merits of the various breeds of dog most suited to the close cover that we hunted.

Much more learned persons than I have written volumes on the subject of upland bird dogs, but at our lodge in New Brunswick we seemed to attract a half-dozen main breeds. Probably the most prevalent at that time were the English setters; graceful in action, beautiful in pictures, they could almost be termed the "classic" upland gunner's dog.

Visitors from the Deep South, Mexico, and Oklahoma had brought various pointing dogs to our part of the world, but in general these dogs, used mostly on quail and pheasants, ranged much too far for the type of cover we hunted, and the guide had to spend most of his day looking for them. One guide called them "advertising dogs": You turned them loose on Monday morning then advertised for their return in the local weekly paper.

We had a passing acquaintance with German shorthairs, none of which impressed me except the one that dove out through a closed window in our "outback" camp on the Mamozekel River. His owner had left him behind because he was too thickheaded to work woodcock cover beyond simply barging through it and out the other end. Probably there are many good shorthairs, somewhere.

One can only generalize when talking about dogs. After all, every owner thinks his dog is the best in the world, and even the most incorrigible knee-shagger has someone who loves him.

As a guide you soon find out that dogs are very much like people. Regardless of breed, they generally range from terrific to terrible. We have seen individual dogs from somewhat dubious bloodlines perform mightily, and others with papers going back to the Magna Carta not worth a damn.

With a mixed bag of dogs in camp that week, I was somewhat hesitant to put forth the virtues of the only bird dog that we owned personally, old Brittany Joe. Before long, though, one of my senior guides brought him into the conversation.

"You know, there are only three things worth a damn that ever come out of France: champagne wine, Brittany spaniels and that movie actress—what's her name. Fred, you know, the one with the big tits!"

"Yes," I had to agree, "you're right. But champagne gives me heartburn and the lady you refer to is one of the most fanatical antihunters in the world, so I guess I'll have to shorten the list down to Brittany spaniels."

This observation elicited a bit of discussion, especially with the two lawyers from Montreal, but in general it summed up my feelings on the matter.

The little Frog dog—though perhaps gracing fewer calendar covers than the English setter with its long, flowing lines and lacking the drive of the bug-eyed, hyper pointers we had tried to work with—was supreme in our country. When it comes to thick cover, where you need a dog to work with the guide instead of freelancing off into the next county, it is just about impossible to beat the Britt.

I came to be acquainted with Brittany spaniels by the sort of roundabout situation that often arises in the hunting business. Previous to the middle 1960s our guiding season was mainly two months of spring bear hunting, three months of Atlantic salmon fishing, and then two months of white-tailed deer hunting. Bird hunting was something you did sort of by accident—shooting the heads off grouse with your .30-30 deer rifle.

Then the government discovered game management and proceeded to upset a system that had worked for decades. The first thing it did was to start tinkering with the deer seasons. The fact of the matter is, it never did improve anything. Habitat changes due to clear-cut logging done via access roads dictated the level of the deer herd, and nothing done by the government had anything except negative consequences. Had they possessed enough guts to regulate the pulpwood industry instead of the hunting industry, New Brunswick would be a different place today. However, the deer seasons were cut back and we had to find alternative employment. Bird hunting seemed to be one option.

Around 1967 there was only one famous woodcock lodge in New Brunswick, Loon Bay Lodge, owned by George Whelock, down in the southwestern corner of the province. George was kind enough to help us become established in the sport of grouse and woodcock hunting, as done properly with pointing and flushing dogs, a generous gesture that we never forgot.

Although the Tobique River Valley in which we operated had a good population of ruffed grouse—albeit cyclical in the extreme—it was far from the ideal hunting ground for woodcock. The only decent habitat for this migratory bird was right along the course of the river, the rest of the country being covered by dense woods and unsuitable for the purpose. This, of course, meant that along about seventy-five miles of river, there was barely enough decent cover for one outfitting operation. Fortunately we had it to ourselves for several years until imitators inevitably got into the act. Besides overhunting the available cover, this development caused the dreaded No Trespassing signs to go up, and the sport as a commercial venture of any import was ended forever.

One of the most important things Whelock did to assist us was to send up a genuine woodcock-hunting and dog-handling expert. Russ Carpenter, a gunsmith and writer from Newburgh, New York, brought the first Brittany spaniels to our outfit at Nictau.

Thus began an annual tradition that lasted for as long as we were in the bird-shooting business. Russ and Anne would arrive at the first of the season with their two outstanding

Brittany spaniels. I would guide them personally, and we would eventually hunt, evaluate, and catalog every possible woodcock cover from Nictau Lake to the Saint John River Valley.

From this start I was able to acquaint the other guides with the basics, and the rest, as they say, is history. We ran the first and for a while, the only and definitely the best operation of its kind in northern New Brunswick. We hosted and guided the wealthy, the famous, and hundreds of just plain nice people until "progress" overran us. And the start of it all was Russ, Anne, and their Brittany spaniels, Muffin and Cookie.

One fall day about 1970, we set a record that I doubt has ever been broken, certainly not in that part of the world. The cover below the mouth of Little Cedar was stiff with birds. On the first eight flushes, Russ downed eight woodcock with eight shots from a double-barreled 28-gauge shotgun. This being the bag limit of woodcock for the day, we celebrated by going up on the ridges for grouse.

Hunting with Russ's dogs, Muffin and Cookie, could spoil any guide, for they made it look so easy. Masters at working close, they held point so staunchly that once, when making a movie, I was able to creep up and film the bird crouched in front of the nose of one of the dogs. Neither I nor the other guides doubted that Britts were the champions in the thick stuff.

Although learning the game with someone else's dogs is fine, we were hoping someday to get a dog of our own, especially since many of those brought up by our clients left much to be desired. I was gratified to receive a call one evening from a lady down in southern New Brunswick. Her husband, who had been a long-time guide for Whelock, had just passed away. George had kindly told her that perhaps I would appreciate having her husband's top bird dog, a Britt related to those of Russ Carpenter. I was on my way downriver the next morning.

Despite sharing bloodlines with Muffin and Cookie, Joe was nearly twice as big as any Brittany we had ever seen. Typically colored—white and red—he was easy to spot in the brush and immediately proved to be a close worker.

I took him into a cover the first time with Bob Cook, a client in whose shooting I had confidence. We managed six points and flushes, and Joe retrieved the four birds that were hit. Pretty good for a trial run with a far-from-expert dog handler. We soon found out it was no accident, and Joe quickly became the hero of the camp as far as the guides were concerned.

It seemed that he simply liked to hunt woodcock. Far from being the legendary One Man's Dog, Joe had no loyalties except to whomever he was working with at the time. I could send him with any of our guides and any gunner who had not brought a dog of his own, and Joe would turn in a hard day's work. If the birds were in the cover and the guest could hit them, Joe's crew would be right up there with the best at the end of the day.

One of the skills in woodcock guiding is simply to recognize potentially productive cover. This most migratory of birds spends its life looking for earthworms. As far as I could discover, worms are about its only choice of diet. Ideal cover had a black soil conducive to good worm picking, not soaking wet, but not dried out too much and not too overgrown with grass. In our country this usually meant stream margins.

Brittany Joe

Farther south, good cover existed on partially grown-up farmland and old cow pastures growing up in alder bushes.

Old Joe seemed to know good cover, and he knew when he was wasting his time. If he started out casting back and forth within your sight, but then ranged out farther without flushing any birds, he would come back and almost tell you: "Hey, this isn't worth a damn today. We're wasting daylight. Let's head somewhere else!"

According to the guides, Joe was a critic of marksmanship as well. After about the third miss, he would give the gunner a scornful look as if to say, "What the hell's the point of all this running around if you can't hit the goddamn thing?" As you can tell, in our outfit even the dogs were blasphemers.

We had many offers to buy him, and once or twice, when we were hard up during the winter, we probably wished that we had taken one. Many clients would bring their own favorite dogs, only to see them go lame or wear out within a couple of days in the hard going. Joe would be called in to take up the slack and invariably impressed the visitor.

It may sound foolish to say so, but in many cases that dog taught not only the guides but also the hunters a lot about the game of woodcock hunting.

Campfire Lies of a Canadian Guide

It has been said in the hunting business that if a man has one good bird dog in his life, he is indeed fortunate. Joe was such a dog, but he did have a couple of faults. He was a fighter. Not only did we have to keep him chained when other bird dogs were visiting, but on one occasion he crippled a Husky and on another left a German shepherd in stitches at the vet's.

Joe also fancied himself a lover. Whenever he was approached by persons of the female gender, whether our kitchen staff or the wives of millionaire clients, old Joe would roll over and proudly display what my Mum termed his "accoutrements."

I guess if those were the only two faults that I was accused of, I would not consider myself too bad a fellow.

Brittany Joe was killed at the peak of his career, a victim of careless gun handling by a fool from Philadelphia. We buried him up on the hill behind the main lodge at Nictau.

The lodge is gone now, along with the woods we hunted for grouse. There are few woodcock covers left worth mentioning. All along the river are No Hunting and No Trespassing signs where we once ranged freely. Once in a while I meet an old client at one of the conventions, and we talk about how it used to be.

It was good while it lasted.

BIG FLOOD ON MAMOZEKEL

Tom Hennessey —

Ordinarily a fairly tame little stream, the Mamozekel had risen in the night and was rapidly filling the half-mile-wide valley.

Standing in the stern with a pole, I started to let the canoe swing out into the current when my bow man decided it didn't look too promising.

"My God, man, that looks pretty rough," exclaimed Leigh. A statement of the obvious, as any fool could see. I was about to shove her on out when he continued: "You know I can't swim a goddamn stroke, and if it's all the same to you, I would just as soon stay right here and split some wood for the cook." Not wanting to put too much faith in a reluctant helper, I pushed back ashore and went to look for my chief guide, Coleman. I knew he was game for anything.

Less than twenty-four hours before, we had left the camp, driving the truck easily across the ford above the footbridge in water barely up to the top of the tires of the four-wheel drive. It was a beautiful sunny afternoon, and with six bear hunters on the back of the pickup we were headed up into the Red Brook country to man the stands for another evening. It's a good thing we were always prepared for just about any-thing in the woods.

By four o'clock we had placed the last hunter. As we walked back to the truck we could feel the wind shifting and noticed that black thunderheads advancing from the south were rapidly driving off the big, white, puffy summer cumu-lus clouds. We had just reached the truck when the first big drops hit the windshield, and within seconds you couldn't talk in the cab for the rain beating on the roof.

"I'm going to pull to hell off this ridge before it gets any worse," I yelled. Although by this time I could barely see the hood, let alone the trail, it was not very smart to sit where some big old beech or maple could come crashing down through the roof.

"Yes," Coleman agreed. "I'm glad we've got a can of gas for the chain saw. Before this evening is over these roads are going to be filled with blowdowns."

Coming into a logging yard big enough so that no tree could reach us, we decided to eat our lunch early and wait it out. It was going to be a busy evening. The rain abruptly stopped. The wind slackened somewhat, then increased to near hurricane force, and this time hailstones as big as golf balls were hammering the paint off the hood of the old truck.

Big Flood on Mamozekel

Lightning split the near-darkness, striking several trees on the ridge behind us. Fortunately, with so much water coming down, none of the strikes managed to start a fire.

"Man, oh, man," Coleman said, "I have seen some bad storms in seventy years in the woods, but this is sure one of the dandies."

"Yeah," I replied. "I hope those guys had enough brains to get down out of those tree stands and take shelter in some even-height growth or we might be shipping them home in the same bag as their bear skin."

By seven o'clock it quit, moving off north toward the headwaters of the river. We decided that we had better cut down the blowdowns so we could get down to the main Little Tobique Road. Then, when we picked up the hunters, we would not be cutting trees out of the road all night.

Unless you have done it, there is no good way to describe what it means to wade into a tangle of downed trees, some of them still hung up in the air, and cut a hole through the mess without being killed in the process. Doing it in the night, lit by the headlights of a truck, with a bunch of dudes getting in the way and offering advice, certainly adds to the entertainment.

Cutting our way down to the main road, we took time to boil a kettle of tea and figure out the plan for the pick-up. For once we did not have to go to the brook for water. Coleman filled the boiling kettle full of hailstones, which even two hours after they had fallen were still half the size of a hen's egg.

As always, I was thankful to have Coleman with me. Even though he suffered from ulcers so bad that he couldn't zip up his pants because of his swelling stomach, he would take a handful of pills and keep on working. If I had ever had ten guides like Coleman, we would have taken over Canada.

Right up until darkness obscured the sky, it was apparent by the rumbling and black clouds to the north of us that we were going to see a hell of a lot of water come daylight. Gathering up the hunters, soaked but safe, by two in the morning, we were back at the river crossing going over to the camp.

After sending the guests scurrying with their flashlights across the footbridge, now ominously close to the water level, Coleman and I got ready to ford the truck. After unhooking the fan belt and putting a garbage bag over the carburetor, loose enough to contain sufficient air for a short pull, we eased her into the river. Oh-oh, too light. The current started to shove the rig downstream. Hastily I backed out.

On the bank, waiting to cross later, were three drums of gas and a couple one-hundred-pounders of propane. With those aboard we were able to cross without being floated down broadside to the footbridge. That would have been a disaster for sure—losing the truck and going for a midnight swim at the very least.

While having middle-of-the-night coffee with the somewhat shrunken dudes, we figured out the morrow. Leigh and Arnold had hunted on foot right up behind the camp; their men had killed a bear that evening, so they had a bearskin to flesh in the morning. We had lots of grub in camp, but unfortunately our cook, Eleanor, had gone out to the settlement the evening before and would be stuck on the wrong side of a flooded river when she came back at daylight, by now only a couple of hours away.

"Good thing I left a canoe on this side," offered Leigh. "I went out and tied it up high and dry when I first came in."

Big Flood on Mamozekel

"OK," I said, "I'll move the old truck up higher. Surely the water won't be in the cookshack come morning. We'll figure this all out come daylight. If we don't get out hunting too early tomorrow, I don't think those guys drying their clothes in the guest shack are going to complain too much."

It seemed I was in the sleeping bag about two minutes when I woke to find Coleman shaking up a fire in our rusty old tin stove in the guide shack.

"I guess Eleanor made it back," he said. "I heard her blowing the horn over on the other side of the river. The footbridge must have gone down in the night."

After pulling on still-wet jeans and cramming dry socks down into wet boots, I was ready to face another day, whatever it might bring.

"You and Arnold go ahead and start the cook's fire and put the bacon on," I said. "I'll take Leigh to man the bow. We'll be back in half-an-hour with Eleanor."

Now, having replaced Leigh with Coleman, who was kneeling in the bow with a paddle at the ready, I pushed her off again. On the flooded flat the current was sluggish, almost placid, but out in the river channel it was a roaring flood, rounded up in the middle like a haystack.

God knew what lay down around the bend. I could only hope the bridge had gone completely out, because if we swept down upon it half submerged and rolled under it, then we'd be in trouble for sure. Or as the old guides say, "Strangers in hell for breakfast, and no place set for them."

"Coleman!" I hollered down the roar of the water. "Leigh told me he can't swim. Can you?"

Looking back briefly with a grin, the old guide replied, "Surely we aren't out here to go swimming. Are we?"

That's the kind of guts I admire. Forget weighing the chances, forget figuring the odds, let's get the hell into it and get it done!

No bottom to snub with the pole—all I could do was use it as a sweep. We rode the crest. A split-second glance ashore gave the illusion that we were higher than the tops of the alders rushing by in a blur. We careened around the bend, charging down on the crossing. I could see Eleanor in yellow raingear waving from the south shore. Nothing remained of the bridge except the center pier. If we ran down on it, we'd be goners.

I swept her around so the bow was upstream, and Coleman paddled like mad. We slipped alongside the bank, I snubbed it in, and Coleman held it with the paddle—parked like a taxi at the curb.

"Boys," said Eleanor, "I would have bet fifty dollars on who would show up in this kind of water. Let's get over to the camp and start laying on the pancakes."

Eleanor was glad to see us.

We'd soon have the dudes dried out and ready to go again. Come hell or high water, it was another day in the Mamozekel bear camp.

MEDIA STARS

Töin Hennessey —

(Appeared in *Victoria County Review*, March 1977)

Have you ever noticed how the guys in the hunting magazines seem to have only successful trips? The weather is always beautiful and the game cooperative. The guide is expert, cheerful, and dignified, and the shooting is superb. Well, sometimes. Maybe.

A few years ago, one of the major outdoor publications sent its eastern field editor to make a movie and gather material for a magazine article on bobcat hunting. He brought along another outdoor "personality" to portray the role of hero in the film and story.

At that time, cats were plentiful and we were taking them on a regular basis, so I foresaw no problem whatever in turning out a story that was bound to make us all rich and famous. After all, there is really nothing much to cat hunting, aside from finding a track in the right snow conditions and having the proper dog and the ability to snowshoe to where the cat is treed.

Simplest thing in the world, a natural for filming. The only thing bothering me was that on a properly conducted cat hunt, nothing very exciting ever happened, except perhaps a poorly adjusted snowshoe harness. Guides just hate "excitement and adventure," both of which are usually the result of things getting screwed up. Anyway, I thought that with my dog Ben we'd be able to pick up a cat easily enough. LeRoy Johnson, one of the more colorful guides in that or any other country, was there to help me. Surely we could fill in the visitors with enough "background material," as they called it, to make up some kind of a story.

We had a few snags to work out, though. To begin with, the Writer and the Hero weren't quite as much at home on snowshoes as we had been led to believe. However, within a couple of days we had them getting along after a fashion, and of course during this warmup period we were able to film lots of camp and woods scenes and provide all the background material they could handle. Everything else aside, success still hinged on being able to bag a cat, and when the perfect chance arose, we could hardly believe our good fortune.

A fresh track across the Trousers Lake road, a short run, and old Benny was barking treed. Less than two hundred yards from the road, there he was, a great big old tomcat, too fat and full of deer meat to run far, right at the top of a four-log spruce. LeRoy arrived, herding along the Writer and the Hero, and pretty soon we were all set up.

The tree was photographed, including the patch of fur way up in the branches, the dog at the base, and the Hero looking up. He was holding my cat gun, a good old single 12-gauge loaded with a dose of magnum No. 4s.

"OK," said the Writer/Photographer, "now just where is the cat going to land?" I showed him the spot about ten feet out from the tree, right in the sunlight, perfect for the picture. He set up the tripod and carefully focused. LeRoy collared the old dog and held him between his knees.

I instructed the Hero. "Now, you see that little patch of fur up there? That's his head; try to shoot him in the chest. When you fire, turn around and pass me the gun. I'll have another shell ready just in case."

"Fine," said the Hero. "Action," said the Photographer. "Shoot," said I. *BOOM!* went the old gun. Turning frantically, the Hero pushed it into my face, stepped onto my snowshoe, and fell on top of me, jamming the gun barrel down into the snow. At the same instant, the cat, hit in the ass, launched himself straight outward, soaring down like a flying squirrel to hit the snow eighty feet away.

As I struggled to get up, old Ben tore loose and was after the cat, bellowing his guts out. LeRoy was hollering, "Take him, Benny, get the bastard!" The Hero was hollering, "Where, where?"

Screaming something totally unprintable, I at last got straightened out and raced after the action with a gun full of snow. The cat started up a tree. Ben lunged and pulled him back down, and the cat jumped straight into my face. I swung in a dead panic, hit the cat, and broke the stock off the shotgun.

I had not quite demonstrated the cool professional manner of the storied white hunter, but we had the cat, and I figured enough film for the most exciting cat hunt ever. Our fortunes were made.

But, you guessed it; there stood the cameraman, looking through the viewfinder, faithfully focused upon that little patch of sunlight where the cat was supposed to land. Never took a frame.

So that is one story you will never read in a magazine, and a film you will never see. We still aren't rich and famous, but if you ever need any "background material" for a cat story, just ask me or LeRoy.

SHORT-ORDER CATS

Tom Hennessey —

Hunting bobcats was always exciting. The big challenge was going out at daylight after a new snowfall, especially one that had quit early in the night so the game had had some time to move. For the hound hunter, anything from a couple of inches to a foot, on top of a solid base, was good news indeed.

The mysteries of scent tracking will never be completely understood by anyone except the hounds, but a few tips can be picked up by an alert observer. It is quite apparent that temperature and humidity play important parts in how long scent will stay in a track. We have seen times when the dog was happy to nose down and cold-track three-day-old trails, and others when either extreme cold or rain seemed to make it much more difficult.

The very best conditions seem to be when the thermometer reads a few degrees above or below zero, the wind is calm, and the cat is stepping into at least three inches of snow. The scent apparently comes from the hair around its "wrists," because when bare tracks are laid on an ice-covered road or the critter doubles back and gets on your snowshoe track, confusion can result even with the best dogs.

On an ideal morning in February 1970, we started out at daylight from our main camp at Nictau. Tom Everett had been up from Riley Brook, four miles away, the evening before and on the way home had tramped out any cat tracks crossing the road. Now, with about four inches of new snow, which had stopped in the night, we were in business.

"The first track I saw on the way up is right here a half-mile away on top of Vanderbeck Hill," Tom observed. "By the looks of it, he crossed there only a couple of hours ago."

"That's great," I replied. "Old Streak is just busting for a run. I had a hell of a time stuffing him into the box back there. Let's hope we can round this one up in time to try another one later." I liked to start out with a hopeful but cautious frame of mind, knowing it could always go either way.

From where we stopped the truck we could almost look back and see my house. Daylight was just a few minutes old, and the school bus, coming up to capture the boys for another day's torture, passed while we were getting ready to hit the track.

Sometimes we would keep the dog on leash for a while until we got lined out on the track. This time, it was impossible to hold Blue Streak back. Unhooked, he was off on the run, pausing as usual to relieve himself of last night's rations. After the initial few bawling roars to let us know he approved of our choice of tracks, he was silent on the trail. Tom and I wasted no time in getting started. Equipped with the best available snowshoes, we were good for a long, hard day's travel once limbered up.

We'd been brought up on homemade ash-and-moosehide shoes harnessed up with lamp wicking and had managed with them for most of our lives. However, in a magazine ad we had

Short-Order Cats

discovered a tremendous improvement. The new shoes, made by a family named Iverson in Michigan or Minnesota, were constructed with ash bows but with half-inch-wide neoprene rubber-coated nylon filling. Complete with an improved harness, these were the Cadillac of snowshoes. They never sagged or bagged, and you could step in a brook and then right into new snow and just knock it off, a vast improvement over what Grandfather had to work with. These shoes—complete with harness, shipping, and duty at the border—cost us the princely sum of twenty-five dollars, the equivalent of three days' wages at the time or the bounty from two bobcats.

This morning we were dressed as usual—long johns, wool Murphy pants, and red-plaid wool jacket, all from Phoebe's store right in Riley Brook. Pockets held matches, a compass, and a large fishhook inside a piece of cardboard wrapped in rabbit snare wire. The Humane Society would not have approved, but the fishhook with a hastily cut pole for a handle would fetch the

angriest bobcat out of any crevasse in the rocks that you could reach into.

When we hunted as a team, I carried my old full-choke 12-gauge break-open shotgun and Tom carried the ever-present ax.

Campfire Lies of a Canadian Guide

No self-respecting Tobique guide would be separated from that essential tool of the wilderness.

Regardless of temperature, we dressed lightly, knowing full well that we would be soaked with sweat and snow down our necks within the first ten minutes of any chase. The matches and the ax would keep us alive in any unforeseen overnighter.

Once the dog is out of hearing range or running silent, the only option is to follow the tracks. You learn a lot that way about how a bobcat spends his time, most of it hunting through spruce thickets so dense you couldn't beat a weasel through them. You also learn that if you follow the cat down into a thousand-foot gulch, he will climb right back up again a few feet farther along on the same side. However, if you ever try to outsmart him by walking along the rim, he will go directly up the opposite side and walk right out of the country. Oh, yes, one learns a lot about bobcats, and about thickets, mountains, and gulches.

This chase was destined to be a short one. We soon came to where Mr. Cat had lain down to sleep off a feed of rabbits, and the tracks showed that Streak had jumped him rudely out of his slumber. By the sound of the chase—short, choppy barks—Streak was at this minute within sight of the cat, and very soon he was steady in one spot, bawling out "Cat up a tree," so a blind man could have found him.

That old tight-choked 12, loaded with No. 4 shot, would fetch a cat out of the top of the highest tree in New Brunswick. Bobcats are not hard to kill, but as we always told our clients when we hunted with them, one must respect the cat for how

198

he makes a living, and respect the dogs and the hunt for the effort involved. The killing part is certainly anticlimactic, and would have been regretted had we not ourselves been predators bringing home food—in this case in the form of money—to our families.

On the way back to the truck, we noted that it was only 8:30, a good start to the day. Down the road less than half a mile, another track crossed the road.

"That one wasn't there when I came up," Tom was sure. "Look, his track is right in the tire mark made by the school bus."

We headed back out again, snowshoes on and dog released. This cat had not paused to hunt. He was a traveler, heading off east in the direction of Bald Peak. Two hours later, pretty well lathered up, we hit the Bald Peak Portage at a short, sharp hill called the Ram Down. We could hear the dog down off the road a short way and soon were tracking back to the truck with a thirty-pound tomcat wrapped around my neck. Incidentally, you should check a cat for fleas before carrying it this way—a lesson I learned with this one.

Cutting off the ridge and heading directly for the road, we hit our outgoing track almost back at the truck. Some of the local "experts" always claimed never to need or use a compass or map. Of course, they never left the road, either, and most would get lost in any new clear-cut that didn't have signs on the roads.

After a cup of coffee from the Thermos, we decided to go on down to the village to gas up for the afternoon hunt. We didn't get that far. Just past and within sight of Frank Ross's house, a big cat had crossed. Examining the track closely, we could see that Tom had missed it on the way up. Although fresh looking on the bank, for sure the road traffic had wiped it out.

"What do you think?" Tom said. Looks like he's headed for the river and the open places, or maybe he stayed down on the flat, hunting those thickets."

"Let's see what the dog says," I replied. The dog liked it. I was holding him by the collar; he pulled me into the bank, so I let him go.

"Well, what the hell—this may be a hard one if he crossed the river, but we'll never find out standing on the road."

I opened the back of the truck and was getting the snowshoes out when Streak opened up, coming straight for us! One snowshoe off and one on, I was grabbing for the shotgun when I heard a scrambling noise. I looked around and saw the cat going up an old dead tree right behind the truck. Tom never even got his snowshoes out.

With the dog back in the box and the cat added to the load, I checked my watch: 11:50 A.M., three miles from home, three cats, and never even got to Riley Brook for gas. Testimony to a country literally full of bobcats, a real heller of a dog, and excellent snow conditions. That day, anyone who could snowshoe and have faith in the dog could have been the hunter.

We went back out after lunch with the other dog, Ben, and killed two adolescent cats up the same tree down by the Haley Brook Bogan. We lost a third one—the mother, judging by her track—because we ran out of daylight trying to sort out all the confusion.

BROTHERS UNDER THE SKIN

Tom Hennessey—

Having worked with guides all my life, I have encountered a wide range of backgrounds and personalities. As in a cross-section of any profession, they vary in age, size, ethnic background, ability, and ambition. Most are outstanding individuals, a few perhaps less so, but one thing is certain: There is never a dull moment around a crew of guides.

ENOUGH IS ENOUGH

LeRoy and I were guiding a couple of old Long Island stogies one time, and the week had been pretty slow. Hunting conditions vary, but in general when you have clients unfit to get into the heavy cover, you are pretty well limited as to what you can do on a northeastern whitetail hunt.

We had tried all the handicapped options, including sitting at dried-up deer licks and sailing the river. Now, as a last resort, we were driving the lumber-company roads in hopes that a buck would be suicidal enough to stumble out in front of us. As with many clients, these two could not adjust their expectations to fit their physical ability, so by the end of the week things were starting to get a bit strained. LeRoy, throughout it all, had kept their spirits up with his extensive repertoire of entertaining anecdotes about hunting, fishing, and life in general. Even kept me entertained, and I had heard them all before.

Now, on the last afternoon, with the end of the ordeal in sight, I figured everything was going as good as it could, despite the low kill ratio. Coming around a turn in the Trousers Lake road, I had to slow to avoid running over a varying hare, or snowshoe rabbit as we call them.

Breaking into a bear story already in progress, LeRoy, in his naturalist mode, remarked, "Now, look at that, would you. Going to be an early winter. That rabbit is already starting to turn color, and he'll be pure white in another couple of weeks."

From the back of the van, one of the Yankees erupted, "Jesus Christ, man, I have listened to your bullshit for an entire week, but enough is enough! Do you take us for a couple of idiots, telling us that rabbit is going to turn white?"

Never at a loss, LeRoy rejoined, "Well, sir, now, there you go. That's the only goddamn true thing I have told you all week, and you don't believe me!"

RIGHT ON TIME

We were hunting moose and caribou at the head of the Robinson River in Newfoundland. At that time accessible only by floatplane from Corner Brook, this country was full of game.

With a party of four mill owners from West Virginia, we were having a very enjoyable hunt. Though the camp was somewhat rustic, the crew was one of the best I have ever worked with. All guests had filled their tags for moose and caribou with the exception of Jim, leader of the party, who was still looking for a trophy moose.

On a typical Newfoundland October morning, guide Loman and I decided to hike old Jim up the mountain once more to a spot from which we had spotted a good moose the evening before. By late morning, despite the rain and fog, we were hunkered down on a pinnacle from which we could see several moose of varying dimensions within the range of our binoculars.

On the interior plateau of Newfoundland the terrain varies from sections of open tundra to some of the most impenetrable black spruce thickets on the continent. An added impediment is the tangles of low-growing spruce that I have encountered nowhere else across the North, locally called tuckamore or "the tucks." This stuff will eat up the most expensive raingear, entangle and discourage the most hardy hiker, and hide a full-grown bull moose upon occasion.

Sitting rounded up in the rain, your feet wet despite the claims of the boot manufacturers, wiping the fog from the binoculars with your damp shirttail, and trying to score a moose a mile away makes you wonder at your choice of profession. Then in two seconds the scene changes entirely.

"Look, Wibb, does you see him?" Loman hissed. "There's our bull, right there in the tucks this side of that yellow grass clearin'!"

Jim—the client—and I strained to see what Loman had seen. At last I spotted the tip of an antler; then, with a slight movement, more of the rack was exposed. Yes, out there about three hundred yards and downhill from us lay a mature bull, nearly completely hidden in the tuckamore. There was no way of further evaluating the rack, and no shot was possible from our position.

We looked it all over and decided there was simply no way to approach without losing sight of the bull once we descended to his level, and every chance for him to simply step into the nearby thickets before we could have a look. The wind was constantly swirling and changing, and the weather front passing through was almost certain to bring the wind in the wrong direction if we tried to get closer.

"What do you think?" I asked Loman. "Can we move him by calling?"

"Noo, scare 'im off, I thinks—bulls quit callin' two weeks past."

We sat and waited, and as the mist swirled and cleared, we could see more of the rack, very decent for an Eastern moose.

"Yis, Skipper," said Loman, "good pams, lots of pints—ee's a good bull, all right. Jim, can you take he from here, do ye think?"

Jim had a brand-new 7mm Remington Magnum—not my favorite caliber for moose-sized critters in the brush, but we had seen him kill a caribou with it earlier in the week. With the help of my knapsack rolled on top of a rock, I knew Jim could put a round into the bull at that range if it would just stand up.

Lunchtime came and we were still waiting. Nothing fancy— can of Vienna sausage, (little, slimy, cold frankfurters, a Newfoundland delicacy) plus a couple of perspiration-soaked sardine-and-molasses sandwiches from inside our rain jackets.

And still we waited.

"OK Skipper," said Loman to Jim, looking at his watch, "lay your rifle over that rock and be ready. Comin' on three o'clock. See them two cows there, up and startin' to feed? Old Mister Bull goin' to stand up and piss. That's when you shoots 'im, before he steps off into the woods. Don't let 'im stop pissin' or we lost 'im!"

"OK, Jim," I advised, "clear the fog out of the scope. Loman knows what he's talking about."

A few more minutes, and up he stood, a great bull. *Kawhoom!* The 7 Mag echoed through the hills, the bull sagged, and then was down. A great bull, super by Eastern standards, nothing to be ashamed of even in Alaska.

Sometimes a good guide knows there is nothing to do but nothing.

EVERYONE'S AN EXPERT AT ONE THING OR ANOTHER

Tom Hennessey

Rand Smith was guiding for me one fall during the mixed deer and bear season of early October. His sport on the second week of the season was a young man from New Jersey who had read every hunting book and magazine he could put his hands on and fancied himself something of an expert woodsman. No problem, we always admire enthusiasm in a client—wouldn't be much fun otherwise.

By the end of a couple days, though, old Rand was becoming a bit tired of the constant second-guessing and the expert opinions being offered, especially about the game sign they encountered. "I don't mind his Davy Crockett impersonations and his arguing about every track I try to explain to him, but every time we come across any fresh deer droppings, he has to finger and fondle them and lecture me upon the consistency and moisture content and when he figures the buck passed through. It gets a bit wearing after a while."

Next evening at the guides' table, I could see that Rand had a story he was bursting to tell. "Well, Rand," I said, "and how did you make out today with the New Jersey Shit Expert?"

"I have finally taken back my job of interpreting sign and doing the guiding," he said with satisfaction. "This morning I cured him of his fascination with deer and bear sign.

"We had just left the main road and started up the trail at Four Mile Brook when we came upon something that really excited him. Right in the middle of the path was evidence that he claimed proved we were on the track of a big bear.

"'Look here,' he explained to me. 'The size and the way it's cross-piled indicate it came from a large male bear.' Stirring it around with the toe of his boot, he proclaimed, 'Yes, you can see that he has been eating in a cornfield somewhere nearby.'

"I didn't bother telling him," said Rand, "that the nearest cornfield is probably a thousand miles away and that corn comes from other sources as well. When he stooped over and stuck his finger in it to test the temperature, I knew he was a true crap detective.

"'There,' he says, 'it's as plain as day. This is from a large male bear. He traveled here overnight from a cornfield, is heading up the mountain, and must have passed this way just before daylight. We better get after him!'

"Yes," I told him, "and if you notice what has blown over here and caught in the bushes, you'll see he wiped his ass on pink toilet paper!"

Sometimes even the experts need a lesson or two in observation.

GUIDES' DREAMS SOMETIMES COME TRUE

Herman was one of the old-time Tobique salmon guides. About seventy years of age when he worked for me, he had seen the river from one end to the other, back in the glory days of the big clubs. He fully understood that the first day of the week—when the luck of the draw and the outfitter's judgment match up the guides with their sports—is the most important.

This week we had about twenty guests at the lodge, including some couples, all longtime Atlantic salmon devotees. Most of the guests were from the traditional salmon states of New England, but we also had a doctor from Miami and his attractive wife from Argentina.

Watching her practice-casting on the lawn in front of the camp, one could see that she was really adept with the fly rod and would be a pleasure to guide. She had other attributes as well.

The guides had gathered around, as guides do, to swap lies and figure out the coming week. They did not notice a gentleman who had come around behind them and opened the trunk of his Buick to take out and assemble his rod. The topic under discussion was who they were going to guide.

"Well," said Noah, "I guess Fred will want me to guide old Russ again, like I have for the past few years."

"Yeah," chimed in Leigh, "old Wid from L. L. Bean and I always seem to get partnered up. I don't mind—he isn't going to work anyone too hard at his age."

"Well, Sir," piped up Herman, "none of my regulars is here this week. I hope Fred teams me up with that little short woman with the big tits. That's the one I want in my canoe. She can cast a mean fly line, too."

The gentleman behind them closed the trunk and cleared his throat. "Boys, that lady is my wife. And indeed you are right—she IS an expert angler."

Herman got his wish, they hooked and released more salmon than any other crew in camp that week, and we all came away with good memories, even the husband.

FREIGHT-TRAIN CAT

Tom Hennessey —

After we had been catching bobcats with hounds for a few years, we found that a bunch of local legends had been built up. Although no one in the area except Ab Higgins, Tom Everett, and myself had ever seen a cat hunt, that didn't stop the emergence of several local "experts" who knew all about the game.

We decided one day to take out one of the most vocal of the "experts" and actually let him see a cat being killed, mostly because the idea tickled our sense of humor. We agreed that the perfect candidate was Weasel Parish. Known fondly around the country as The Weasel, or simply Wease, he was a man of many talents. Without peer as a rum drinker, banjo picker, and hillbilly mechanic, Wease was not the least hesitant about expressing his opinions on everything from the sporting business to Nixon's successful landing of a man on the moon.

Ash Peasley was up visiting, and we decided to give his dog Warrior the first chance, so we spent some time switching dog boxes around in the Blazer to make room for an extra passenger. Getting away to a late start, made later by having to wait for Wease to get up and put his clothes on, we started up the Little Tobique road. We were going to run only one cat, so we kept going, checking tracks and looking for what appeared to be a good, big, fat, lazy male cat.

Around noon, after passing up a couple of dozen runnable tracks, we picked up what looked like a sure thing up beyond the Left Hand Branch of Little Cedar Brook. Heading off the hill and down into a cedar swamp to hunt, our cat had crossed the road a couple of hours ago and was probably close-by, the perfect cat on which to break in our "sport."

Sure enough, by the time we got the snowshoes out and harnessed up, Warrior had jumped the cat, and being fresh and eager for a fight, was really putting the push to him. Before long the dog was bawling at a tree, and we figured it was all over with. But no, after a short time the cat bailed out of the branches and the chase was on again.

A bit later the bawling and barking indicated that the cat was cornered on the ground and fighting. Suddenly the noise stopped, then started again. This sequence was repeated as we got closer to the action. Cedar swamps are notorious for low branches, blowdowns, and trees growing at odd angles—hard to pick your way through, going fast on snowshoes. Finally, as we drew nearer, the sounds intensified, then became mute, then loud once again, but old Warrior never quit to catch his breath.

Warrior had the cat cornered on the ground, and as we came up, we could see at last what had been going on. There was a big leaning cedar, a couple of others blown down over it, and the entire mess was snowed under. The cat had gone down a hole under the leaning tree, clear to the upturned roots. Warrior, by now dripping blood from his muzzle, rushed roaring down the sloping hole, giving frantic tongue to what could only be hound-dog threats and obscenities. He then came scurrying back in reverse, even madder.

It was quite a struggle to get him by the collar and tie him back out of the way while we thought this situation over. We could see that his approach was not working. Unless we were going to simply walk away from this fight, someone was going to have to crawl down into the hole and dispatch what had to be a very upset bobcat. We offered our guest, Wease, the shotgun and the honor. Gentleman that he is, not wishing to hog the glory, he politely declined.

Ash was just too big a man to fit into this tight space, so Tom and I flipped a coin. I won, or lost, whichever way you might look at it.

As I slid down, headfirst, into what I now saw to be a tunnel at least ten feet deep, I had to roll onto my side to try to let a little daylight enter, as I had no flashlight. As I pushed the old 12-gauge ahead of me, the thought occurred that should the cat decide to leave, the only way out would be by clawing his way the whole length of my carcass. I advanced on my elbows, trying to keep one arm in front of my face while poking the gun ahead with the other. The cat, meantime, was spitting, snarling, hissing, and generally carrying on to let me know he wasn't too pleased with all of this.

At last I could make out why the dog was at such a disadvantage. The cat was wedged down behind a root, a perfect ambush spot from which to whip out his wicked claws at any intruder. Blindly jabbing the gun ahead, I let her rip— *KABOOM!* Powder, smoke, dirt, and blood flew. The gun, half-full of snow and not on my shoulder properly, hit me full in the face, splitting my upper lip and bloodying my nose. Dazed but trying to pretend to keep my cool, I made as dignified a retreat as is possible when one is hampered by being deaf, blind, and propelled only by toes and elbows. At last some kind soul grabbed my ankles and flung me out onto the snow.

Drying off my hands and shakily rolling a smoke, which I could stick only into the left side of my mouth, I joined the discussion as to how we were now going to retrieve the supposedly deceased cat.

"Wease," I managed to mumble, "seeing as this is your cat, probably you will want to get down in there and see whether I have ruined it with a face full of Number 4s."

"Well, now," he allowed, "I've been thinking about this, and really, as much as I would like to have the cat, there just isn't anywhere in the house that I would have room to put a bobcat rug. You boys just go ahead and do whatever you would do if I wasn't here."

Having got a glimpse of how that cat was forted up, and not entirely sure that I had even hit it, I didn't know whether to crawl back down there and feel around behind that root or not. The problem was solved by old Warrior, who had chewed through his rawhide leash while we were talking it over. With a lunge and a roar, he was back down the hole and seemed to be in possession of the trophy.

Finally, with Warrior ahold of the cat, I slid down and got the dog by the tail right close to the body so I wouldn't hurt him. With Tom ahold of my ankles and Ash and our reluctant guest pulling on his legs, we all eventually backed out, bringing the cat with us.

On our way down into the swamp, we had come across a freshly killed doe the cat had been feeding upon when Warrior jumped him. Now he lay dead, a big old male bobcat, later weighed at over forty pounds. One more old deer-killer accounted for. Secretly, we all would have had more satisfaction bagging a few of the market-hunting poachers of the two-legged species. Unfortunately, the $15 bounty was for bobcats only, and we needed the money to feed our own families.

A few weeks later I stepped into Phoebe's store in Riley Brook, where The Weasel was holding forth on bobcat killing. "By Jesus, boys, I didn't know whether to go down that hole or not, but someone had to save the dog. He was a fighter and roaring like a freight train blowing for the Salmon River Bridge, but I figured the cat would have killed him for sure if I hadn't been there to help."

No one noticed as I backed out, not wanting to spoil the birth of another Tobique legend entitled "How Wease Saved the American Champion Bobcat Hound." After that, Tom and I just referred to that trip as the one on which we killed the Freight-train Cat.

214

COLEMAN

KaBang! The sound of a rifle shot echoed across the ridges.

"That's our man," declared Coleman. "If he is where he's supposed to be, we can drive right to him. I sure hope that shot means a dead bear!"

I was born in 1935, and Coleman McDougall was guiding before that. On this day, although I was the employer, Coleman and I were guiding together and he was the senior partner. For about twenty years we guided in the Tobique River country and trapped together several winters. I could always depend upon Coleman to excel at any guiding assignment. He could handle sports that were young or old, rich or poor, man or woman. Coleman was the guide I turned to when I had either a famous or a potentially difficult person visiting. He could handle them all. He once remarked that he could spend at least a week guiding the Devil and probably part friends.

On this late May bear hunt, we had placed two hunters on stands a few miles apart in an immense area that had been clear-cut about ten years previously. No credit to the logging company—through mechanical logging, they had turned the land into something resembling the surface of the moon. However, after a few years a recovering cutover starts to green up and the roads grow up in grass and dandelions, which the bears love in the spring.

Tactics were simple enough. We placed hunters where they could see long distances, then carry out a stalk when and if they spotted a bear. It was easy enough to have up to a half-dozen hunters situated and under control without the guide actually sitting with them at all times. This allowed us to scout new areas during the long evening hours of waiting.

As we came to a fork in the hauling road, Coleman directed me: "Take the one to the left. That should put us downhill from where our sport is waiting, and if he killed the critter, we won't have to drag it too far or skin it in the dark."

Sure enough, as we rounded a turn in the road, the camouflaged hunter appeared, and frantically flagged us down. After stopping, we calmed the guy down, made sure the rifle was unloaded, then listened to his story. Any guide who jumps out and forgets to check the sport's rifle is probably going to be shot through the guts with a Weatherby sooner or later. There is something about bear hunting that turns even the most stolid individual into a raving lunatic. Adrenaline, testosterone, and gunpowder make a lethal combination. For some reason the lady hunters are always easier to handle.

"The bear came right along here, a real big one!" the guy blurted. "I was up there on the hill when I first glassed him, and I got about halfway down when he took off. I had the scope full of bear hair when I pulled the trigger."

Coleman

Coleman and I have heard some version of that story several hundred times at least. Most of the time it means that half the night we will be crawling around looking for blood, hair, and tracks, for nothing. Sometimes we are lucky enough to find where the bullet struck a tree twenty feet too high and convince the guy he has missed.

This time the client was right. Within a few minutes we found sign where the bear had swerved in the road, taken a couple of panic-stricken leaps, and dived into the bushes.

"Just put the rifle in the case and wait by the truck," I told him. "No thanks. We don't need anyone backing us up." I was never anywhere near as afraid of a bear as I was of the clients.

Less than a hundred yards downhill, in thick bush, the animal lay dead, facing back along his trail. This is the way we found most wounded bears. It was a nice, ordinary black bear, probably 140 pounds—funny how much they shrink when the air goes out of them. Coleman and I grabbed it by the ears and half-dragged and half-carried it back up to the road. The happy hunter jumped out of the truck, fumbling with his camera.

We congratulated him on taking a nice bear. Any fairly won trophy is a record in our book, as long as the client is happy. After ten minutes of posing and picture taking, now with the flash as it was rapidly getting dark, came the inevitable question:

"Coleman, you've seen a lot of bears. What do you think he weighs?"

217

"Well, now," Coleman said, looking at the ground, scraping his toe in the gravel, and finally finding just the right reply, "what would you like him to weigh?"

"Oh, surely he must weigh four hundred, doesn't he?" the guy pleaded.

"Well," replied Coleman, "we could take him to the scales tomorrow, but I would rather skin him early before the flies get to him."

Bending over, the seventy-year-old guide picked up the bear by the slack skin on his back and tossed him over the sideboards into the back of the truck. End of the discussion on what the bear weighed!

In all the years we guided together, I never knew Coleman to tell a client a lie. When we quit outfitting in New Brunswick and moved to the Northwest Territories, how I wished that Coleman was twenty years younger and willing to go with us. But as he put it, "When Fred Webb is done outfitting on the Tobique, then I am done guiding."

Honesty, integrity, and loyalty: virtues much appreciated in a world where they are becoming extinct.

FAME ONLY STRETCHES SO FAR

It was a change over Sunday in the bear camp in northern New Brunswick. Always a stressful day, new people arriving, supplies going out to the outpost camps, guides to assign, and always the ten thousand questions to answer for the fifteenth time.

By suppertime in those years, I was usually half full of beer, simply in self-defense. Now it appeared that one expected guest was missing. Held Martin and the rest of the crew going up to a spike camp as long as I could, then had to tell them to go without him.

Supper at the main camp cleared away and despite me going to look down the road for the hundredth time, he was nowhere in sight.

Worrisome evening. Maybe an accident, maybe trouble at the border, finally it's bedtime and he is still missing. How in hell could anyone get lost coming up Interstate 95 from Pennsylvania, with all the directions I had given him.

At two o'clock in the morning, on the first ring of the phone I snatch it up.

"Mr. Webb, this is John Smith from Philadelphia."

"Yes," I say, starting to get dressed, "we will have to keep you at the main camp tonight and send you up in the morning, but no problem, how soon will you get here."

"Well, that is the problem. I am at the bridge here and no one can give me directions to your place, in fact no one knows you."

"That's funny," I reply, "Are you at the bridge in Riley Brook, five miles away, or the bridge in Plaster Rock 30 miles away, or the Saint John River bridge in Perth 50 miles away? Someone there has to know the way up to my camp."

"Just a minute till I ask the man here." Comes back on, "The Customs man here says this is the Thousand Islands Bridge, and he has never heard of Fred A. Webb & Sons."

"Jesus Christ man! There's a good chance he hasn't! Did you look at that goddamned map I sent you? You are over two thousand miles away, heading up into Ontario!"

Long pause, "Oh! This happened to me one time before. Maybe I better just get a motel and head back home tomorrow."

"Good idea," I concede, "and tell that Customs bastard that I have never heard of him either!"

Fame only stretches so far, I guess.

EVENING AT KINGFISHER POOL

It occurred during the annual visit by my favorite group of clients, the sporting gang known as Rikhoff's Rangers. As usual, the salmon fishing for most of the week had been simply terrible.

A veteran Atlantic salmon guide will have an excuse to cover any fishing disaster. This time it was simply a long stretch of hot weather, warming up the already-too-low water. As one of the old guides said, "Any self-respecting fish has long ago gone ashore to hide in the shade."

After supper we decided to try another part of the river, and despite the lowering skies and the hordes of no-see-ums that usually warn of a coming storm, a group of us were on our way downriver to the Oxbow. Here a couple of pools, well away from the road, might produce results. At least we would be fishing over salmon that hadn't already seen everything we had to offer.

Gene Hill was driving his well-equipped "sporting wagon," with Jimmy Rikhoff riding shotgun. Noah and Bernie Ruff and myself completed the crew. Two canoes had already been trucked down by Martin and Rick, so all we had to do was rig up the rods and set sail for the evening's effort. A half-hour later, Noah and I, with Gene in the bow seat, had anchored at the head of Kingfisher Pool.

Hilly was the kind of sportsman that guides revere. He was always enthusiastic, not only interested in the quarry but having a quiet appreciation of all the world around him. Whether conversing with the wealthy and famous among our guests or discussing just the right fly with a Labrador Inuk on the George River, Hilly was always in his element. A legend for being happy with very little, Gene could have more fun on a one-rise fishing trip than most people could by filling the boat. Definitely a valuable attribute while angling for salmon in low water.

This evening Hilly lived up to his reputation. To see one fish roll was all the encouragement he needed. We proceeded to try cast after cast and fly after fly as we progressed in short drops down through Kingfisher Pool, then poled back up to try again.

Some wet flies, some dry flies, a white and then a brown Bomber, straight-hitched and Portland-hitched: the fun had to be in the trying, for nothing offered seemed to fit the mood of the King of Fish.

Evening at Kingfisher Pool

Lightning started to play along the horizon. Soon a fresh upstream breeze brought a welcome respite from the sticky heat, and Gene kept on casting. About the time the first raindrops arrived, big enough to splash back up when they hit the bottom of the canoe, he removed the ever-present pipe from his mouth long enough to ask Noah and me if we minded getting a bit damp, as he figured the cooling rain would entice the fish into striking. I remember his smile and mumbled thanks when Noah informed him that Tobique guides were not made of sugar and we probably wouldn't melt in a little rain shower.

The storm hit with a suddenness and a violence sufficient to make me wonder if indeed we were crazy to be sitting in the middle of a river, waving around a graphite fly rod. The canoe heeled over on the anchor line.

At last! A fish rose and struck. No time now to take down the rod and go ashore to shelter. We were here to stay.

The rain increased in ferocity. We could but pull our hats down like turtles and shade our eyes from the lashing fury of the storm. The line disappeared into the mist, the bend in the rod and the intermittent scream of the reel guaranteeing that we were still fast to a considerable fish.

The gloom was split when a bolt of lightning struck a big "cow-shade" spruce at the side of the pool, just where we would have landed had we quit and gone ashore. Perhaps our lives had been saved by the salmon—old tales tell of such things.

The crash of thunder and the smells of ozone, pitch, and smoke, brought to mind stories of the dreaded Other Place. Despite the plastered-down cowboy hat, the hair rose on the back of my head.

"Evil spirits," said the part of me that is aboriginal. "Static electricity foretelling the next lightning strike," said my white-guy education.

Whichever it was, it was enough to recommend getting out of the middle of the river in such a maelstrom. But we were fast to a great fish, and with the canoe having blown halfway across the pool, the anchor had wedged into a ledge. It was better to just hang on and bail. No words were needed between Noah and myself and couldn't be heard anyway. We agreed instinctively that sometimes the best thing to do is nothing.

The wind abated, the lightning moved up the river, but the rain increased in intensity. As we sat at anchor, almost becalmed, we could not see six feet beyond the tip of Gene's rod, but the fish was still on.

I hunched in misery and thought: *Here I sit with two friends who have faced extreme danger in their journey through life—one on a far-away Pacific island, the other as he fought the long road through Sicily, Italy, France, Belgium, Holland, and across the Rhine into Germany. Two men of the generation who had gone to war to save the world from evil. Surely we will not be killed by something as commonplace as a thunderstorm on a salmon river.*

And then, as if in a dream, I was reminded of the Malecite elder, Peter Paul, who had told us tales of the river from long ago. I remembered his brown hand dropping the tea leaves into the black boiling kettle before putting it aside to settle. I remembered him lighting the short old pipe with an ember from the fire before sitting back to tell us young ones of how, in the days of his grandfather's father, the mighty Mohawks had come down from the north to take scalps and capture slaves among the people of the Saint John River Valley.

On the headwaters of the great river they had captured the daughter of the chief of the Tobique Malecite, the northern guardians of the valley. Her husband—Moween, the Bear— died under torture. Malabeam, the Princess of the Nation, then agreed to lead the Mohawk raiding party down the river to the village of her father, and farther to the bigger fort at

Tom Hennessey —

Medoctik, which sat on the end of the warpath leading down into the New England settlements.

As they sailed down the broad and serene river, Malabeam convinced the Mohawk leader that the river continued on in the same docile way clear to the mouth of the Tobique. She persuaded them that they could tie their canoes together and sleep as they floated down the gentle current.

No one except Malabeam was awake when the water started to quicken, the trees on the bank began to speed by faster, the long, oily swell turned inevitably into the head of the rapids, above what the English came to know as the Grand Falls.

Malabeam stepped quietly from one canoe to another until she had removed all the paddles, except one that she took into her own canoe, which she then cut loose. When the raiders awoke, they were already doomed, caught in the clutches of the current and speeding to oblivion in the gorge.

Two women, tending a fish trap at the foot of the cataract, saw the Mohawk canoes dash down into the rocks, where none of the occupants survived. They also saw Malabeam, in her canoe, ride upon the torrent and rise from the mist, never to be seen again. It is said she went to sail with her lover upon the waters in the Land Beyond the Earth.

As we sat in the downpour, our canoe as well seemed to float upon the mist, as if suspended between water and sky. My white blood said it was an illusion, but some of my genes said we were one with Malabeam of the legend.

The spell at last was broken. The rod tip sprung up, the line went slack, the angler's shoulders slumped momentarily. Hilly turned to me. Taking the long-dead wet pipe from his mouth, he grinned and said, "Boys, that was a grand fish, but I guess we were just not meant to kill him."

Noah and I did not argue the point. The rain had at last slacked off, gone with the salmon. It was time to retrieve the anchor and pole up to the landing where we were to meet the other boys and load the canoes for the trip home.

Starting to dry out a bit, with a good slug of brandy from Jimmy's flask in our bellies, we were in the van heading back up to Nictau, where a hot shower, dry clothes, and more serious refreshment awaited the weary angler. Bad storm. No fish, but a wonderful evening!

As we drove along, talk was subdued as we all remembered the ferocity of the lightning and Man's insignificance when measured against the forces of nature. From the stereo speakers, Mary Travers provided a heart-catching rendition of the fine old hymn "Amazing Grace," the perfect accompaniment to such an occasion.

Now, years later, every time I hear that hymn—whether bagpipe instrumental or sung by Inuit artist Susan Aglukark or by Willie Nelson—my heart goes back to that evening in the mist and my two companions Gene and Noah. Sadly, both are gone now. I feel that they sail now on tranquil waters with Malabeam and the Ancestors. They await the guides and canoe men left behind.

TUNDRA GRIZZLY

Tom Hennessey —

"Hold it, Gerry! Take a look at that black dot way over there across the valley."

Setting down his cup of tea, my fellow guide steadied his binoculars and finally focused in on the object I was glassing. "Oh, yes, now I see him. Big, big bear! Now all we have to do is get over there without killing our sport hunter."

It was mid-May and we were hunting barren ground grizzly out west of Coppermine in the central Arctic. We had left town nearly a week earlier, four guides looking after two sport hunters from down south. Days are long at this time of year, just about twenty-four hours long. Snow-machine travel is good most of the time, although it can get hot enough during the day to cause problems. We don't pay much attention to the clock, sometimes traveling all night when conditions are better.

This method of hunting offers an excellent chance for success on big bears. That is, if everything goes right—if there are not too many breakdowns, if sufficient fuel is cached or hauled along, and, most of all, if your client can handle the conditions and keep his spirits up. Although we have often killed bears almost within sight of town, and most times take them within a few days to a week, you can occasionally go the entire ten days that are usually planned for the hunt.

Such an operation can be carried out properly only with good planning and, most of all, a dependable backup crew in town ready to send out snowmobile parts, fuel, or food when needed. In this case my partner, Martin, with many years of experience in the business, manned the radio at our permanent base in the community.

Hunting this fairly rare and unique member of the bear family is a privilege not to be taken lightly. The barren ground or tundra grizzly, as the name implies, exists mainly across the western and central Arctic above the tree line. Although not as big as the salmon-stream bears on the west coast of the continent, they are as large as or larger than the average woodland or mountain grizzly. In the spring the fur is long and luxurious; colors range from the traditional silvertip to reddish blonde—magnificent as either a rug or a full mount.

Reading the accounts of the early explorers on the western plains and their encounters with savage bears, it is quite apparent that the open-country grizzly, having fewer options for concealment or flight, is generally much more aggressive toward man than its cousins in the woods.

The adage that there are two confrontation options—flight or fight—is true. When you take away the opportunity of flight, then you are much more likely to have a bear in your lap. Such has been our experience, both when hunting these animals north of the Arctic Circle and when they consistently raid our caribou-hunting camps in a more southerly area, where we cannot as yet obtain tags to kill them.

Back in the mid-1980s, when the first bear tags were issued, we tried hunting in the autumn. That was a disaster. Unlike Alaska, our small communities do not have any local flying service, so the use of aircraft for scouting or travel is ruled out. This means that in the fall, before snowmobile travel becomes possible, you can get over the country only on foot. Needless to say, walking on tundra and being unable to cross major streams seriously limit the number of bears one might run across. On those first fall hunts, although we managed to kill some bears, the clients were extremely glad to take the first bruin encountered.

A commonsense argument presented to the Game Department resulted in getting the season changed. We simply pointed out that given the strictly limited number of tags available and the desire to properly manage the resource by taking only mature males, a change in season was required. We were not long in proving that late April to May is the proper time to be out there. The mature males come out of the den a couple of weeks in advance of females and cubs, and tracking on snow helps guides to disregard small, immature bears. The excellent travel conditions and long days allow the hunters to range far afield, thus spreading the pressure over a wider area. This makes for both better hunting and better management.

Our guiding companions are Inuit from Kugluktuk, or Coppermine as it appears on the maps. With a background of centuries of Arctic hunting, these men provide a living for their families by hunting, trapping, fishing, and guiding visiting sport hunters. Like most guides anywhere, they are sometimes hard to handle in town, but out on the land there are none better.

Going into the grizzly season, the guides will have already spent a couple of months hunting muskox, during which time we often take the opportunity to haul out extra gas and spot it in places where it will come in handy later. Close watch is kept via the "party line" radio frequencies. Local Inuit out hunting and family camping will report to us any grizzlies or tracks they run across in their travels.

On the day of a visitor's arrival, all is ready for a quick start. *Komatiks* carrying all the equipment, food, and fuel are loaded and lashed down; the guides are ready to go. The visiting sport is soon dressed and his license made out. He is out of town in a couple of hours—no hanging around the hotel burning time and money waiting for things to happen.

On this particular hunt, we had two first-time guests. I will call them Dave and Tom. As we left town that late afternoon, we were two crews that would travel out together until a base camp was established approximately 150 miles to the west. Gerry Atatahak hauled a shorter sled with extra gas aboard. Andy Atatahak pulled Tom on his sled, with McCauley Niptanatiak ferrying extra gear and more gas. In the face of a snowstorm, we made about sixty miles before camping on the shore of No Name Lake, a good start to our journey.

The following morning it was clear and cold, probably around minus twenty-five, ideal traveling conditions. By shortly after noon we arrived in the area from which we would hunt for the next few days. Tents were soon up and sleeping gear stowed away. Then we stripped down the *komatiks* for faster scouting. Gerry and I would take Dave and head west; Andy and Mac with their hunter would range south toward Great Bear Lake.

Traveling initially up the valley of the Richardson River, the three of us gradually ascended a plateau and were now in an area of small hills and gentle valleys, easily hunted by glassing and then moving to the next high point. The first afternoon's hunt was unproductive as far as bear sign was concerned. We did, however, encounter three herds of muskox complete with a half-dozen decent trophy bulls, something to keep in mind for next year's early hunt.

Andy and Mac, already cooking supper when we arrived back at camp, had made a big swing to the south, where they had encountered some difficult and rocky country. They had seen one fairly old bear track not worth following, and run into some sizable herds of caribou, now moving back north from their winter spent in the tree line around Great Bear. Andy had picked out a young bull in reasonable shape, providing meat that the Inuit guides always prefer greatly to "white man grub" out of cans.

Over the next couple of days the weather remained clear and both crews expanded their area of search. On the third afternoon, coming around the end of a high hill, Gerry spotted two black specks far in the distance. Getting up on the sidehill, we set up the spotting scope, which revealed what looked like twin bears. Of less than medium size, they were working directly away from us, stopping once in a while to dig and roll in the snow. Going on down with the machines, we came to their tracks, definitely a pair of two-year-olds in the 175- to 200-pound class. Maybe we'll run across them again in a few years. Those bears provided little encouragement, at least, for our patient guest, who must have been thinking that the rest of his life would be spent bouncing around in a box, interrupted by occasional snowbank picnics.

When the other crew got in that night they reported having had a bit of excitement also. They had made a wide circle in the area west of Dismal Lake. Late in the afternoon they had cut the track of a fairly large bear and attempted to follow it until it got into broken, hilly country full of sheer cliffs and dead-end canyons. They gave up the pursuit temporarily, and were hoping to go back to solve the problem in the morning.

We therefore decided to give it one more day at this location. Thereafter, a decision would have to be made whether to split up totally or move the base camp farther south, where we'd had a report that a bear had approached a party out from town, ice fishing for the weekend.

When it's daylight nearly around the clock, time loses its meaning. We didn't get away to any record-breaking start in the morning, but instead took time to pack extra food and fuel for the machines as we intended to go straight west, well beyond the area we had been covering.

On trips like this, I always record the reading of the snow machine's odometer, not only to keep track of where we are but also to figure out gas consumption. By noon, after driving fast through the area we had already scoured, we were forty-some miles farther west, toward Bluenose Lake.

On a beautiful day, we were in extremely scenic country. Looking across the frozen plain was almost like viewing an ocean, with high, steep islands appearing here and there. But these "islands" were hills, some of them rising straight up from the flat land in cliffs three or four hundred feet high—ideal country for bears to den up on the rocky hillsides and in snowdrifts at the base of the cliffs. In climbing the hills on some of the easier slopes to glass beyond, one had to be careful not to get stuck in a position where the only route was either a free-fall to the plain below or a retreat along our tracks.

We would work our way up one hill, set up the scope and glass, then travel down across the valley to the next range of hills and look around some more. It was exhilarating and enjoyable for Gerry and me, traveling over new country where very few, if any, had ever hunted before. Our guest, bouncing along in his padded box, got little more than an occasional glimpse out either side. The rest of his attention was taken up just hanging on.

Sometime in the middle of the afternoon, during one of the stops, we took out the Coleman stove and made a cup of tea to wash down our lunch of bannock and dried caribou meat that Gerry had brought from home. Not exactly a gourmet dinner, but in those circumstances and surroundings, nothing could have been better. Gerry was glassing some mountains over across from us, three miles or so away, when he spotted some kind of disturbance in the otherwise unbroken expanse of snow in the lee of a mountain.

Curious as to whether it might be a bear den, we headed off in that direction after lunch. Sure enough, it was a den, and all the sign pointed to the fact that a very large bear had only recently broken out. Just to make sure nothing remained in there, as the tracks in the immediate vicinity were fairly confused, we set the hunter up in a good position with his rifle uncased and loaded. Gerry and I went over to prod around and throw snowballs down the hole, to satisfy ourselves that the bear had indeed departed for parts as yet unknown.

When these old males come out of hibernation, they have two things on their mind: They want something to eat, and they are coming into the season when they want to meet up with a friendly, unattached female; both reasons will set them to walking right out of the country.

This guy was no exception. After quite a bit of circling around to unravel the tracks, we finally came to where the bear had lit out in one direction. We could now get down to some rapid follow-up. I checked the odometer to figure out how much gas we were burning. It's surprising how much it varies with terrain, load, and snow conditions. The last thing I wanted to do was get stuck way out somewhere short of gas, and have to sit around for a day while Martin sent out another barrel to rescue us. However, we seemed to be heading back in a northeasterly direction, closer to an area where we had gas cached and could contact Andy and Mac for help instead of someone coming clear out from the settlement.

In any decently flat country, even when hauling someone on the *komatik*, it is usually possible to average ten miles an hour without undue hardship. Now, because we were stepping up the pace, it was going to be a lot rougher for our hunter. People sometimes get confused about the difficulty inherent in this kind of hunting, whether for grizzly, caribou, or muskox. We try to tell them that although it is not strenuous, it does indeed demand a considerable degree of stamina, strength, and positive mental outlook. It is not quite like the "animal rights" idiots would portray it: tooling along in a limousine shooting bears out the window.

In Dave we had one of the good ones: At each stop to check on him, his reply was, "Let's go!" The track continued generally north and east, mostly sticking to flat country but occasionally striking up into the hills. Each time this happened, Gerry and I would drop the sled and take off up into the rocks until we had the track sorted out again.

Finally, about six in the evening, heading almost straight north, we topped a range of hills from which we could see the track was headed out across a valley probably ten miles wide. Taking a gamble, we lit out across the flat plain by the easiest route. When we headed down parallel with the next ridge, we picked up the track again almost immediately. The gamble had paid off! The track was considerably fresher; we had gained a few miles on him for sure.

Again I checked on the mileage and the gas: We had come about fifty miles on the track and were now getting down to the "hot pursuit" phase of the operation. Each machine had about half a tank of gas, plus another five gallons on the back. It was going to be close; we couldn't go forever, but this chase was too good to give up. Besides, although Gerry didn't know it, I had put another five-gallon can into the box in front of the hunter, just for emergencies.

A half-hour at a fast pace, and we came over another range of hills. Facing us was a long expanse of frozen prairie heading downhill for a couple of miles, then gradually rising toward another string of mountains that were just a blue smudge on the horizon. We stopped to fuel up the machines and have a hastily prepared cup of tea with some bannock and peanut butter.

It was time to make up our minds whether to quit or continue on the track. We knew at this point that we were about forty miles from our camp and the rest of the gas, food, and sleeping bags. However, the weather was good and daylight was no problem.

While we talked over the options, I got my binoculars out from my parka and scanned the country before us. There he was! Heading up the opposite slope with about a five-mile head start on us. As we were packing up the grub box, I could see that Gerry was thinking this situation over carefully.

"I recognize this country," he said. "Two years ago I trapped up here. That dip in the land ahead is the headwaters of the Rae River, and usually by this time of the season either there is overflow on top of the ice or the ice is gone altogether. I hope we can get across with Dave and the sled. All we can do is try it."

No sense in hurrying now. I took the time to set up the spotting scope to look the situation over. It was too late in the day to make any mistakes. With the temperature dropping, the haze and heat distortion were clearing up. I could easily see it was a good big bear. He wasn't hurrying but was walking steadily away from us, headed for that range of mountains in the distance. Once we got down off the plateau, we would lose sight of him, so I took a real good look at the mountain ahead and those behind us; we would need something to line up on if we got over there.

We were soon packed up and on the trail down into the valley. Stretching across in front of us was the Rae River; as Gerry had feared, it appeared to be running wide open. About a hundred yards wide at that point and with twenty-foot vertical banks on both sides, it was impossible to cross. I took off downstream, but after a mile the terrain got worse, if anything. Heading back, I met Gerry coming for me. "Come on, we'll try it up here," he said. "Looks a little better." He had found a spot where it was fairly level down to the shore and an island split the river into two channels. On the near side, the ice appeared to be intact but with about a foot of water on top of it.

We had experienced this kind of situation before; the only way to cross water with a snowmobile is to hit it wide open and hope to skim right across. This is usually successful for a limited distance, but neither of us had tried it while towing a passenger. Gerry made it down over the bank and took it with a rush, splitting the water and hauling the sled right through. With no load behind, I skimmed right over—no problem. We were now at least halfway across and looking for a place to cross the other channel.

This crossing would be more hazardous. Not only was there overflow, but against the far bank was a ten-foot stretch of totally open water, with rocks sticking up here and there. There was no way of telling if the water between those rocks was six inches deep or six feet. We would just have to try it and see.

Only one way to do it. Gerry took off at full throttle with me right behind him. With water flying everywhere we made the other bank. Our passenger was soaked, thanks to a big wave that had broken right into the box, but he was laughing and ready to go. We got up on the land, spun the water out of our machines so they wouldn't freeze up, and were on our way again.

The first thing to do was get high enough on the slope so we could see both mountain ranges and line up with where we thought the bear was headed. Cutting back and forth, we soon struck the track; he was still heading in the same direction.

Stopping for a moment, we agreed that with a limited amount of gas we couldn't keep on following the track forever. The way this bear was going, he might travel clear to the Arctic Ocean before we came up with him. We decided to gamble again and head straight for the hills facing us to try to cut him off or at least get up on top where we could set up the scope again.

As we approached the line of cliffs, I could see that this was not going to be as easy as I had thought. They had looked like fairly gentle, rounded hills from ten miles away; up close they were anything but—jagged and rocky with steep cliffs and narrow canyons that led up into the mountains. Our only chance was to try to get around the end and up an easier slope to where we could glass again.

Ten minutes later, I was leading. I came around the end of one bluff, and here came the bear running straight up the narrow canyon toward us. About 150 yards away, he had no idea that we were anywhere in the country. I guess the wind had kept the noise and the smell of the snow machines away from him. I had time to swing back out of sight, flag down Gerry, and start dragging our hunter out of the box.

In a panic, we got Dave unloaded, rifle out, and a round in the barrel with more in his hand. I grabbed him by the elbow and started towing him around the corner of the hill to see if the bear was still coming. He was coming straight on, full out, snow flying back from his pads! Dave got off his first shot when the bear was about thirty yards away, still headed right for us. At the crack of the .300 magnum the bear hit the snow and started spinning around and biting at his left rear foot, snow and blood flying in all directions.

Fumbling around, Dave got another shell up the spout. I was a big help, hollering, "Christ, man, give him another one quick!" Gerry took off back to his sled to grab his rifle from under the lashings. The bear got himself unwound and had made about three long jumps in our direction when Dave's second shot flattened him out on the snow—stone dead, as it turned out.

As I look back on those few seconds of furiously exciting action, I figured this might be made into another dramatic bear-charge story. However, I tend to think the bruin was totally disoriented, and once he stopped spinning like a top and got his feet back on the ground, he simply went in the direction he was headed and we happened to be standing in the way. That's one of the things we will never know for sure because obviously the bear isn't talking.

Old Dave was pretty happy with it all. He kept walking around the bear, asking, "What do you think? Is he a big one?"

"Yes, he's a better than average bear," I assured him. "By the way, how does this hunt compare to others you have been on?"

"Well," said our hunter, "to tell you the truth, this is the first hunt I've ever tried, except one time pheasant hunting in South Dakota."

Nothing like starting at the top, taking a trophy that few will ever hunt and fewer still will ever better. This bear turned out to be one of the best we have ever taken, squaring out within an inch of nine feet and with a skull that scored well above minimum for entry in the record books—that is if someone had had the good sense to enter it. But that's another story. I guess you can't have everything.

We set up the radio and contacted Martin in town; he had already heard from our other crew. They had been successful and were back at camp working on their bear skin. By the time we got finished with pictures and skinning our bear, we would be lucky to reach camp in time for breakfast.

It was a long, hard night. We did have to use that extra gas I had hidden, but no one was complaining.

OLD FRIENDS ARE THE BEST FRIENDS

Tom Hennessey —

My friend Gordon Birgbauer phoned me the other evening, and we had our quarterly rant about how the U.S. and Canada and the world in general are turning to shit and nothing is the same as it used to be. I think it is therapeutic for both of us, as God knows we can't do much about it.

Gordon and I are exactly the same age, both born in the depths of the Great Depression. Although he was in Michigan and I was in rural New Brunswick, we both inherited the stories and the attitudes from parents and grandparents who had come to North America, started in poverty, and by hard work managed to ensure that each following generation would have it better.

We are both of the generation that missed involvement in the horrors of World War II by a scant half-dozen years, and thus are in the enviable position of enjoying the fruits of all that our parents worked, fought, and sacrificed for.

Unashamed believers in hard work and free enterprise, we will never win the U.S. Democratic nomination for president or rise high in any of the quasi-socialist parties currently bent on destroying the once-free country of Canada. We both hate communism, socialism, unionism, and any other cult that saps the lifeblood of the true working man.

We share a lot of history, attitudes, and concern for where we are headed. Thankfully, we have also shared a lot of good times in the pursuit of sport afield.

Gordon first came to hunt black bears with us in northern New Brunswick back in the 1970s. At that time we were running mobile bear hunts all over the province. Having been on one of our remote hunts, the logistics of which I had trusted to a supposedly honest man-and-wife team, Gordon took me aside one day and told me how we were being robbed blind by two people I had taken off welfare and given a chance to earn a living. As a businessman himself, running a chain of lumber and hardware stores back in Michigan, Gordon was no stranger to this phenomenon.

We both had what I term a "missionary complex"; we were inclined to give everyone—client and employee alike—the best deal possible. It was about then that I began to realize that not everyone was as devoted to looking after my interests as I was to looking after theirs.

When our family company became involved in developing the new caribou camp, Akuliak, up on the shores of Ungava Bay, Gordon was one of our very first clients. Akuliak in those years was one of the best hunting destinations in North America. Bill Tait, then tourism manager for the Federation of Cooperatives of Northern Quebec, myself, and a number of friends from George River took an exploratory party into the area, where the Inuit had told us there were always big caribou. They were right!

Old Friends Are the Best Friends

The following summer, working under contract for the Federation, I went up the coast with the Inuit again, this time to build a caribou camp and pace out an airstrip because the first hunters were due to arrive in less than a month. We had booked eight hunters a week for the six best weeks, and were anxious to get started. The camp was a banner success from the start.

Those first years generated many record-book entries, amusing stories, and a fund of memories. Not amusing at the time, for sure, but a well-remembered story anyway was Gordon's departure from camp on an Air Inuit Twin Otter— a classic example of why flying regulations have been tightened up in the North.

Eight hunters were in camp that early September week and each had taken two big bull caribou. Unfortunately the party included a butcher from Wilkes-Barre, Pennsylvania, and a fat, greedy, old bastard who arranged to take home all of the meat from all of the hunters. Normally, each sportsman took out his duffel, his trophies, and one reasonable box of meat, the remainder being given to the families of the native staff.

This week was to be different.

The butcher and the self-appointed Pope of the Week spent every waking hour and half the night boning out and packing every scrap of meat, from the cheeks to the ankles. They used all the meat boxes that we had thought would last the rest of the season, and as the pile continued to mount, I informed them that there was no way in hell one aircraft would be able to take off from our short little tundra strip with all of that weight.

When the plane arrived, the two French Canadian pilots looked over the mountain of gear and the ton and a half of meat and shook their heads. *Good*, I thought, *the captain of the aircraft is the boss. He'll back me up on this!*

The pilot and I talked things over in my broken French and his more broken English, and we decided that the only smart course of action was to load the hunters and gear, fly them sixty miles down to George River Village, where there was a 1,200-foot gravel strip, and put them off to wait.

He would come back for the meat, then go pick up the hunters again. This time he would be lifting this excessive load off a decent hard-surfaced strip instead of nine hundred feet of rocks, moss, sand, and snow. The Akuliak International Airport amounted to something over three hundred of my short-assed paces. Built with two shovels and a wheelbarrow, it abutted the base of a sheer mountain on one side, and the other side dropped off about fifty feet into a dry lake bed.

When I explained the plan to the dudes, Gordon and about three others could see the good sense in this maneuver. But then old Greedy Guts spoke up and demanded to know whether they would still make the Nordair 737 flying south that evening or be stuck in Fort Chimo overnight.

I should have lied to him, but I didn't. They probably would have to overnight. I pointed out that a night in the hotel in Fort Chimo was certainly preferable to a trip to hell wrapped in aluminum and burning diesel fuel.

After a bit of a huddle, the Meat Scroungers took the pilots for a little walk and an earnest talk. I saw a number of hundred-dollar bills change hands. Money is one thing that bridges the gap in Quebec and everywhere else, crossing all language lines, and overruling common sense.

The plane was loaded—all the people, all the gear, all the trophies, and all the meat right down to the last scrap. A Twin Otter, as a rough rule of thumb, can get away with about a ton of payload, plus fuel for the flight, even off a soft strip. In this case I know damn well it was half again overloaded.

Nothing I could say had any effect. The pilot is the captain. Whatever he says goes. I took some comfort in the fact that they had all signed waivers of liability. This might help somewhat during the crash investigation and the subsequent lawsuits, but I would miss Gordon if anything happened.

Regardless of wind direction, there was no option but to take off toward the west, over the dry lake bed. The plane would never make it the other way, over the mountain. Stanley Annanack, the Inuit elder, and all the native inhabitants of Akuliak were watching when the attempt was made.

With engines straining, the pilot started down the strip. Right in the middle a soft section dragged down the speed, and at the last possible second the props were reversed. No go! He started to taxi back toward us. "Good," I indicated to Stanley. "*Nakooyuk*! Coming back to unload the meat."

Alas, he had no such intention. With the overloaded plane waddling like a goose, he proceeded past the east end of the strip, moving out among the rocks to get another fifty feet. Then, "balls to the wall," swerving around the rocks, turbines screaming, he tore down the strip toward the inevitable plunge over the cliff. Stanley and several of the Inuit onlookers threw themselves on the ground with hands over their eyes!

The last thing I saw disappear down the hole, amid a whirlwind of snow, sand, and uprooted bushes, was the flashing strobe light mounted on the tip of the tail section. They were gone!

Miracle of miracles. No explosion, no pillar of jet-fuel flame. With engines still maxed to the limit, the plane appeared, gradually gaining altitude, across the flat land to the west.

We all ran over to the end of the strip, and I photographed the wheel tracks in the foot of snow where he ran off the edge. Across the lake some part of the aircraft—I assume the tail skid—had cut a groove as big as a trailer truck in the snow atop a rock. Someone was looking after things that day.

Later, I heard from our expediter in Fort Chimo that the pilot had commented that he would not want to take off there with very much more aboard! Who says French Canadians don't have a sense of humor?

Tom Hennessey

Old Friends Are the Best Friends

Despite the fact that we had nearly killed Gordon on his first visit to the coast of Ungava, he returned for a number of years thereafter and helped us with bookings and plans for expansion.

Sometime in the early 1980s, we made our first safari to the island of Newfoundland. I had previously worked there for several years, first before there were recognized outfitter areas and later with a couple of resident license holders.

This time we were to try out a new area and explore the possibility of a working arrangement that would make sense to ourselves, the local outfitter, and our clients. The Webbs refuse to be simply booking agents; if we cannot have an active hand in management, we are not interested in being involved.

Our first exploratory trip with a well-established outfitter who later became our partner for several years was supposed to be a combination of business and pleasure. Porter Hicks, then living in New York, was not only a good friend and client of ours but also owned the advertising company that helped produce our promotional ads and literature. With his wife, Mary Jane, a most avid hunter, we had enjoyed many adventures together. However, this was the first time we had taken Mary Jane along in such a close-knit trio of "dominant males"— Gordon, Porter, and myself. Porter and I were used to Mary Jane's inclination to outdo the boys, and she usually made the best shots and took the biggest trophies, just to rub it in.

We were to meet at our camp in Nictau, then drive across New Brunswick and down through Nova Scotia to North Sydney, take the overnight ferry across to Port Aux Basques, Newfoundland, and drive up to Robinsons, where we would meet our new outfitter friend, Gerry Pumphrey.

Campfire Lies of a Canadian Guide

Porter and Mary Jane, in from New York, were already at our place when Gordon drove in from Michigan with his big "moose hauler" trailer towed by his powerful LTD station wagon. A great outfit, it handled like a limousine, even when loaded with meat, antlers, skins, and iced-down beer coolers.

I had the pleasure of driving, which I thought I handled fairly well, even without Mary Jane's instructions from the back seat. As it became apparent that we would have plenty of advice on all subjects pertaining to the trip, I settled into my truck-driver mode, concentrating on the road, and Gordon took refuge in the bottle of Scotch that he hadn't intended to open until we had a dead moose to celebrate.

I always enjoyed the trip to Newfoundland in those days. There was always a sense of expectation as the vehicles lined up on the ferry dock in North Sydney. All through September and October there would be a steady stream of trucks, trailers, and pickups headed to the island for the fall hunt.

You could always tell by the appearance of the vehicles, how the occupants were costumed, and the amount of bragging and beer talk, which ones were going to the quality fly-in outfits and which were headed over to hunt the roads, sleep in some hovel, and pay the guide a quart of rum to kill them a moose.

Usually the ferry was jammed full for the overnight crossing, and this trip was no exception. Only one cabin was still available, which Gordon and I were happy to leave to our companions while we sat in the bar with the rowdies. I sort of think Porter would have preferred that as well, although at that time he didn't drink.

Despite a few minor hitches, it turned out to be an excellent trip. It afforded me the chance to work out a deal with our new associate, and all of us took a moose. Mary Jane's, of course, was the biggest one. The male members of the party took it all in good spirit and probably benefited from the advice, as we all did better on subsequent trips without her.

Gordon had managed to contain himself during the trip over and in the close quarters with all of us together in a small camp. But he finally rebelled when Mary Jane started to instruct him upon the proper method of loading the moose meat into the moose hauler.

His comment, "Jesus Christ, woman, I think I can tie a f—rope on my own trailer!" made the rest of the trip anticlimactic.

Gordon and I made annual trips to Newfoundland for probably ten years, bringing many hunters to the operation and taking many good trophies. The best trophy was taken in October of 1984 on a combination moose and woodland caribou hunt.

I had finished the seasons in the NWT and Ungava and driven to Newfoundland, meeting Gordon upon his arrival. For the first few days he went out spike-camping and took a pretty standard eastern moose—nothing to enter in the book, but good eating.

Our partner and pilot, Gerry, brought him back to the main camp at Hungry Grove Lake, and after a day's resting up and drying out, he was flown with guide Tom Childs and a bit of camping gear over east a few miles. Here they expected to intercept caribou coming down through the area. Before he boarded the plane, I told him, "Gordon, forget about those big bulls we hunt in Quebec. This woodland caribou is a smaller critter. So if Tom tells you it is a pretty good one, you better take it."

As things turned out, that's exactly what happened. Glassing a herd the next day, they spotted a stag that Tom recommended. On the ground he looked even better. Gordon, though still a bit doubtful, having been used to the big Quebec-Labrador caribou, was beginning to think he had a real trophy. Upon his return to camp, I thought so also when I got out a tape and added it up on a beer box.

In June of 1986, in Las Vegas, Nevada, the panel at the Boone & Crockett Club's 19th Big Game Awards agreed. Gordon was presented with the First Award for Woodland Caribou, an honor that does not come along every day in the life of a trophy hunter. I was proud to be there with Gordon. His trophy put our area in the book for the third awards period in a row.

Frosting on the cake was the fact that our hunters were also well represented in the Quebec-Labrador and Central Barren Ground caribou classes. The 19th Awards of Boone & Crockett was as important to our companies as the 23rd Awards, when we took the top muskox of all time.

Gordon and I shared many more trips, from Newfoundland to the Northwest Territories. For many years he put on an annual game dinner in his hometown of Algonac, Michigan, and I would fly in from whatever part of the world I happened to be at the time. At the last dinner I was able to attend, I had the pleasure of presenting him with a portrait of himself and the Boone & Crockett caribou.

With his gracious wife, Mary, Gordon has been generous host to many outfitters at his home over the years. I hope to make it again one day, while we are both still young enough to enjoy complaining about where the world is going and reminiscing about when it was a whole lot better.

SALMON WARS

One of the most precious resources put on this planet is the Atlantic salmon. Salmon angling, long held to be the "sport of kings," was the main source of guiding wages in our country for several generations.

By the late 1950s this traditional sport fishery began to change and decline as hydroelectric dams were built, first on our river, the Tobique, and later on the main Saint John River. This most gallant of fish, returning from the ocean, now faced almost insurmountable obstacles on its way to the spawning grounds.

During the 1960s and 1970s, the tremendous runs dwindled to a few hundred fish. Having run the gauntlet of the commercial deep-seas fishery, the Indian "food fishery," and three power dams, the salmon now arrived in the river of their birth to face a regulated sport fishery. But here, in their most exhausted and vulnerable state, they fell prey to the commercial poachers.

As fishing guides and outfitters on the river, it was natural for us to cooperate with the fish-and-game wardens to protect this valuable resource. Although this was a deadly serious problem, it did have its lighter moments.

The heavy-duty poaching was done at night, mostly by net, but the practice of "jigging," especially in the smaller pools, also killed plenty of fish on their way to the spawning grounds. We had managed to have the river declared "fly fishing only," so at least some of the crooks were deterred from belly-hooking fish with four-inch Dardevles and other treble-hooked hardware.

However, some of the more innovative poachers could do a pretty good job of killing fish by using fly-fishing tackle, but with a few alterations. One of these experts, well known as a poacher, was able to extract fish from the pools with great regularity. This was particularly galling to the professional guides, who, working with expert sport fishermen, were unable to catch fish during the low water of mid-August.

This "expert" arrived at the Forks Pool one weekday afternoon when not many people were fishing. With his wife in the canoe in an attempt to look like an innocent sport fisherman, he poled up to the foot of the Ledge Pool, anchored, and proceeded to lay out his line. Here was our chance.

Following a hastily made plan, a couple of us crossed the river down below and came up through the woods to overlook the pool. Junior, the warden in charge, drove around, hid the vehicle, and worked down through the woods on the other side. With a portable two-way radio, and well-camouflaged, he would crawl through the bush to a perfect point for observation.

Our gentleman fisherman was truly a master in the art of jigging while appearing to be angling legitimately. He used a good-quality fly rod and reel, but with a sinking-tip fly line and a very short leader. He was fishing for sure, but with a No. 4, double-hooked Cossaboom, which, when handled properly, would sink deep into the pool and could be worked across the current. Although it was impossible to actually see into the pool, he stood a better than average chance of foul-hooking a fish.

Fishing for Atlantic salmon, even with a jigging rig, takes a fair amount of time. After a half-hour of looking through binoculars, I observed our man increasing his chances a bit by squeezing a strip of lead solder onto the line. The added weight would get the hook down a bit deeper in the current; surely he would soon snag onto a salmon. In that pool, once he hooked a fish, he would be forced to go ashore on one side or the other to land it, at which time we'd be ready to pounce.

Lying in the deep grass and weeds, besieged by midges and black flies, I had to wonder if it was all worth it. There was lots of time to think about places I would rather be and how good a nice cold beer would taste. All of a sudden there was action and loud conversation in the canoe—in fact, as far as we could tell, quite an argument. The lady occupant, having finished her book, her lunch, and a large bottle of Pepsi, now apparently wished to go ashore.

With great reluctance, it was obvious, her husband pulled up the anchor and poled the canoe to the far bank. The moment the lady jumped out, he pushed off again, to anchor in midstream and resume casting and jerking across the current. An experienced poacher, he was gun-shy, not taking any chance of a warden showing up to check his gear.

While we were trying to figure out what the next move would be, three clicks came over the radio, repeated three times—the signal to break off and meet downriver. What could have happened?

At the rendezvous a half-hour later, Junior arrived. Covered in mud, sweat, and grass stains, he was wiping the camouflage paint and fly dope off his face with his under-shirt. "What happened?" we asked. "We had the bastard dead to rights. The minute he hooked a fish and went ashore to net it, we would have had him!"

"Boys," said Junior, "I hated to let you down, but I've just been through the goddamnedest experience that any warden has ever had to face. I was lying flat down in the weeds and stinging nettle, looking straight out that path, when the ca-noe came ashore. Before I could move back farther into the bushes, the woman jumped off the bow and ran straight up into the woods. I was afraid she was going to tramp on me. It's a damn good thing I had pulled in the binoculars and the radio. Right in front of my face, she turned around, jerked down her pants, and then I knew why she come ashore.

"So help me, Jesus! She gushed out a swath of piss as wide as a handsaw blade! Had force enough to cut the heads clean off the fiddlehead ferns! Blew sand right in my face. Good thing I closed my eyes at the last minute. I never saw nothin' like that in my entire life!

"There I was, stuck to the ground. If her husband had jigged the biggest goddamn salmon in the Tobique, I couldn't have moved a muscle. Now, that's enough to blow any stakeout!"

RONALD

We were hunting from the camp at Hungry Grove Lake in the Long Range Mountains of Newfoundland. This was before the lumber company put a road in and turned the entire area into a desert. It was a wilderness in those days, reachable only by floatplane from the coast.

Having come in from hunting early, I was standing out on the veranda savoring a cold beer when about six shots rang out down in the corner of the cove, in the area we called the Yellow Grass Bog. Half an hour later, guide Ronald Biggen and his client arrived in the gathering darkness.

The client from New York was really pumped up: "Boy, we walked thirty miles today and never saw a thing. Then, as we were halfway down the hill, this great big bull moose took off across the flat. Must have been four hundred yards away, but I hit him six times with this .338 Magnum."

"That's fine," I observed. "I guess Ronald has him all quartered out, ready to take the boat down and pick him up. What do you think, Ronald, do you want me to give you a hand after supper?"

"Well, to tell you the truth," drawled Ronald, "we haven't exactly got him yet. I came in for a lantern so we can go and have a better look around."

Besides being an energetic and expert moose guide, old Ronald was also a Pentecostal lay preacher, so when he said "to tell you the truth," you could depend upon that!

After asking the cooks to hold supper for a while, we rounded up flashlights and went down the lake to look for the moose. Upon reaching the spot where the action had taken place, I soon detected that there were two vastly different versions of the event.

The client insisted, "We were coming down off the mountain, way back there," and he pointed out the crest of a hill barely discernible against the darkening horizon. "The bull was running through the bushes ninety miles an hour. I could barely see him, but I am sure I hit him right through the heart. We must be looking in the wrong spot."

I knew that old Ronald would try to be diplomatic and not hurt his hunter's feelings, but I didn't want the cook to keep supper half the night while we figured this out. "Ronald," I said, "can you remember where the moose was running, and do you think he is hit mortally?"

"Oh, yes, Sir!" says Ronald. "I saw him take the fourth bullet, right through the shoulders. Sure, we were only fifty yards away, and he was standing still as a statue, right up here on the short yellow grass. Why, he was that plain I could see every hair on him and even his hoofs. He must be right around here somewhere."

Ronald

Two minutes later, as Ronald predicted, we found the first blood and hair. Walking right up the track, we soon found the moose, not a tremendous trophy but a decent enough bull. One straight through the heart. Guess the other five shots went elsewhere.

Ronald, like my friend Coleman, would never tell me a lie.

WAITING FOR WEATHER

I'm sitting in Kugluktuk on the shores of the Arctic Ocean, looking out the window at the blowing snow, waiting for the weather. On this particular hunt we are flying guests across to our camp at Nagayuktok on the south coast of Victoria Island. We always expect unsettled weather in mid-October, in the transition from late autumn to full-scale winter. Ice is forming, but most of the ocean is still open, adding to the weather problems.

In ten years of doing this hunt, we have encountered everything from twenty-five below zero with high winds to the dreaded ice fog and freezing drizzle. This time, for the past four days we have endured what the weatherman is calling a full-scale Arctic storm with hurricane-force winds and zero visibility in blowing snow.

Waiting for Weather

The clients are camped comfortably in the Coppermine Inn—good rooms, satellite television, great meals—but probably they would prefer to be freezing to death in a flapping tent somewhere closer to the game. So far they have not questioned my judgment or that of the pilot, but give them time.

We have done all that we can. Last summer we transported snow machines, fuel, food, and the makings of a tent camp to the island by ship. Our Inuit partners, Charlie and Marion, and two other guides are waiting patiently. We have brought up a $2 million Twin Otter aircraft from Yellowknife. The two pilots are installed at our base, driving Martin crazy as they insist on watching hockey games on our television.

We are all anxiously awaiting a break in the weather so we can fly. Despite the benefit of every modern electronic aid, satellite technology, and hourly surface charts faxed to our base, it still comes down to waiting for the weather.

I remember with fondness an old guide friend of mine and his statement that in fifty years of guiding he had spent about forty of them waiting for something to happen. That, I guess, has been my experience as well, and I have spent my time waiting in some far-flung places. But it all boils down to the fact that modern science and the plans of humans must often take second place to nature.

Windbound one time on a large wilderness lake, we huddled under a tarp in a black spruce thicket in a location nearly devoid of any decent dry firewood. Somehow we managed to keep body and soul together for three days.

My Micmac trapping partner joked about it, saying, "Back in the days of the Creation, Indians were white, but they all got smoked brown hanging over a green spruce fire." I guess he knew what he was talking about. Although only partly aboriginal myself, I was at least three shades darker before the wind quit and we got off that desolate shore.

While I was employed on an Arctic expedition in the early 1960s, our ship was attempting to traverse the key portion of the Northwest Passage, through Bellott Strait, into the Gulf of Boothia, and south through Fury and Hecla Strait, thus completing a portion of the Passage never before accomplished.

Unfortunately that summer a steady north wind had packed multiyear ice down into the Gulf so not a lead could be found to allow us to proceed south. We were stuck for seventeen days, waiting for the wind to change and hoping that another ship with better icebreaking capabilities would be able to relieve us.

Finally I received word on the radio that the brand-new *John A. MacDonald*, second largest icebreaker in the world, was proceeding to our rescue. The only larger icebreaker, the nuclear-powered *Lenin*, belonged to our friends across the Pole and was not at our disposal in those days of Cold War politics.

About ten hours before the *MacDonald* arrived after an extremely rough passage and major damage to her rudder and propellers, the wind shifted and blew a real gale out of the south. Within hours the ocean, which had previously looked for all the world like an unbroken frozen prairie, broke up into individual ice floes and islands. We were at last able to proceed southward, down through Fury and Hecla into Foxe Basin and Hudson Bay, thus becoming the first ship ever to do so. We were reminded once again, however, that although technology had changed over a couple of hundred years, we still faced the same obstacles and dangers as had the early Arctic explorers over the previous three centuries.

Those who run hunts in Newfoundland and Labrador are beset with some of the most miserable flying conditions in the world. Besides the shortening of the days as autumn advances in that part of eastern Canada, the ocean influence results in some of the worst weather on the continent. Just as northern coastal British Columbia and Alaska flyers experience terrible conditions for days on end, a pilot in Newfoundland must develop a great deal of patience and an outfitter must have a thick skin to turn aside the idiotic demands of the clients.

Each trip began when I would meet the jet flight into Stephenville, pick up the party and their ton of gear, and truck them sixty-odd miles out to the float base at Mitchell's Pond.

Here our partner Gerry had a shack and what passed for a dock where we could tie up the Cessna 180 and various other aircraft leased or chartered for the season.

On the trip out to the Pond, I would always try to prepare the clients somewhat by explaining that although the weather at present was flyable down at sea level, up on the interior plateau it was socked in solid. I would explain that sometimes it cleared just before dark, so we would be on standby at Mitchell's waiting for a break.

Their comments on this first day were usually reasonable, such as, "Oh, well, I've had a long day, so if we have to go to the motel overnight, it won't bother me a bit."

The next day, Gerry and I would be up by 5 o'clock, calling the camps by radio to get their local weather. By daylight we would be out at the Pond, the aircraft would be checked over, and once again we would be waiting for the weather.

Again we would bring the clients out to the base just in case we got a break in the clag. This day would pass with the boiling of countless pots of coffee, going out to look at the sky every five minutes, and, when the whining became too intense, drives out to the top of one of the local hills to try and see into the mountains—a useless exercise, of course, but at least it got the clients out of our hair for a while.

Comments this day would range from, "It looks good enough to me" or "I can't stand hanging around; just get me in there and I'll stay until Christmas" to "I flew in a lot worse than this in Alaska, B.C., Africa, or Vietnam."

At this point, trying to be diplomatic, I would say something like, "In a lifetime of guiding I have met two kinds of people: one kind on the outside begging to get in and one bunch already in the camp begging to get out. It's too bad we just can't trade places, but we do not intend to kill anyone today. Not that you would bother me dead, but your wife's new boyfriend, the lawyer, would harass my ass for the next ten years."

This usually worked with even the most high-pressure executive. We did our best to entertain them and assure them that traditionally it had always cleared up, even in Newfoundland, and when it did, we would be ready to fly.

Only once did the pilot crack under the strain and go against his better judgment. With an abnormally obnoxious insurance agent from Chicago, who was an authority on everything in the world including bush flying, we went to Plan B. Taking him up in the 180, Gerry flew up the narrow valley, then climbed over onto the plateau, which was totally engulfed in ice-filled cloud and turbulence. After groping around blind for a while, he had to fly back out over the Gulf into weather clear enough to descend to visual limits and pick his way back into the Pond. It was foolhardy in the extreme, but our expert, after being helped out of the airplane, did not express any further opinions upon flying and weather. He was a nice guy the rest of the trip.

In general, though, we did not succumb to the pressure and kill clients, as a few of our competitors have done over the years.

During late-winter hunts in the central Arctic, here again you are faced with the awesome forces of nature. You are dealing for the most part with temperatures down into the minus forties and wind chills that make it considerably colder. Most of the tales you hear from the clients are exaggerations, but for sure it is good and cold.

Here we make no exceptions: Only when we figure it is safe to travel do the hunters hit the trail. When in the judgment of our older Inuit guides it is unsuitable for travel, they hole up in the tents or in igloos. The guides are well aware that the number one priority is getting the client back alive and on the airplane; everything else, including bagging the world record, takes a lower priority.

A lifetime of experience has made me fairly tolerant of clients' complaints, but on one memorable occasion I may have blown my cool. We had booked a gentleman from Mexico on a caribou hunt in the Barren Lands. Because he had a full command of the English language, without which I will not accept a client, I thought that he understood my reluctance to put a boat out to hunt on a lake churned up by a near hurricane. Everyone else in camp did.

After some grumbling around the breakfast table, he tracked me down to where I had hidden in the manager's shack. In an apparent attempt to impress me, he listed the names of about five northern outfitters, all good friends of mine and all well known in our business. It hurt me to listen as he described how all of them had let him run things to his satisfaction when he had graced them with his presence.

"Hold it right there!" was my reply. "I know every one of those guides, and they all have one thing in common. Every goddamn one of them is *DEAD*. Every one of them was pushing weather, pressured into it by some demanding old ——," and here I used a word even I will not put into print, "such as yourself! You will notice that I am goddamn well still alive and I intend to stay that way, and I intend to keep your worthless old ass in one piece until we deliver it back to the dock in Yellowknife!"

Needless to say, this outburst ended the discussion. He has since approached me to take him to the central Arctic, but he does not have enough money to tempt me.

Regardless of how tired we all get of hanging around, we believe in the logic of our Inuit friends: that everyone has to be somewhere, and it may as well be this place as another.

Until it changes, we'll be waiting for the weather.

INUK HUNTER

Tom Hennessey —

Arctic Hunting: Coronation Gulf, Central Arctic, 1993

The whining drone of the snowmobile engine has a hypnotic quality. With visibility down to about ten feet in blowing, billowing snow, the world is reduced to a frigid envelope where nothing matters except keeping to the trail and catching an occasional glimpse of the sled in the lead. The lunging of the machine over hidden drifts, the never-ending strain on the arms, and the constant jolting that tells you the rope-towed *komatik* astern is still attached seem to bring all of life down to the basics.

Squint into the blinding snow, disregarding the growing numb spots on the face as cold seeps in around the goggles. Try to thaw the thumb on the throttle by sliding it back into the wolfskin mitten. When this doesn't work, reach across and hold the throttle with the left hand to ease the aching shoulder and tuck the right one under the armpit. Awkward, but it gives relief for the moment.

And once again and most important: do not lose the trail! Stick with the leader, old Atatahak, who is hauling most of the supplies and the radio. Without him, you and your passenger in the *komatik* behind are going to be in a lot of trouble if this turns into a three-day blizzard. Let the mind wander, but don't forget that the life of your passenger depends upon the sled staying hitched to the machine, and your ability to stick with the trail.

We have been out nearly a week with two *kabloona* (white) sport hunters from down south. After leaving our base at the mouth of the Coppermine River, we had traveled west in clear but cold weather, crossed the eastern end of Dolphin and Union Strait, and hunted inland on Victoria Island. Two snow machines hauled two *komatiks* with the guests and all the gas, food, camping equipment, tools, and spare parts needed for such a journey.

We'd been five nights out in the tents, and luck had been with us. Only minor breakdowns had occurred, and the hunt was successfully concluded with two trophy muskox heads and skins added to the load.

Each day had seen miles of travel and glassing until the herds had been located. Now there was the work of skinning the animals in 40-below-zero temperatures. Hides must be chilled out, then rolled into manageable packages before they freeze into something as difficult to carry as sheets of plywood.

The *kabloona* stand around blowing on their fingers as they try to make their frozen cameras work, and they wonder how anyone can skin barehanded in such harsh conditions. Routine for Atatahak, Inuk hunter, and trapper—just part of the job of staying alive in the Arctic.

It is late evening before the tents are pitched, food and tea prepared, the evening radio call to base completed, and everyone turns into the sleeping skins. Gossip from town had mentioned a general deterioration of weather, forecast on the government radio. However, one learns to rely more upon observation and the knowledge of Inuk hunters like Atatahak than upon official forecasts.

In the intense clear cold of the night, under the star-filled roof of the heavens, it is hard to believe that bad weather might be on the way. However, something in the sound of cracking ice, or maybe the haze growing around the moon, or the shift of the wind, which had been consistently from the north but is now backing around more to westerly, brings a brief comment from Atatahak: "Maybe tomorrow not so good for traveling."

One hates to leave the warmth of the sleeping bag in the morning, but it is time to remelt the ice in the teapot and feed the guests. Better get going. Warm up the machines, break camp, and load the sleds—time to hit the trail. It is noticeably warmer, the wind has come clear around to a more southerly direction, and the horizon is somewhat obscured in ice fog.

TOM HENNESSEY —

"Sort of whiteout," we tell the lady on the radio. "Yes, same here in Kugluktuk," she says. "Wind starting to blow more out of the east. Can still see Seven Mile Island, but maybe not such a good day to travel."

Atatahak agrees. It isn't going to be as pleasant a crossing of the ocean as we had coming out. In the carefree days when we hunted for ourselves, on this kind of day we would seriously consider staying in camp. Maybe chop out a fishing hole, work on skins, repair gear, and generally relax until things settled down. Now, catering to visitors, we must think about such things as airline connections and whether there are rooms available at the hotel over the weekend.

Watching the *kabloona* pacing impatiently, waiting for us to pack the *komatiks*, removes any doubt about whether or not to travel. Happy though the guests are with their hunting experiences and their trophies, a two- or three-day stay in the tents is not an option we want to consider.

It won't be comfortable, but no one will die unless we are really unlucky. On sunny days, I could cross the ocean by myself if there weren't too many open-water leads. On the kind of day this is going to be, I am glad that "old man Atatahak" is leading. Loaded at last, the *kabloona* snug in the boxes on the sleds, we string out, heading southeast across the frozen ocean.

We can still look back and see the flat shore of Victoria Island until the surface-blown snow picks up into a real blizzard. Now it's a matter of hanging onto the track. There will be stops occasionally to check the passengers, warm our faces with our hands, inspect each other for white frozen spots, and have a mug of hot, black, sweet tea from the big Thermos. An indescribable luxury, that hot tea. A lot different from the old days when a tea break meant building a snow house and melting ice over a *kudlik* soapstone lamp fueled by seal oil to obtain a luke-warm mixture somewhere between tea and seal broth. Now, if one is smart enough to melt ice, boil water over the gas stove, and fill his Thermos, he can enjoy tea and biscuits at his convenience.

As the miles and hours pass, we occasionally see the dull glow of the sun to the south, but at the level of the sea ice, the whiteout is total. I can only wonder at the stamina of the "old man." Jack Atatahak is seventy-three years old. Born in an igloo, he saw his first *kabloona* or white man when he was about ten years old. Lived as an Inuk hunter and trapper, and then, with the coming of the Cold War, worked with the builders of the Distant Early Warning (DEW) radar sites across the central Arctic.

Now, a year after going down south for an operation on his spine of the kind that often cripples people for life, Jack is once more living on the land by hunting, trapping, and guiding for our company. Some of the younger people find guiding too difficult and would rather take endless government-sponsored courses in everything from computer science to driving a bulldozer, but there are still men who would rather live like their ancestors, traveling the land and sea.

When I ask him to take on a difficult trip or a potentially troublesome client, Jack always shrugs, smiles, and says, "OK. No problem. You the boss!"

Now, as we travel, there is no doubt in my mind that out here, the old man is the boss.

While I am thinking about these things, the *komatik* ahead looms up in the blow. I swing wide to avoid a collision and come up abreast of the leader. Looking around, I can vaguely see a low shoreline rising out of the snow. "Dead Man Island," Atatahak informs me. "Maybe better stop for tea and gas machines. If sport hunters OK, we be in town maybe three hours."

I can only take his word for it. I know it is around thirty miles or so. In smooth going—no blizzard and no guest on the sled—it's less than an hour's run. Under present conditions, it's considerably longer.

That night, at home in Kugluktuk after delivering the sports to the hotel, we have time for dinner sitting at a table and enjoy a hot shower. I have time to nurse my frost-burned nose and cheeks, phone my wife down south, and reflect once more upon how an age is fast disappearing. The people who live on and from the land are passing into history. Although Atatahak's sons and grandson have worked for our company, it will never be the same without the "old man." Crossing the ocean safely, pinpointing an island a half-mile wide, and arriving on the shoreline in Coppermine before we even see the lights on the radio towers: this is the kind of confidence that comes with being at home on the tundra and the ocean.

One may navigate by modern electronic means or by digging out the map and compass, but give me the guides who follow the sun, the stars, the wind, and the patterns found in the drifting snow, and I will trust them with the lives of our clients any day.

I salute my friend Jack Atatahak and all the Inuit of the old ways. They are the real Arctic hunters.

KITIKMEOT, THE CENTRAL ARCTIC, MARCH 1987

Toin Hennessey —

As I lie snug in my sleeping bag upon a mattress of caribou and muskox skins, my Inuit partner hangs our *kamiks* to dry in the peak of the tent and we settle down for the night.

John Kapakatoak and I are guiding Bob Milek, on assignment for the magazine *Petersen's Hunting*. We are in search of a trophy muskox and a story to excite the imagination of prospective clients in the land down south. Now, at the end of our fourth day on the trail, seventy miles west of our home base in Kugluktuk, we have seen *Omingmak*, "the bearded one," in several herds. As yet, however, we have not chosen to end the quest.

"Maybe tomorrow, the big bull." We are content, each in his own fashion. For myself as a professional hunter, it is always encouraging when the hunt goes smoothly and animals are present in sufficient numbers to keep alive the dreams of the client. Kapakatoak, old in the ways of traditional subsistence hunting but new to guiding trophy hunters, is secure in his knowledge that his guest is enjoying the hunt. Milek, sitting up on his sleeping bag with a last cup of tea, is making notes, the better to recall the events of the day.

The hiss of the Primus stove, its light playing on the canvas walls, reminds me of other trails, and I wonder anew at how travelers can come from distant parts of the world but all become equal in the wilderness. Here in one tent are three men . . . one originally from eastern Canada, one from the western United States, and the third of the Copper Inuit race from the central Arctic. Besides a shared love of the land, we are all three—first and foremost—guides.

Having met Bob Milek a few years earlier on a hunt in the central Barren Lands, which left a lot to be desired, I had been impressed by the way he handled adversity. Rather than throw fits or sulk because of the poor hunting, as I have seen some clients do, Bob had taken it all in stride.

His comment that, "Hey, this is why they call it hunting. No one can control the weather or the game migrations, so we'll just keep on plugging and see what happens," was much appreciated. As things turned out, we did manage to bag a more-than-decent caribou and a magazine article that told it like it is—what hunting in the subarctic is all about. I subsequently learned from a mutual friend that Bob had been a guide himself, was an expert at western mountain hunting, and was one of the finest pistol shots in the country.

When contacted by the magazine and told they were interested in an article on muskox, I was glad to hear they were sending Milek.

My other friend, Kapakatoak, is a true Arctic hunter. A member of the generation spanning the gap between the Stone Age and the Space Age, he retains the traditional skills of his ancestors even while handling modern snowmobiles, radios, and other equipment.

Make no mistake about it: Arctic travel and survival, even at the end of the twentieth century, rely as much upon inherited knowledge as the latest inventions of civilization. You can fly to just about any Arctic community in a day or two—journeys that used to take months within my own life-time—stay at a modern hotel, enjoy electric heat and satellite television, and pick up the phone and call anyone in the world. Many changes over the past forty years. However, beware! A couple of miles out of town, and you are in exactly the same environment as our ancestors experienced. Have your snow-mobile break down or get separated from your sled load of food and equipment—even in good weather—and you must be able to survive in the old ways. Otherwise the foxes and ravens will be quarreling over your bones come spring.

Having been a guide all my life, I can appreciate the things both large and small that go into a safe and comfortable ex-pedition, and I knew Milek did too. Most of his writings were a combination of the adventure itself and expert insight into the equipment and methods involved. Judging by the volume of notes and photographs taken, evidently this was the plan for the current trip as well.

Aching muscles now remind me that I have been away from snowmobile driving for a couple of years, getting soft since I gave up the traplines. Kapakatoak is pumping up the extra-large tank on his gas stove and closing down the tent door for the night. Inside clothing is hung to dry, melted ice water in the large pot is ready for remelting in the morning, and small holes are open in the tent peaks to protect against the deadly carbon monoxide. I can relax knowing that John has everything under control and think about what it takes to stay safe on an Arctic journey. There is a reason behind every action and a proper use for every piece of equipment.

Knowledge of the land, the animals, and the weather is all-important and gained only over years of experience. While modern maps, compasses, and the satellite navigation systems are certainly welcome, they will never replace the ability to navigate by traditional knowledge of the land, the sun, the stars, and the effects of wind on snow and water.

When it comes to predicting changes in the weather, the country is so vast and the weather stations so few that even with all the scientific support available, the official forecasts cannot be relied upon totally. Many times weather systems in the Arctic are so localized that only experience gained over centuries will tell you when to travel and when to stay in camp.

Leaving Kugluktuk at the start of the hunt, Kapakatoak with his new snowmobile had hauled a twenty-foot *komatik* loaded with gas, food, camping equipment, spare parts, tools, and a closed-in box in which rode Milek, the hunter-writer. On a second machine I hauled a sled with a drum of gas and extra supplies.

The traditional *komatik*, the best sled yet developed for Arctic travel, is basically unchanged in design from the ones used a century ago. It is simply two long runners with crosspieces lashed rather than nailed or bolted, providing enough flexibility to ride over the roughest ice or terrain without breaking into pieces. The old-time sleds were built from salvaged wood, sometimes using bone or antler, while the present-day runners might be ordinary planks, especially laminated spruce, or even aluminum.

The old ones sometimes had runners shod with whalebone or covered with a coating of frozen mud. In the eastern Arctic forty years ago, I traveled with one party that used oatmeal porridge when mud was impossible to find. This all-important coating would be planed smooth or even filed, then water would be sprayed on by mouth and polished as it froze with a piece of polar bear fur. This coating had to be renewed at least daily, but more often in rocky country or on rough ice. Most modern Inuk hunters will have a set of steel runners for rocky conditions and the new Teflon plastic ones for general winter travel.

Dogs originally hauled *komatiks* with much help from the people. As a general rule, most teams in the eastern Arctic employ the fan hitch, in which each dog is on an independent line. This applies in some communities in the central and western Arctic as well, especially when the journey is on sea ice. However, the most popular setup in recent years is a single main line attached to the leader dog, plus pairs of short side lines for the rest of the team. Positions closest to the sled are reserved for lazy or inexperienced dogs so they are within reach of the driver's voice and whip.

Most old-time drivers employed some kind of anchor to keep the team from running off and leaving the driver afoot in the middle of the frozen world. Some relied upon turning the rig on its side when it was not too heavily loaded.

Nowadays the *komatik* is still hauled on a long line, but in most cases by a snow machine. Many drivers will use about six feet of chain hitched below the curve of the runners, not only for added strength but also to help ease the sled downhill. You just slack off and let the runners ride over the chain, thus slowing the descent. From there out will be fifteen to twenty feet of strong rope hooked to the hitch on the machine.

Most sleds are equipped with side ropes and hooks, and a tarp cover. Under the load, caribou or muskox skins not only cushion the ride but also help in holding the load in place, without which one would be constantly retying the lashing ropes. These skins also serve as sleeping pads.

Watch a skilled Inuk traveler loading up, and you will think he is taking a long time. Everything has its place. Ideally, when totally loaded the sled should be slightly lighter in the front. The lashing is done as skillfully as a mountain cowboy loads his packhorses. The Inuk may take longer to load his sled than the *kabloona* driver, but the white guy will stop many times to retie his load, and often go back to pick up lost equipment.

Making camp requires the same precision, the aim being to construct, in as short a time as possible, a warm shelter, a home away from home for the weary traveler. If weather and time permit, a site is carefully chosen. Ideally, it will be a location sheltered from the wind and close to a lake or river where ice for water and possibly a fresh fish can be obtained.

The snow is carefully probed. It must have a certain consistency to provide the best insulating qualities and ease in cutting blocks for windbreaks or an igloo if no tent has been carried. People I have been with on the trail carried a special slim stick a couple of feet long to probe for good snow and to beat the frost from tents and clothing. Some guides have room on their sleds for a short-handled snow shovel, and some use a carpenter's handsaw, but just about all, especially the old-timers, carry the traditional snow knife.

In most cases today, a double-wall tent is used. Deliberately kept small and low to conserve heat, it will be pitched

TOM HENNESSEY -

with two end poles and a ridgepole. The bottom and sides will be tied to rocks, gas cans, or the sleds.

Inside, caribou and muskox skins go down on top of the insulating snow, then the sleeping bags and small gear are arranged around the sides. Sometimes the sled tarp will go over the tent as a fly, but one must always be conscious of the dangers of warm air forming frost that will soon be dripping on your bed.

Vents must be left open to regulate the temperature and guard against fumes from the stove. As in a snow house, it is best to keep the temperature below the point of melting and let body heat supply the needed warmth.

Heavy outer clothing, rifles, and cameras are best left covered on the sled and not allowed to warm up, causing condensation, then freezing solid. Boot liners and socks must be dried out in the peak of the tent every night or frozen toes will be the result.

Although it is sometimes hard to convince visitors, you are always better off removing all clothing and sleeping naked in the big sleeping bags. I personally keep my underwear and light socks inside the bag to dry out and avoid some of the shock in the morning. The person who insists upon crawling into the bag fully clothed not only never gets the sweat dried out of his inner clothing but also destroys the insulating qualities of the bag. The rule in Arctic traveling is simple: Stay dry or die!

The sleeping platform takes up two-thirds of the small tent. The grub box with the gas stove on top becomes the kitchen, taking up one corner. Directly in front of the door, snow blocks are removed to a depth of about two feet. This serves a couple of purposes. It forms a cold trap, like the sunken entrance to an igloo, allowing cold air to sink and thus making the level of the sleeping bags marginally warmer. It also allows you to sit on the sleeping mat with legs hanging down, especially appreciated by the *kabloona* guests who are not comfortable sitting with legs outstretched.

In windy weather, snow blocks are cut and stacked as a windbreak and snow is shoveled around to seal the tent bottom. Sometimes it is possible to camp where ice is not too thick, and you can chisel down to obtain water and do some ice fishing. Otherwise ice is chipped and melted on the stove. Once a visitor has experienced a good hot mug of sweetened tea made with ice water and a chunk of fresh bannock with jam or peanut butter, he will never forget it.

The modern Inuk will always carry his high-frequency radio, and our party is no exception. Across the Arctic, the Spillsbury SBX 11A is by far the most popular model, thanks to rugged construction and long battery life. It is universally known as the Orange Radio as opposed to the Black Radio working on the CB band, which many people have in their homes for local communication.

In our tent, the radio hangs from the ridgepole, the antenna tied out between the snow shovel and a gas can, only a couple of feet off the snow, but it always seems to work. It is comforting to know that someone somewhere along the coast is always listening for calls on 5046.

John has signed off the evening contact with the other hunting parties and the folks back in town. The lantern is turned off, the stove is turned back a bit, and we zip up the big sleeping bags. The tent is rustling, wind is coming up, maybe blowing snow tomorrow: we'll worry about it in the morning.

In the meantime, we'll dream of a big muskox and a safe journey home. Like the Inuit of old, we are at home on the Arctic tundra.

MY FRIEND DOOLEY

During the early days of Safari Club International (SCI), one of the real sparkplugs of the organization was my friend Dooley. Whether serving on committees, helping at the auctions, or refereeing the famous Duck Drop Derby, Dooley would be in the middle somewhere. Big and boisterous, he was always audible even if you couldn't see him, and you could not mistake the fact that he counted Dixie his home territory.

Perhaps I am old-fashioned, but I still remember those early years of SCI with great fondness. The group was new and exciting, maybe a bit rough around the edges but with a real feeling of companionship and shared goals, which simply does not come across the same now that SCI has become a mega-fundraising industry.

I guess everything has to change and progress cannot be denied.

I first met Dooley through a mutual friend, Lester Grant of the New England chapter. Lester had hunted with us up in New Brunswick and that winter had kindly invited me down to a chapter meeting at his spectacular home and trophy room outside Boston.

Leigh Everett—one of our guides—and I would be on the road most of the winter in those days, coming down from the North by truck to set up the booth at all the major sports shows in the eastern circuit from Maine to West Virginia. Visiting a Safari Club chapter would be a new experience. We were used to dealing with the sport-show audience and didn't ordinarily suffer from stage fright, but rubbing elbows at a cocktail party with the safari crowd was something else again. I intended to show some films of our hunting operations, and hoped that some of these high-level, world-experienced hunters might be interested in what we were doing up in Canada.

A bit rattled as we tried to set up a screen and projector in the middle of such a gathering, among many magnificent trophies from the far corners of the world, old Leigh and I felt just a little bit shy of it all. As he put it, "This goddam necktie is strangling me. I'm sweatin' like a pig at a quiltin', and just about as comfortable as a turd in the punchbowl at a high-society wedding."

"Well," I said, "I ain't much better. I'd take one of those beers they keep offering me, except I'd probably piss myself before I could find the bathroom in a place as big as this."

Out of the crowd came our hostess, towing a big dude in a blue suit, string tie, and cowboy boots. "Boys," she said, "this is Dooley. Came clear up here from Mississippi to watch your movies."

We hit it off right away. After helping us set up the equipment, he ushered us to a quiet spot at the bar for a cold draft, showed us where the bathroom was located, and generally put us at ease.

"I want you to remember," he assured us, "you are welcome as the flowers in May. Don't worry about all these doctors and lawyers and millionaires. Every single one of them would give all he has to be able to lead the kind of life you all do, and not a one of them could do it. You are among friends that just admire the hell out of you!"

And he was right. We made friends that night that have lasted for all these years. And none better than Dooley.

A couple of years later I got a call one night and it was Dooley, wanting to book a caribou hunt with us up on the shores of Ungava Bay. Said he'd be all alone, as that was the way he preferred to hunt most of the time. We made the arrangements for early September. He would fly from Mississippi to Montreal and on up to Fort Chimo, meet our Air Inuit charter, and fly into camp. We had opened Akuliak only the previous year, and it was still top trophy country for Quebec caribou.

I was on the strip when the Twin Otter came in from Chimo with Dooley and seven other guests, among them Tink Nathan with his bow and bags full of promotional hats and stickers advertising his Doe in Heat deer lure. For a year later I was taking "I love Tink" stickers off the tents, the boats, and the toilet seats, and probably some of the Eskimos are still wearing the hats and T-shirts showing the famous buck sniffing the doe's ass.

It turned out to be a very entertaining week, all in all.

At Akuliak, as all along the Ungava Bay coast, the tides govern your travel. They average over forty feet: Twice a day the water was up to the tents at high tide and out of sight beyond the horizon at low water. When you told newly arriving guests that they would not necessarily be up and away at dawn, some figured we were dragging our feet, but before the week was over, most conceded that you had to wait for the water before you could float the canoes.

Dooley was relaxed and took it all in stride when I told him that we would launch the guys who had lain awake all night as soon as we could; then old Stanley, the Inuit camp boss, and I would take him out for the day.

Heading up the coast, we turned into the first long inlet and started glassing. Within five minutes we saw a very passable bull on the skyline. "Boys," said Dooley, "that's the bull for me right there."

I tried to tell him that we were only starting to hunt and that for sure we would see better ones before the week was over. However, he was certain that with two tags in his pocket it would be better to get rid of one of them right off.

Securing the boat on a long anchor line so it could pay out with the tide, we hiked up over the top of the mountain. In the valley beyond, right on a nice grassy spot, stood the bull. Looking him over at this closer range, I told the anxious gunner that although the animal was OK for a start, we would surely find better ones.

In our business, the man paying the bill is the one pulling the trigger. Now that I'd given my advice, it was up to Dooley. Soon Stanley and I had the bull caped out and cut up to carry to the boat. Coming down off the mountain laden with cape, horns, and four quarters of meat, we stopped to admire the view of the valley and take a breather.

Around the side of the hill came another big old bull. Glassing him all over, Dooley couldn't resist asking, "What do you think of that one, boys? Looks like a real heller to me!"

"No good bull!" Stanley was the first to answer.

We sat there enjoying the view and glassing across the inlet to the hills beyond.

"What do you think, Fred, isn't that a good one?"

"Christ, no, Dooley! The old man is right; there's hundreds around here better than that." We got back to glassing. I looked to my left, and the stupid caribou was still coming toward us.

"Boys, if you all don't mind, I really want to shoot that caribou. He is just the one I want. What about it?"

"Dooley," I told him, "that sorry son-of-a-bitch has great brow shovels and tremendous bez, but he hasn't got a goddamn thing up top. However, you are the guy paying for the shot, so if he comes past that white rock there, I guess you could say he was charging and shoot the bastard."

And that's exactly what happened. On a week-long caribou hunt, we were all done before noon on the first day. Maybe it was fortunate, since old Stanley and I had to pitch in and help the younger Inuit guides a bit with some of the other clients. It's not that the guides didn't know how to run a motorboat and kill caribou, but they lacked a few of the refinements in keeping the dudes under reasonable control.

As for Dooley, he was happy as a clam at high tide just to hang around with the guides and preside over the dinner table with tales of hunting in the wilds of Africa. It certainly was entertaining to me at least. He and old Tink between them apparently knew every bend in every river on that immense continent and were on a first-name basis with at least two-thirds of the indigenous population, human and otherwise.

We met again at the SCI conventions for a couple more years, and then I received another midnight phone call. Dooley wanted to return to the scene of his triumphs in Ungava, and this time he wanted to bring along Lester Grant and some other guy whose name now escapes my memory.

By this time, we had expanded into the Northwest Territories, and for me to go back and guide a party in northern Quebec required a five-day nonstop drive across the continent. I would not have done it for anyone else except my friend Dooley.

I left Martin to finish the caribou season 200 miles north of Yellowknife in the middle of the Barren Lands, and after an exhausting trip I arrived in Montreal late at night and checked into the Airport Hilton. In the morning I was to meet Dooley and his party, take the early flight 1,500 miles north to Fort Chimo, charter a Twin Otter, and fly east on the Ungava Bay coast to the newly established camp at Weymouth Inlet. Dooley would have preferred to return to Akuliak, but he had booked too late, and I convinced him that the new area was just as good, and a change in scenery.

It was too late to contact them that night, so after a few hours' sleep I was in the airport, standing in front of the Nordair counter awaiting their arrival. One hour before flight time, I called the hotel in desperation. After several rings I got a muted, hung-over answer—seemed they'd been out celebrating last night.

"For Christ sakes, Dooley, I drove four thousand goddamn miles to meet you bastards. Now you better get your asses over here because if we miss this flight, we miss the charter out of Fort Chimo and will have to wait a week for the next one." I hung up none too gently.

They called the flight. I went through security and proceeded to the designated gate down on the ground floor because the 737 was boarding on the tarmac. I anxiously waited at the gate as the passengers gathered. Usual load for those days—mostly Inuit, many of whom I knew, heading back up home to the coast after visits to the southern metropolis for medical reasons or meetings, plus the usual gaggle of long-haired, bearded, frog-hippie civil servants returning from their paid vacations with enough weed to do them for the next six months on the frontier.

As far as I could see, I was probably the only one paying for his own ticket. Now, if we could only get the three American dudes rounded up, we might yet bring enough free-enterprise dollars aboard to pay for the flight.

They started boarding the airplane, and although I hung back at the end of the line, there was still no sign of Dooley and company. About the time the flight attendants were counting heads and getting ready to pull up the gangway, I heard a noise approaching. It was Dooley, and in his wake, a little sawed-off red-faced dude. They were trying to argue, in Mississippi Delta accents, with the French Canadian chief flight attendant, to further delay departure. A communication problem in the extreme.

Knowing better but having no choice, I left my seat and went to the rear to see what in hell was going on, since at least I knew what both sides were talking about.

"Fred, am I ever glad to see you!" Dooley said. "We lost Lester somewhere, and no one can find him. He went through security ahead of me and what's-his-name here, but when we got to the gate he was nowhere to be found. They called all over the airport, but mostly in French, and as far as I can figure out, this little lady here says they are already twenty minutes behind time and they just gotta take off without him."

A few minutes of earnest conversation with the attendant confirmed that the flight did indeed have to depart for Fort Chimo with or without our buddy Lester.

"Dooley," I told him, "there are some problems that I can solve, but this is not one of them. You and your buddy here better take your seats. If it is any comfort to you, I can tell you that this is a first for Fred A. Webb. I have lost clients in the woods, in the mountains, and once at sea, but this is the first goddamn time I have ever lost any sonofabitch in the Montreal Airport!"

The rest of the trip was somewhat of an anticlimax. We did get to Fort Chimo, met the charter, and flew way up the coast nearly to the Labrador border, to the camp at Weymouth Inlet. Dooley and I managed to kill a couple of record-book caribou. I managed NOT to kill his buddy from Jackson, Mississippi, and sure enough old Lester eventually turned up in a Twin Otter load of gasoline and propane—three days late but still in time to kill a good caribou.

So I guess the old saying "All's well that ends well" would apply in these circumstances.

Although this turned out to be the last hunt I shared with Dooley, who knows . . . we may get a chance to do it all again someday.

CLIENT MANAGEMENT
AND THE LAW OF AVERAGES

Tom Hennessey —

Jimmy Rikhoff and I were sitting around one time on the rocks by the rapids on a river in Arctic Quebec, watching some of our salmon-fishing clients perform. We had been discussing one of the guests, to whom I had felt called upon to explain the facts of life in a northern camp.

This young man was a seven-foot football hero from Texas, living off the money that his daddy and granddaddy had made in the ranching and oil businesses. He had, I suspect, little knowledge of what it means to do a day's work himself.

His arrogance in dealing with our Inuit guides and camp staff over the course of several days had started to get under my skin a little bit. It all came to a head when he foul-hooked a salmon and was trying to drag it ashore broadside to the current. Approaching the net with it, he put on too much pressure. The leader parted and the fish escaped.

He immediately threw a real screaming tantrum. Tossed his rod down on the rocks, and accosted his young Inuit guide, blaming him for being too stupid to net the fish. He scared the kid half to death; Inuit are taught from birth to fear the mentally deranged, and this guy showed all the symptoms.

While attempting to be at my diplomatic best, I remember saying something conciliatory such as, "Listen, Buddy, you can forget this 'Hey, José' horseshit. You're dealing with friends of mine here, and without them we wouldn't be here fishing. Just because these people are brown doesn't mean they are wetback slave labor on your daddy's farm back in Texas."

This seemed to resolve the problem for the rest of the week.

So Jim and I were discussing public relations and client management in general. After a few minutes' thought, he made this observation: "You know, Fred, over the past ten years of these Fraternity trips to one place or another, we have handled just about a hundred people from all over North America. When you come to think about it, the only problem cases we've run across are this overgrown spoiled rich kid from Texas and that oil-company president who tried to impress us with the fact that he went to college with the Kennedys. Now, when you consider the fact that I can step out on the sidewalks of New York City any day of the year and at least 80 percent of the people I encounter are going to be assholes, then our 2 percent isn't such a bad average."

I could only agree. Looking back forty years at literally thousands of clients, the "asshole ratio" would be a mere fraction of 1 percent of the total. This, I think, speaks highly of the people who go on hunting and fishing trips.

That is not to say there haven't been some criticisms and a few of what may be charitably termed "personality clashes." However, as one of my guides, Coleman, used to say, "They're mostly nice guys, and if they ain't, you and me'll make them into nice guys."

Frank, another veteran guide, always kept his eye on the bottom line. When I apologized for the sport I had saddled him with, he told me, "Don't worry. I can put up with Satan himself for a week, just as long as he's a big tipper!"

As the "boss guide," I have always felt that among my more important duties are seeing that the guide does his job without abusing the guest, and likewise seeing that the guest doesn't totally bulldoze our staff. This latter situation has led to the occasional disagreement, mostly settled amicably.

Running a caribou camp one time in Ungava, we were dealing with Inuit who had never been around visiting sport hunters, and we also had guests making their first trip to the Arctic. Keeping everyone happy in a situation alien to both sides, with language and culture barriers to overcome, made for an interesting first season. To the Inuit, a good caribou was a nice fat cow, preferably standing right beside the canoe, and any caribou was a caribou to kill.

It was a total mystery to them why the crazy *kabloona* would want to turn down hundreds of nice animals, leave the shore and climb the mountains, and then, when as far away from the boats as possible, shoot some rangy old critter with big horns but poor meat. After a while this was straightened out, and I was able to convince them that *"Tuktuk aaniook"* were what we were looking for, and that cash tips and nice knives and binoculars were bestowed upon the guy who brought in the biggest racks. This certainly worked, as confirmed by any look at the record books showing caribou taken from the late 1970s to the mid-1980s.

In the years we ran Akuliak, there was never an unpleasant incident between guests and ourselves, once everyone learned that we were lucky to be hunting in a brand-new area with genuine Arctic hunters for companions. It was simply a matter of education for all concerned.

It is always the responsibility of the "boss guide" to pair up the guests with the most appropriate guides. This judgment call occasionally leads to some amusing situations. I like to think that this is an art only learned over many seasons, and the variables that aid in making the decision are endless. Sometimes, however, when all else fails, I'll get out of sight and simply pull names out of my hat.

On one trip I had a dear-friend lady guest who had hunted with me in many parts of Canada. She had the reputation of always being cheerful, a great shot, never a whiner, and incidentally, a nonstop talker, even when climbing the side of a mountain. I paired her up with Norman Annanack, one of our greatest guides.

Norman, a native Inuit from George River, not only did not speak any English, he did not speak at all, being a deaf mute. Nevertheless, he was one of the finest guides I have ever known. Pairing him up with Mary Jane was a stroke of genius. They set out at high tide on Monday, had an excellent week, and took two great animals. On Thursday at dinner, M.J. made the observation, "Boy, that Norman is a great guide, but he doesn't say much, does he?" It had taken her four days to realize that Norman was only smiling and nodding his head.

Just about 100 percent of the matches I have made over the years have had equally positive results. In a couple of instances, giving in to the clients, I have put them with guides upon whom they had insisted, based upon previous experience or recommendations from friends who had known the guide for one week out of their lifetime. Both of these occasions turned into complete disasters.

The most recent occurred when a client from California insisted upon going on his ten-day hunt for barren ground grizzly with his "good buddy Jerry," with whom he had enjoyed a previous hunt. Against my better instincts, I gave in to his wishes.

The result was that "good old Jerry" took him out for a couple of days of snow picnics and wandering around in the fog, brought him back to town, got drunk, refused to continue the hunt, and in general acted just exactly as I had feared. It was only because Martin was successful in finding the guide with whom this client should have gone in the first place, and got him geared up and back out on the trail, that the hunt resulted in this man taking a good bear. So much for letting the client dictate who should guide him.

It would be impossible for me to relate all of the successful and enjoyable trips we have shared with clients, most of whom became lifelong friends. The people we will never allow back for any amount of money share a much more exclusive list. Each of them has been left with no doubt whatsoever as to my feelings in the matter.

Yes, I am glad to say that I heartily agree with my friend Rikhoff. The few bad experiences are so far outweighed by the many, many friendships made and cherished that the Law of Averages, helped along by a little judicious Client Management, comes out overwhelmingly in our favor.

SIGHTING-IN

First day with a new group of hunters and we are sighting-in their rifles. Different faces, different rifles, but typical of what we have done for the past forty years. Nothing much changes.

Aside from the obvious necessity of checking sight alignment, after the gorillas working for the airlines have done their damndest . . . it is also the chance for the guides to assess their chances for success on the upcoming hunt.

For myself, it is the first opportunity to see if any of them are in the habit of waving the weapon around at waist level.

Ducking and dodging gun muzzles is as much a habit as sticking my fingers in my ears, twenty years too late. Decades of exposure still haven't made me enjoy looking down the mouth of some cannon. I have been places where I got paid extra for being shot at, but this isn't one of them. Besides, I am a coward when it comes to being paunched by a Weatherby Magnum.

It never ceases to amaze me that people who brag about firearms being such an important part of their culture, still go around pointing them at my belly button. In my most diplomatic manner, I give them the Message. Better a minute of humiliation, if it can forestall a lifetime of regret.

In our camps we have a proper setup to find out where the rifle is shooting. A bench, with sandbags and targets at a measured one hundred and two hundred yards, takes the mystery out of it. Better to sort out the problems now than next Thursday after missing the new World Record.

In this, the first few hours in camp, the clients always act like a team of sled dogs coming into a strange community. Like one of my old Guides used to say, "Walkin' around stiff-legged and pissin' on the bushes". They scrape their toes in the dirt and watch one another out of the corner of the eye. Not quite sniffing asses but establishing the order of dominance for the week. This is important stuff, no doubt about it.

I give them the little lecture. "Welcome to the Arctic. I know you can all hit a dime at a thousand yards, so just show me that you can hit a beer box at a hundred and the guides and I will be happy. Use the bench and the sandbags, we will then know what the rifle is doing . . . what you do with it is a different matter.

If you use handloads, be sure to run them all through the action to see if they chamber properly . . . we have seen plenty that didn't. OK, who goes first?"

Usual foot shuffling and hanging back. One of them is finally forced out of the herd and reluctantly comes to the bench. No one ever wants to be the first.

He removes the scope covers, adjusts the earmuffs, hat and glasses, squirms around on the seat . . . finally comes the squeeze . . . "Click!"

Embarrassed little grin. "OK, now put a cartridge in the thing."

"*Bang*!" Guide at the spotting scope hollers, "One inch high at 12 o'clock. Perfect, leave it alone."

"OK!" says The Expert Marksman, now out to show off his prowess before the gang, "I guess I'll try one more."

I cringe and turn away. Have seen this scenario a thousand times at least.

Bang! Two inches low and to the right. Frig with the adjustments. *Bang!* Six inches high and to the left. *Bang!* Four inches low.

At this point he wants to keep screwing around with the scope.

"Hang on a minute," I tell the rattled Marksman, "please let me fire one shot if you can spare the ammunition."

Most graciously concede, those who don't can go to hell.

As much as I hate having the piss kicked out of me by magnums with poorly designed stocks, here we go again. First with the rifle unloaded and muzzle pointed at the ground, I try the trigger pull. It is surprising how many thousand-dollar fancy rifles have a lousy trigger release.

Then from the sandbags, one solid shot. While my ears are still ringing, the scope man shouts out. "Two inches high at 12 o'clock." Plenty good enough to kill an animal, leave it alone.

The Expert Marksman having been subdued and his rifle back on target, the rest of the cast falls in line.

Rambo with the cammo outfit he has worn all the way from New Jersey to the Northwest Territories, steps up with his Remington Burp Gun. Wants to touch off a burst off hand.

"OK," I say, "let me fire one round till we see if it will hit the piece of paper, then you take over."

The Gunsmith comes next, gets out the Bore Sighter and ballistic tables, both of which he should have used at home . . . neither of which has a hell of a lot to do with hitting something as big as a caribou at a hundred yards. After awhile he is happy.

The Re-loader comes next. He finds out that half of his "roll your owns" are not seated properly and will not come up out of the magazine. If it is some Whacko Wildcat, we are in trouble, but if it is some sane caliber I will have a few cartridges to fit it in camp. "Here, take three of these and go hunting."

The Old Vet with the WWII Springfield, shakes them all over. "A Flyer!" he says after each miss. I try it . . . lousy trigger, scope with zero eye relief, but it hits somewhere around the middle of the paper. "Here," I say, "nice rifle, right on!"

The Guide will get him close to a convenient rock and he will kill the caribou just as dead as the best marksman in the outfit.

The Four Bad Boys perform. Kibitzing, grab assing, smart talking, betting on who can hit a rock way over on the hill half

<u>Sighting-In</u>

a mile away. The assigned Guides look at one another . . . it's going to be a long week. "Don't let them cripple something by shooting at stupid distances and don't let them load the goddamn thing until it is pointed at a caribou," I tell the guides.

Last one to step up is the Lone Lady Hunter. The males have all hung around to advise and sympathize. She carries a lightweight, short stocked Remington 660 in a .308 caliber.

Bang! "Dead on!" shouts the guide at the spotting scope. "Guess that will do," she says.

We're ready to go hunting in the morning.

LAST GENERATION OF GUIDES . . .
TRANSITIONS

Toom Hennessey

We have finished another hunting season in the Barren Lands and the central Arctic. At this time of year we always look back, try to assess where we have been, and make some attempt to figure out where we are going. My partner and son, Martin, commented the other day how enormous the changes have been during his thirty-five years on earth. This set me thinking about what the next century might bring.

Our family history illustrates to some extent what has gone on in Canada over the past hundred years, including tremendous changes in demographics and lifestyle. Some branches of our family have been in North America for over three hundred years, some branches forever. The Webb lineage is the most recent—now into its fifth generation.

At the end of the nineteenth century, my grandfather and three of his brothers were shipped out from England to sink or swim in the New World. Working first as farm laborers in eastern Canada, some of them made their way west to the Great Plains, where they established farming families, some branches of which still exist in the West.

Our direct ancestor, Harry Webb, worked in the woods and on the streams of northern New Brunswick and settled at the mouth of the Tobique River. His diary shows that in 1904 he brought his new bride over from the Old Country. They later moved fifty miles down the Saint John River, but never went back to England.

At that time, the majority of Canadians lived a mainly rural life in such time-honored professions as farming, logging, trapping, and later guiding visitors to the area. The first guides on the Tobique River were Maliseet Indians, but by my grandfather's and father's time this had gradually changed, and "white settlers" made up most guide crews before World War I.

Back then the sports came by train, mainly from the eastern U.S., in pursuit of moose and woodland caribou. In the Boone and Crockett all-time record book, two entries from 1899 and 1900 appear, animals taken in the Serpentine Lake area on the Tobique River watershed.

Later the moose and caribou declined because of habitat changes brought about by lumbering, the resulting inflow of white-tailed deer, and other inroads of civilization. By the time my generation started guiding, it was for whitetails, black bears, bobcats, and gamebirds. During the summer months, employment on the river with the big Atlantic salmon Clubs and outfitters kept the guides occupied.

Campfire Lies of a Canadian Guide

Right up until the end of World War II, one-hundred-acre farms along the Tobique River provided a living for most families. Cutting logs in the winter, driving them down the streams in the spring, and guiding in summer and fall supplied wage employment. The small farm with homegrown vegetables, a cow, a couple of pigs, and a flock of hens added to the larder, and fish and game helped keep the wolf away from the door.

Tom Hennessey —

Early on, people lacked the complications of taxes, telephones, and electricity, and the only oil purchased was to fuel lamps and lanterns, so cash expenditures were kept to a minimum. Energy was supplied by horse power, and fuel was cut from the woodlot. People were self-sufficient in the extreme, far better off than the less fortunate starving in the cities during the Great Depression.

In the case of my generation, born in the middle 1930s, none of us ever considered employment except in the out-of-doors. Practically from the time we could walk, we headed for the woods. My younger brother Gary and I, only in grade school during WW II, with Dad away overseas for five years, ran traplines and helped in the woods and on neighboring farms. That we would do so was simply taken for granted. By the time Dad came home, I was ten years old, had already inherited a .22 rifle, and was adept at handling an ax, camping out, and generally taking care of my brother and myself.

Throughout the course of my life to follow, the majority of my living, after a short stint in the Army, was made in such pursuits as truck driving, logging, trapping, and guiding. Even the span of years spent as a communications specialist and guide on scientific and exploration expeditions was broken up by periods of working in the woods. I never had any interest in anything else, and most fortunately had Irene as a wife who worked right along with me.

By the 1960s, with two daughters, Cindy and Janice, of high-school age and two sons much younger, Irene and I launched our own guiding business and never

305

looked back. The period of the steady paycheck was replaced by the feast-or-famine cycle common to seasonal outdoor employment.

This is the era in which my sons grew up and inherited the skills and traditions of all the generations that had gone before. They were country boys with country aims and attitudes, hanging around with and helping the guides in our family operation.

Traveling seventy miles a day on a school bus to avail themselves of the blessings of a marginal school system did not encourage them to become scholars by any means. Their daily goal was to get home to change their clothes and take to the woods. Year-round, the wilderness was as close as the edge of our clearing. Whether it was hunting and trapping, building log camps, cutting wood, or making maple syrup, the boys were learning far more there than they did in school. And the guides, men who had fought in the war and been in the woods all their lives, were better mentors than some of the draft dodgers, dope smokers, and would-be hippies who made up a good proportion of the educational establishment.

Fortunately, the system also included a few very admirable and dedicated professionals, including one who encouraged Rick to become involved in things military and a lady who helped Martin obtain his private pilot's license at the age of seventeen. The boys learned to relate to visitors from all walks of life and how to drive a truck, pole a canoe, and handle the tools of the woodsman's trade . . . all through exposure to the influence of the senior guides.

Now, at the turn of a new century, we are in an entirely different country. For almost its entire history Canada was a largely rural nation, but over the last two decades more and more Canadians have been forced into the cities to find employment. In the case of eastern Canadians, our family included, the last migration westward was thrust upon us by the failing opportunities for employment in the land of our family graveyards. We are economic refugees within our own country, as surely as the ones from other countries driving taxis in Vancouver or picking lettuce in California.

Daughters Janice and Cindy now live with their families in the Vancouver area of British Columbia. Rick, when not serving overseas with the military, is based in Edmonton, Alberta. Martin and I, still maintaining the family outfitting business, now operate totally in the Northwest Territories, and even that immense area is getting smaller as civilization advances.

Irene and I have six grandchildren ranging from kindergarten to high-school age. We are extremely proud of them all. They are talented, involved in organized sports, and educated for life in the computer age. I can only wish them well as they prepare to enter the workforce of the twenty-first century.

However, they will never have the skills or even the desire to chop down a tree, snare a rabbit, trap a muskrat, or live in a self-sufficient manner unsupported by the technology of civilization. They will never be hunters and woodsmen, or know the satisfaction of guiding a city alien in our wilderness world.

Thus, like the majority of people in Canada and the U.S., our family has crossed the divide between rural and city lifestyle in just one generation. It is hard to contemplate, but with my passing and the retirement of Rick and Martin, the Webbs as woodsmen will have vanished.

Epilogue

A few weeks ago I received an important-looking letter from the hospital in Vancouver where I underwent open-heart surgery. They were inviting me to participate in a follow-up study of survivors of their coronary bypass program.

The first question was, "How are you adjusting to your retirement?" This provided Irene and me with an ironic chuckle.

Retirement! Guess they don't know a hell of a lot about making a living in the guiding business.

It brought to mind the time a lady magazine writer had asked Irene, how come in this era of multiple marriages, we had managed to start out as teenagers and remain married for over forty years. The logical answer was, "Because he has been away about thirty of them!"

In the early 1950s, I had left school, joined the Army, acquired a tattoo, got married and started a family . . . all in one eventful season. Shortly after the War, when some of the returning veterans were very little older than I was . . . taking on responsibilities at an early age was nothing out of the ordinary in our part of the country.

Now, as we race toward the millennium, we are once again facing changes in our lives as hunting professionals. Civilization, this time in the form of diamond mining, has caught up with us clear out in the middle of the Barren Land of the Northwest Territories. In the Central Arctic, no one knows what effect the new native government is going to have upon existing business.

The sporting industry itself is rapidly changing and perhaps having seen the golden years of exploration and development, it is hard for us to settle down to the more mundane aspects of the business.

I remember one time thirty-some years ago when we had come down the river on the log drive, into the village of Riley Brook. Having picked apart a jam, which had threatened to take out the bridge, Herb Stevenson, Blake Sutherland and I were boiling up a pail of tea and watching the logs go by.

Just then a couple of the local young ladies were crossing the bridge, both of them pushing baby carriages.

"My God how time flies," observed one of my companions, "why I can remember taking that blonde girl's grandmother out in the grass behind the dance hall one night forty odd years ago. Do you suppose that kind of stuff still goes on in the village?"

"Yes sir," replied my other friend, "I imagine it does. But for damn sure it's a different bunch a doin' it!"

Epilogue

So I guess it's all a matter of perception. While we long for the "good old days," to others new in the business, it is all fresh and exciting. What is one man's back door yard, is another man's wilderness.

The Webbs may very well shift areas of operation once again, but for the foreseeable future we will still be "a doin' it!" Going into the new century, one thing is certain . . . the journey is not yet over.

Pritchard, British Columbia
New Year's 1999